Faroe Islands

THE BRADT TRAVEL GUIDE

PUBLISHER'S FOREWORD

The first Bradt travel guide was written in 1974 by George and Hilary Bradt on a river barge floating down a tributary of the Amazon. In the 1980s and '90s the focus shifted away from hiking to broader-based guides to new destinations – usually the first to be published on these places. In the 21st century Bradt continues to publish these ground-breaking guides, along with others to established holiday destinations, incorporating in-depth information on culture and natural history alongside the nuts and bolts of where to stay and what to see.

Bradt authors support responsible travel, with advice not only on minimum impact but also on how to give something back through local charities. Thus a true synergy is achieved between the traveller and local communities.

*

There is something appealing about a place where visitors are advised to pack woolly hats and gloves for an August holiday! The Faroes are not for conventional holiday-makers, but then nor are Bradt guides. This group of islands offers a blend of the exotic and the familiar (at least to listeners of BBC weather forecasts), but where nature is the main attraction and there are more puffins than people. Sounds like my kind of place.

Hilary Bradt

19 High Street, Chalfont St Peter, Bucks SL9 9QE, England
Tel: +44 (0)1753 893444 Fax: +44 (0)1753 892333
Email: info@bradtguides.com
Web: www.bradtguides.com

Faroe Islands

THE BRADT TRAVEL GUIDE

James Proctor

Bradt Travel Guides Ltd, UK
The Globe Pequot Press Inc, USA

First published November 2004

Bradt Travel Guides Ltd
19 High Street, Chalfont St Peter, Bucks SL9 9QE, England
www.bradtguides.com
Published in the USA by The Globe Pequot Press Inc,
246 Goose Lane, PO Box 480, Guilford, Connecticut 06437-0480

British Library Cataloguing in Publication Data
A catalogue record for this book is available from the British Library

ISBN-10: 1 84162 107 2
ISBN-13: 978 1 84162 107 4

Photographs
Front cover: Puffin (Cornelius Nelo)
Text: Trevor Codlin (TC), Dan Powell (DP), Lance Price (LP), James Proctor (JP),
Geoffrey Roy (GR)

Illustrations Dan Powell
Maps Alan Whitaker

Typeset from the author's disk by Wakewing, High Wycombe
Printed and bound in Italy by Legoprint SpA, Trento

Author/Acknowledgements

AUTHOR

James Proctor first visited the Faroe Islands in 1992 on board the Smyril ferry sailing from Aberdeen and has been back and forth ever since. Accompanied half of the way by a pod of dolphins and buffeted by gale-force winds and stormy seas during the rest of the journey, James's love affair with the North Atlantic got off to a flying start. Whilst working as the BBC's Scandinavia correspondent, he produced a series of television and radio reports about the islands, concentrating on the issues of independence and whaling. James now divides his time as a freelance travel writer between the south of France and his native Yorkshire. He has also co-written the *Rough Guide to Iceland* and the *Rough Guide to Sweden*, and contributed to the *Rough Guide to Scandinavia*.

ACKNOWLEDGEMENTS

I would like to extend heartfelt thanks to Hildur and Unn at the Faroese Tourist Board in Tórshavn, without whom this guide would never have seen the light of day. Their patience, good humour and endless supplies of coffee were much appreciated. Thanks are due also to Ingigerð at the Kunningarstovan in Tórshavn for her exhaustive knowledge about the Faroese capital, woolly sweaters and weather forecasts. Lance, the man with a devotion to duty – even on his birthday – is the cause of singular adoration. Kate and family in Tórshavn also deserve extra special mention for their kindness and generosity – and their superb fish suppers! Kate's help and attention to detail were second to none. I am also indebted to Magni and Kent at Atlantic – who, quite remarkably, didn't catch my appalling flu. Elsewhere in the Faroes, I'd like to thank Christian in Klaksvík for help and expertise regarding the northern islands, Esbern in Mykines, Gunnar and family in Vestmanna, the Paturssons in Kirkjubøur, Richa in Saksun – and everybody who approached me in the street having heard me on Faroese radio telling the nation about this book – the first travel guide in English to cover solely the Faroe Islands.

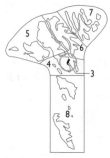

Contents

LIST OF MAPS

KEY TO STANDARD SYMBOLS — Bradt

— · — ·	International boundary
- - - - -	National park boundary
✈	Airport (international)
✈	Airport (other)
+	Airstrip
	Helicopter service
	Railway
	Pedestrianised street
	Footpath
	Car ferry
	Passenger ferry
	Petrol station or garage
P	Car park
	Bus station etc
→	One way arrow
M	Underground station
	Hotel, inn etc
Ⓐ	Campsite
	Hut
♈	Wine bar
✕	Restaurant, café etc
☆	Night club
✉	Post office
☏	Telephone
ⓔ	Internet café
⊞	Hospital, clinic etc
	Museum
ⓘ	Tourist information
$	Bank
	Statue or monument
MW	Male/female toilets

⊞	Historic building
	Castle/fortress
✝	Church or cathedral
	Buddhist temple
⌂	Buddhist monastery
	Hindu temple
ς	Mosque
▶	Golf course
	Stadium
▲	Summit
△	Boundary beacon
◉	Outpost
⨯—⨯	Border post
	Rock shelter
	Cable car, funicular
	Mountain pass
○	Waterhole
	Scenic viewpoint
	Botanical site
	Specific woodland feature
	Lighthouse
	Marsh
	Mangrove
	Bird nesting site
∭	Waterfall
✳	Source of river
	Beach
	Scuba diving
	Fishing sites

Other map symbols are sometimes shown in separate key boxes with individual explanations for their meanings.

Introduction

Attention all shipping. The Met Office issued the following gale
warning to shipping at 17.25 GMT on Monday 23 January. Fair Isle,
Faroes, southeast Iceland: northerly gale force 8 expected soon,
veering northeasterly, increasing storm force 10 later.

Shipping forecast, BBC Radio

Arguably best known for their dramatic appearance in the BBC shipping
forecast, the Faroe Islands are one of Europe's best-kept secrets. Wild, wet and
windy, these 18 volcanic islands, far out in the North Atlantic, are mercifully
still off the main tourist trail. Travel here and you'll discover a different world
– a world of austere beauty where crystal-clear mountain streams cascade
down verdant hillsides dotted with turf-roofed homes, their timber walls
painted a mêlée of reds, yellows and blues; a world where sea cliffs, teeming
with birdlife, plummet precipitously into the churning Atlantic below; a world
where the sea is all-powerful, giving and taking away.

This geographically isolated land of towering layer-cake mountains and
deep rounded valleys, sparkling fell-top tarns and shorelines gnawed into
countless craggy inlets is of such elemental wonder that first-time visitors soon
become ardent devotees, returning time and again to the Faroes, one of
Europe's last places. True, the weather can be unreliable, even downright
inclement at times – but the good news is that conditions in the middle of the
Atlantic change fast, so you'll never have long to wait for a glimpse of the sun.
There's sound logic behind the Faroese saying: 'If you don't like the weather,
wait five minutes!' The quality of the light in the northern sky, which attracts
countless artists to the islands, and the purity of the air are perhaps two of the
most difficult things about the Faroes to qualify on paper – visit, though, and
you'll soon appreciate this most alluring side of island life.

Thanks to regular air links to no fewer than five European countries and a
new ferry plying the waters of the North Atlantic, it has never been easier to
reach the Faroe Islands. Whether you're looking to hike across tussocky
moorland landscapes to imposing lighthouses perched on rocky promontories,
watch seabirds in their natural habitat atop vertical cliff-faces or simply island-
hop around the Faroes exploring traditional villages and hamlets as you go,
you're sure to find an itinerary to please. This is a country where gliding across
narrow sounds and fjords by mail boat or skimming scree-topped pyramidal
peaks by helicopter are just two of the options for getting around. Travel in the

Faroes is not only well integrated, but also incredibly good value. Given the rigours of the climate, quality of life is important to the Faroese; consequently, the islands' infrastructure is well-developed, accommodation is warm and snug and eating out throws up an array of options – everything from pan-fried puffin breast to whale meat could be on the menu alongside more conventional dishes.

As a Scandinavian specialist, I have not only travelled widely across the Nordic countries but have also lived and worked in the region. I speak several Scandinavian languages and have, over the years, developed an extensive network of friends and colleagues throughout the Nordic area. Based on this experience, it is with great pride that I recommend a trip to the Faroe Islands; this is still one of the few places in Europe where life moves at an enviably sedate pace and where the forces of nature and vagaries of the climate mean everything to the people who live here. A visit to the Faroes is a marvellously soporific experience. All 18 islands are waiting to welcome you. Open your eyes and enjoy.

Part One

General Information

FAROE ISLANDS AT A GLANCE

Location In the middle of the Gulf Stream in the North Atlantic at 62° north, halfway between Scotland and Iceland

Size 1,399 km² (545 square miles)

Area Faroese archipelago, 113km (70 miles) long and 75km (47 miles) wide. Total coastline of 1,100km (687 miles). No point in the Faroes is further than 5km (3 miles) from the sea.

Islands 18 volcanic islands separated by narrow sounds and fjords arranged roughly in the form of an arrowhead. All but one are inhabited.

Neighbouring countries Closest land is Shetland, 300km (162 nautical miles) to the southeast

Heights Highest mountain 882m (2,883ft); average height above sea level 300m (980ft)

Climate Average 3°–11°C, winter–summer

Population 47,700 (and roughly twice as many sheep)

Capital Tórshavn (population 18,400)

Status Self-governing region within the Kingdom of Denmark

Language Faroese. Danish has equal status in all official affairs

Religion Evangelical Lutheran

Currency Faroese króna/Danish krone (kr); £1 = 10.24kr, US$1 = 6kr, €1 = 7.44kr (October 2004)

International telephone code +298

Time GMT (winter); GMT +1 (summer)

Electrical voltage 220V; European two-pin plugs

Weights and measures Metric

Flag Red cross fringed with blue on a white background

Public holidays January 1, Maundy Thursday, Good Friday, Easter Sunday, Easter Monday, April 25, Common Prayers' Day (May), Ascension Day, Whit Sunday, Whit Monday, June 5, December 24, 25, 26, 31

Background Information

GEOGRAPHY AND CLIMATE

The geography – and geology – of the Faroe Islands is remarkably consistent and straightforward to get to grips with. The islands are what remain of an eroded plateau of volcanic basalt which was composed during four periods of rock formation; these different layers of rock help to give the mountains on several of the islands their terraced appearance. During the Ice Age, the Faroes were covered by a vast layer of ice. Gradually, over time, the ice sheet melted and broke up into smaller glaciers which in turn created the glacial features that dominate the Faroese landscape today. The Faroese mountains provide textbook examples of glacial activity: a series of mountain slopes rising steeply from a valley floor to culminate in the sharp ridges (arêtes), cirques and pyramidal peaks typical of the head of a glacier; in parts of the islands, where the sea now covers what would have been a valley floor, deep rounded valleys (originally cirques at the head of a glacier, known as *botnur* in Faroese) are all that remain of the land that once bore the tremendous bulk of a glacier. The tallest and most sheer sea cliffs, often perpendicular in character, are found in the north and west of the country where the land is at its highest and most rugged. The rock strata slopes slightly towards the south and east with the result that the coastline here is much gentler and more eroded. It's a harsh yet austere beauty, repeated throughout the country, though at its most breathtaking in the northern islands where the houses are seemingly stuck on the steep mountainsides, their brightly painted colours contrasting with the grey-brown basalt behind and the deep blue of the sea in front. On the islands further south, the landscape is softer, with lower, gentler hills and larger expanses of farmland.

Climate

The weather is maritime, quite changeable and totally dominated by the Gulf Stream which encircles the islands and moderates the climate giving an annual average range between 3°C in winter and 11°C in summer. In sheltered valleys the temperature can often reach into the high teens; however, the highest temperature ever recorded in the islands is a balmy 22°C. The Faroes also lie in the stormiest part of the North Atlantic, directly in the path of the majority of Atlantic depressions, and as a result are cloudy, wet and windy throughout the year. In **winter**, temperatures are relatively mild for the high latitude (the Faroes are warmer in winter, for example, than Denmark, 6° of latitude

AVERAGE CLIMATIC CONDITIONS FOR TÓRSHAVN

Month	Average sunlight (hours)	Average precipitation (mm)	Wet days
January	1	149	25
February	1	136	22
March	2	114	23
April	4	106	22
May	5	67	16
June	5	74	16
July	4	79	18
August	3	96	20
September	3	132	12
October	2	157	24
November	1	156	24
December	0	167	26

further south), harbours never freeze and although snowfall does occur it is generally short-lived. Winter storms though can rage for days, cutting off some of the smaller islands. Conversely, in **summer**, days are cool and sun-less – daily sunshine in the summer months averages only about four hours, fractionally less than Iceland, but in stark contrast to the ten or 11 hours of sunshine, for example, experienced in the Mediterranean. Throughout the year mist and rain are common, but weather changes are rapid and there are nearly always different conditions prevailing on different islands. The two main southern islands, Sandoy and Suðuroy, for example, have more sunny days than the northern islands and are generally a shade warmer.

NATURAL HISTORY
Other than the vast numbers of seabirds that are attracted to the Faroe Islands, visitors will notice a distinct lack of fauna. The islands have no indigenous mammals due to their isolated location in the middle of the North Atlantic and all animals currently found in the Faroes have been introduced here.

Seabirds
Although there has been a steady decline in the seabird population in the Faroes since the 1950s, with a severe drop in numbers recorded during the '80s due to falling fish stocks, it's nevertheless estimated that there are two million pairs of seabirds in the Faroe Islands during the breeding season. This is unmistakably the best time to watch birds in the islands – simply find yourself a suitable cliff, sit down, remain quiet and watch and smell the spectacle: a cliff-face populated by hundreds of thousands of seabirds is not only an audio-visual delight, but also one that won't fail to leave your nose

Kittiwakes

unstimulated either. Each species of bird has its own favourite spot on the cliff – **puffins** (*Fratercula arctica*), for example, will be found on the steep grassy slopes at the top of the cliff and a colony is easily recognised by the luxuriant green colour of the surrounding vegetation which thrives on the birds' nutrient-rich droppings. They also appreciate grassy tufts on the top of sea stacks. The birds burrow about 1m into the slope where the female lays a single egg. Moving down the cliff-face, **guillemots** (*Uria aalge*) and **kittiwakes** (*Rissa tridactyla*) come next, closely packed together on the narrow shelves towards the top of the cliff. Although there are some cliffs preferred only by kittiwakes, these two species, the former a black-and-white member of the auk family (members of which, incidentally, lay their eggs straight on to the cliff-face or into holes in the rock), the latter a small white gull with grey wings and black wing-tips, are often found nesting together; kittiwakes are among the noisiest of all the seabirds and their nests become a stinking pile of guano by the end of the breeding season. **Razorbills** (*Alca torda*) are similar in appearance to guillemots but have a blacker back and a thicker bill with a white line – they can sometimes be found on small ledges and crevices amongst the guillemots but they are much fewer in number and in smaller colonies. Four hundred years ago, the **fulmar** (*Fulmarus glacialis*) was so rare it was thought to be a bad omen heralding the arrival of terrible weather – today it is the most common seabird in the islands and can be found scattered across the cliff-face. This is one of the most elegant fliers of all seabirds, gliding effortlessly on outstretched grey wings along the top of the cliff. This large seabird is similar to a gull, stout with a thick neck, whitish head, neck and breast. At the bottom of the cliff, you'll find the **shags** (*Phalacrocorax aristotelis*), large black birds with an unusual green eye, whose plumage often looks scaly. In a few locations around the island, you might be lucky (or unlucky) enough to come across the **great skua** (*Catharacta skua*), a massive heavily built bird with dark brown feathers throughout, except light

Great skuas

> **WHERE TO WATCH SEABIRDS IN THE FAROES**
> **Puffins** Northern islands; Eysturoy; Vestmanna bird cliffs; Saksun cliffs; Viðvík bay, Vágar; Mykines
> **Guillemots** Largest colony on Skúgvoy; northern islands; Eysturoy; Vestmanna bird cliffs; Saksun cliffs; Mykines; Sandoy
> **Arctic tern** Kirkjubøurhólmur at southern end of Streymoy; Skúgvoy; Sumbiarhólmur at southern end of Suðuroy
> **Razorbills** Look for them where you see kittiwakes
> **Fulmars** Throughout the islands
> **Kittiwakes** Northern islands; Eysturoy; Vestmanna bird cliffs; Saksun cliffs; Mykines; Sandoy
> **Gannets** Mykineshólmur
> **Manx shearwaters/storm petrels** Largest colony on Nólsoy; Mykines
> **Shags** Northern islands; Eysturoy
> **Great skuas** Svínoy; Skúgvoy

patches on its outstretched wings. Known for attacking other seabirds and forcing them to vomit up their food, this powerful flier will also swoop from the air on anything – or anyone – who comes too close to its nest. Its sturdy bill with a hooked tip is best kept away from your head by holding your arm in the air to distract the birds away from your scalp. Another bird renowned for direct hits on human heads is the **Arctic tern** (*Sterna paradisaea*), a slender, elegant creature with grey and white plumage. Its forked tail, long, pointed wings, black head and blood-red beak are a scene straight out of Alfred Hitchcock when coming in for the attack. The largest seabird in the North Atlantic can also be seen in the Faroes; with a wingspan of two metres, the **gannet** (*Morus bassanus*) breeds predominantly on Mykineshólmur in the far west of the country. These white birds with yellow heads and black wing tips are tremendous divers, sweeping down on their prey from a height of up to 40m.

The largest colony of **storm petrels** (*Hydrobates pelagicus*) anywhere in the world is in the Faroes. As a precaution against predators (they are particularly wary of rats and will not nest anywhere the rodents are found), Europe's smallest seabird can only be seen on land at night; during the day these small black birds, similar in size to a chaffinch but with longer wings, can be seen flitting around bat-like in the half-light.

Other birds

As far as other species of birds are concerned, the small size and isolated location of the Faroe Islands mean that the overall number of non-seabirds is low. There is, however, a good collection of **waders** and **divers** including the oystercatcher (*Haematopus ostralegus*), whimbrel (*Numenius phaeopus*), curlew (*Numenius arquata*), redshank (*Tringa totanus*), red-necked phalarope

(*Phalaropus lobatus*) and red-throated diver (*Gavia stellata*) as well as passerines such as the meadow pipit (*Anthus pratensis*), chiffchaff (*Phylloscopus collybita*) and redwing (*Turdus iliacus*). The most common **duck** is the eider (*Somateria mollissima*) and the only bird of prey is the **merlin** (*Falco columbarius*), or *smyril* in Faroese – a name which launched an entire international shipping line.

Merlin

Birdwatching

The best time to watch birds in the Faroes is in summer.
Although the various species return to the islands at different times of the year, most of them are back in residence for the breeding season between late May and mid-August which reaches its peak between the end of the June and the beginning of July. Not only is the unpredictable Faroese weather at its best at this time of year but you'll also benefit from the long, light northern nights. Make sure you bring a decent pair of binoculars with you as they will greatly enhance your viewing pleasure and the number of species you can see. As for seeing the nocturnal storm petrel, the best bet is to take the tours run by Jens Kjeld-Jensen on Nólsoy since the colonies are difficult, if not dangerous, to find in the dark; see page 80 for details. Remember, too, not to disturb nesting birds as you may cause them to abandon their nests and lose their chicks, and do not collect eggs.

Marine life

Agricultural land has always been scarce on the islands and over the centuries the Faroese have come to regard the seas around their islands as their garden, harvesting the fish and whales found here. Although fish numbers have been falling in recent years due to overfishing, the North Atlantic is still rich in fish. The main species are blue whiting, saithe, cod, capelin, herring, mackerel, haddock and redfish as well as lobster and scallops.

Whales

Several species of whale also inhabit Faroese waters: longfin pilot whales (*Globicephala melas*), killer whales (*Orcinus orca*) and fin whales (*Balaenoptera physalus*) can all be found here, as well as harbour porpoises (*Phocoena phocoena*), bottlenose (*Tursiops truncatus*) and white-sided dolphins (*Lagenorhynchus acutus*). Sadly, though, it is unlikely that you will see large numbers of whales or dolphins whilst in the islands – you will probably have to make do with the odd distant glimpse offshore – since the islands have yet to offer whale-watching tours.

The only whale still hunted by the Faroese, the **longfin pilot whale**, generally lives in pods of between ten and 50, preferring deep water where

Killer whales

squid, its main source of food, is abundant. Jet black or dark grey in colour and weighing around two–three tons when fully grown, the pilot whale can be recognised by its strong blow (often more than 1m high), bulbous forehead, its prominent dorsal fin which is set quite far forward and unusually long flippers. Young whales may breach, an activity which becomes rarer as they grow older, although spyhopping (the technical term for poking their heads out of the water and having a look around) and lobtailing or tail-slapping are regularly observed. Pods of pilot whales are sometimes driven ashore by small fishing boats where they are then forced to beach and are killed for their meat. This traditional hunt has taken place in the Faroes for centuries and is considered an ancient right; over the years the meat produced from the kill has helped to keep many isolated communities alive.

The **killer whale**, also known as the orca, is the largest member of the dolphin family and is easily recognised by its black, white and grey markings (there's a white patch behind each eye) and massive triangular dorsal fin (male) set slightly forward of the centre of the body; this is the whale popularly featured in the film, *Free Willy*. The term killer whale is confusing since they do not eat people, or indeed act violently within their pod. Their main source of food is fish and seals, although they do also eat squid, and they are generally found in deep water but will also enter shallow bays and estuaries, particularly in summer and autumn when herring move closer to the coast. The killer whale is inquisitive and highly acrobatic when on the surface, often leaping out of the water, lobtailing, flipper-slapping and spyhopping. Although individual animals may separate themselves from a pod, they are generally found in groups of up to 25; when fully grown they can weigh up to nine tons.

Weighing up to 80 tons (the equivalent of around 2,000 people standing on one spot), and measuring up to a whopping 26m, the **fin whale** is the second-largest animal on earth. This animal was extensively hunted and its numbers plummeted accordingly; it's thought the fin whale population today stands at around 120,000. It can be recognised by its exceptionally large size, grey body, small fin sloping backwards about three-quarters of the way down its body, and its tall narrow blow, typically occurring between two and five times at intervals of 10–20 seconds. The fin whale also has around 100 throat grooves, which generally reach down to its navel. Occasionally the animal will breach clear of the water. The fin whale is a fast swimmer (around 30km/h) and generally lives in small groups numbering around five. This whale first appears off the Faroes around March, though it's not until late May or early June that it's present in large numbers.

Porpoises and dolphins

Smaller than a human being at roughly 1.5m in length, the **harbour porpoise** is not easy to spot. It's quite shy and is very wary of boats. The best thing to listen out for is its blow, which although not often seen, sounds rather like someone sneezing. This dolphin has black lips (rather than a beak), a chin and a nondescript grey-black body (white underside) with a low fin in the shape of a triangle but with a blunt tip. It is generally found within 10km of the shore and particularly appreciates shallow bays and estuaries where it feeds on shrimp and fish; look out for it rising to the surface about four or five times in a row at 15-second intervals.

Although the **bottlenose dolphin** is relatively rare around the Faroes, it does appear from time to time and usually congregates in groups of ten or so. A classic dolphin in appearance, with bluish-grey flesh, a protracted beak and pointed flippers, it is very active on the surface sometimes breaching and riding on the wake of boats. Its dorsal fin is slightly hooked and is positioned in the centre of the body. Weighing up to 600kg, the bottlenose feeds mostly on fish and squid, though will also consume shrimp.

The **white-sided dolphin** is so named because of its distinctive white and yellow streaks, which stretch from its dorsal fin (slightly forward of the centre of its body) to its tail. This large animal, weighing around 200kg and measuring about 2m in length, can often be seen alongside longfinned pilot whales in groups of anything up to 50, though it prefers smaller pods closer to the shore. It has a gently sloping forehead and a black ring around its eye. The white-sided dolphin is very agile and often breaches and lobtails, surfacing to breathe about every 15 seconds. Its diet consists of squid and fish, occasionally shrimp.

Unfortunately, the exact populations of the above mammals are not known exactly, although it is believed that longfin pilot whales are very common throughout the North Atlantic. It's for this reason that the International Whaling Commission has excluded the pilot whale from its endangered species list, making it legally possible for the Faroese to continue their traditional hunt for the whale whilst still conserving numbers. As far as the conservation of fish stocks is concerned, the Faroese fishing industry has for several years employed a system of 'fishing days' rather than quotas which, it's argued, better conserves fish numbers rather than simply hoovering up large numbers of fish to fill quotas.

Flora

One of the first things that visitors to the Faroe Islands notice is the distinct lack of trees. Although there are a handful of small plantations – mostly of spruce, ash, maple and willow – dotted around the islands, there are no indigenous trees; the islands' 80,000 or so sheep nibble anything they come across putting paid to any chance a tree may have of re-establishing itself elsewhere. In fact, anything that does grow in the Faroes has been brought to the islands either by birds, the wind, the sea currents or since the time of the settlement by people. Today, there are around 400 species of flowering plant (a quarter were introduced by man) and around 30 or so mosses and fungi. The islands are characterised by large areas of hilly grassland divided into the **homefield** (the area immediately enclosing a village), and the **outfield** (everything on the other side of this division, ie: valley sides, mountaintops etc). During the summer months, the sheep are not allowed in the homefield, where vegetables are cultivated, and it's here that you'll find the islands' various buttercups, violets, wild orchids and cranesbill. In the outfield the terrain can often be boggy and peaty, and it's here that you'll come across plants that can tolerate high amounts of water such as cottongrass and rushes. Buttercups are one of the few wild flowers you'll see in the outfield among the sheep because they have a bitter taste and are poisonous. Often in the proximity of bird cliffs you'll find angelica which during previous centuries was once cultivated as a vegetable; it particularly likes soil which is rich in phosphates and nitrates, caused by bird droppings. Faroese mountaintops are renowned for their extensive areas of camomile, knotgrass, lady's mantle and sorrel. Ravines and gorges are the places to look for the several varieties of saxifrage which grow in the islands because here they can grow out of the reach of sheep; five of the most beautiful are the mossy saxifrage (*Saxifraga hypnoides*), alpine saxifrage (*Saxifraga nivalis*), purple saxifrage (*Saxifraga oppositifolia*), Irish saxifrage (*Saxifraga rosacea*) and starry saxifrage (*Saxifraga stellaris*).

During the summer months you should keep to established paths when walking through the homefield and you should take special care not to walk through hayfields which will provide much-needed fodder for sheep and cattle through the long winter months. Although Faroese nature is fragile, there are no special conservation issues as such – nevertheless, you should not import large numbers of cans and plastic bottles which, when discarded, can destroy the delicate environmental balance and endanger birds.

HISTORY

Although the Faroe Islands have never been linked politically with Iceland, 400km to the northwest, their histories frequently overlap. In both cases some of our best glimpses of early life come from the stories or *sagas* written down around the 13th century. Neither Iceland nor the Faroes had an indigenous population to be conquered or subjugated when the first brave travellers arrived from the south and east. Both were visited first, in all probability, by Irish monks but owe their early development to the Vikings. Both had to come to terms with centuries of rule from Norway and Denmark, and both have struggled to establish their independence – the Icelanders succeeded eventually, although the Faroes remain to this day a Danish dependency.

Early settlers

There is still much academic debate about the voyages of the Irish abbot **St Brendan** in AD560–67. According to the stories passed down to future generations, he went in search of 'The Promised Land of the Saints' and had many adventures along the way, but historical evidence of his travels is scant to say the least. His story was long considered a legend, but it spoke of his visit to the 'Island of Sheep and the Paradise of Birds', several days' sailing distance from Scotland. The literal translation of the Faroese word for the islands, *Føroyar*, is indeed 'The sheep islands' and Mykines in particular has a massive bird population, but this wasn't enough to convince the sceptics. Recently, researchers have unearthed archaeological signs of cultivated fields from the same period, and gravestones with what appear to be Celtic crosses have been discovered in an ancient churchyard in Skúgvoy, all of which gives credibility to the theory that even if St Brendan himself never visited, Irish monks were indeed the first humans to set foot here.

The arrival of the Norsemen in the 9th century is not in dispute, on the other hand. These visitors were not Vikings in the sense that most people imagine them. Rather they were farmers and peasants who were either in search of new lands or forced to flee Scandinavia for religious or other reasons.

If the *Færeyinga Saga* or *Saga of the Faroe Islanders* is to be believed, the first Norse settler was a man named **Grímur Kamban** who probably made his way north from Viking-settled Ireland. A Norse system of administration was quickly established, remarkably democratic for the time. There would have been local meeting places for discussion of the islands' development and the settlement of disputes, and the main parliament or *ting* ('people's assembly') sat at Tinganes in Tórshavn. This would have been the final arbiter of the law and the place where any unresolved disagreements were sorted out. It was also the main place of worship to the Norse gods.

The *Saga* tells us of the Faroes' conversion to Christianity around AD1000, around the same time as in Iceland. By all accounts it was a far from peaceful transition. The new religion was brought to the islands by **Sigmundur Brestisson**, a member of the dominant Gøtuskeggjar family, who went to Norway and promised the Norwegian King Olav that he would convert his home people on his return. The Faroese farmers refused, and an increasingly bloody period followed in which the battle for religion became entwined with resistance to Norwegian influence more generally.

The influence of Scandinavia

The victory of the Christians brought many social changes in its wake. Family allegiance was replaced by loyalty to the Church and, in effect, to Norse rule. But, as might be expected, there was a lot of passive resistance and it took centuries before the traditional customs and beliefs had all but disappeared. According to the *Saga*, the *ting* agreed in 1035 to accept Norwegian control and to become a part of the Kingdom of Norway.

It was a dark period for the Faroes because, despite a healthy economic outlook, the islands became more and more dependent on Norway, both politically and financially. By 1035 the *ting* had lost its ultimate power and the traditional, locally administered fishing industry fell prey to foreign intervention, first from Norway and then from the Hanseatic League. The

Church demanded not just the people's faith but more and more of their money too. When the construction of the Magnus Cathedral began around 1300 at Kirkjubøur, the financial demands on the local population to pay for it were so great that there was apparently a revolt against the bishop. By all accounts the fact that the cathedral remains unfinished to this day – it still has no roof – is a testament to the ferocity of the opposition. But that a cathedral should have been contemplated at all is evidence of the growth of the islands both in importance and in numbers of inhabitants. By the end of the 13th century it's thought that around 4,000 people lived here.

The so-called 'Sheep Letter' of 1298 gives a rare insight into the social structures of the time. It was drawn up to regulate the division of land and, as the name implies, to lay down some rules for the rearing of sheep. Remarkably it remained in force until the middle of the 19th century. The Letter suggests that by the time of its drafting, the first settlements, owned by a small number of families, had been broken up into smaller landholdings and farms and that the population was now more spread out across the islands, although by now the Church controlled around 40% of the land. The Faroes were now sufficiently well-established to provide opportunities for trade that its absentee rulers couldn't resist exploiting.

Norway's king, Magnus the Lawmaker, wasn't content with having a cathedral that bore his name. He now tried to establish a trade monopoly too, insisting that all commerce take place through the Norwegian port of Bergen. Here, of course, customs taxes would be levied. But his ships couldn't compete with the much more efficient vessels of the newly formed Hanseatic League in northern Germany. This, coupled with the plague that struck Norway to devastating effect, drastically reduced the king's power in the Faroes and led to a more competitive economic environment.

In 1380 the crowns of Denmark and Norway were formally united, although with the Danes as the dominant partner. Danish law took effect on the Faroes and the *ting* became little more than a talking shop. One of the world's oldest parliaments had effectively been dissolved. At the same time the Catholic Church increased its land-grab; the islands entered a period of economic and cultural decline that amounted to something of a Dark Age with local customs and the local economy being increasingly smothered by the power of Denmark.

After the Middle Ages

The next major landmark in Faroese history didn't come until 1535 when King Christian III of Denmark granted exclusive trading rights to a Hamburg merchant, Thomas Köppen, and with it the right to collect taxes. After a bitter civil war at home, the Danish crown was desperately short of money. The Faroe Islands had already been offered to England's King Henry VIII in return for cash, but he turned them down. If he'd accepted, the Faroes might well be today what many ill-informed people believe them to be anyway – some far-flung extension of the British Isles.

The year 1535 had an even more profound effect on the islands with the advent of the Reformation. Denmark had now adopted the Lutheran

Protestant religion and decided to impose it on its foreign territories too. It was hailed as an exercise in enlightenment, but the impact on the islands was generally a negative one. Danish replaced Latin as the language of the Church and priests, who had been educated until now at Kirkjubøur on Streymoy, had to go to Copenhagen for their training. Before long there were more Danish clergymen than Faroese. By 1557 the local bishopric was abolished altogether and for religious purposes the islands came under the tutelage of Bergen. King Christian III had already confiscated two-thirds of Church lands, leasing much of it to Köppen, and now he grabbed the remainder. This he rented out to tenants known as *kongsbøndur* or king's farmers. Uniquely these lands couldn't be split up among family members, so the tenants who held them went on to become relatively wealthy and powerful. The reform was a major force for stability in Faroese society.

Trade

Over the following century the trade monopoly passed through different hands, almost all of them foreign. The most notable exception was a Faroese adventurer, Magnus Heinason (1548–89), who promised to tackle the problem of pirates in the waters off the islands and, in return, was allowed to build a fighting ship and the fort at Skansin in Tórshavn. He is still regarded as something of a national hero, although he wasn't beyond bullying and cheating his fellow countrymen in pursuit of a good profit for himself. The problem of piracy didn't go away, and the growth of smuggling undermined the monopoly more and more as time went on.

In the mid-17th century the Faroes were all but handed over to one man, Christopher Gabel, who had almost total political and economic control. He passed all of it on to his son, Frederik, on his death. Both men assumed the title of Governor and are remembered for the harshness of their rule and, as ever, their readiness to profit from the islanders' efforts. They tried to fortify Skansin still further, using unpaid workers from Tórshavn. What followed was a mini-revolution. A formal complaint was made to Denmark, but the locals took matters into their own hands and mysterious fires and an explosion in a gunpowder store destroyed many of the buildings owned by the Gabels' company. In 1677 the town was subjected to a violent raid by French pirates, and, once again, the Danes were forced to think again about how best to restore some kind of peace and economic prosperity to the Faroes. A Royal Commission was dispatched to come up with suggestions, but the king's preferred solution was simply to take back power himself.

Faroese historians regard the subsequent period as a distinct change for the better. Corruption all but disappeared and some semblance of fair trade was restored. Unfortunately little was done to improve communications between the islands themselves and people still had to travel to Tórshavn in all weathers to collect supplies. Famine and death on the more outlying islands were not uncommon.

The wealthy *kongsbøndur* were able to consolidate their power still further and in 1777 passed the so-called 'slave law' which forbade marriage to anyone who didn't own enough land to support a family. Despite its obvious unfairness, the law was designed to control the population so the Faroes could remain self-sufficient. It didn't work, and before long new settlements had to be established to house the growing number of islanders and the importation of food, especially corn, became a necessity.

Meanwhile the political upheavals in Europe continued to have an impact on the islands. The outbreak of the Napoleonic Wars disrupted trade and in 1808 an English brig, the *Clio* entered Tórshavn and briefly captured the fort at Skansin. Economically, fishing was growing in importance so that by 1840 fish and fish products made up almost 40% of exports from the islands. The growth of fishing had a powerful social impact, too, with men away from home for long periods of time and women taking on greater responsibilities as a result. Faroese society was entering a period of flux that would help generate a political demand for greater independence. As a first step, the Trade Monopoly was finally abolished on January 1 1856. This had been demanded by the islanders themselves, although the reasons for abolition had far more to do with the fact that the Monopoly was losing the Danish crown money. With its passing, the idea that Denmark was not, after all, all-powerful began to grow.

Political change

These stirrings of nationalist sentiment had been encouraged earlier in the century when the Faroese parliament, already renamed the Løgting to fit in with the Scandinavian system of local government, was finally abolished altogether. Danish law was now supreme. The practical effect was minimal but the psychological impact was far more profound. Add to that the use of Danish rather than Faroese in all official dealings and then, in 1849, the legal assumption of the islands into Denmark itself, and it was inevitable that local noses would be put severely out of joint. The concept of Home Rule was discussed openly for the first time. In 1852 the Løgting was re-established as a kind of regional council with only advisory powers. It had 20 members, 18 of them elected by the various districts. The language question generated the greatest resentment but this led some to start questioning the threat to Faroese culture as well.

Just how much anger lay below the surface was revealed when in 1888 a small group of young men advertised a meeting with the words: 'Everybody is invited to come to the house of the Løgting on Boxing Day at 3 p.m. where we will discuss how to protect the Faroese language and the Faroese culture.' It was standing room only. There were bold speeches about the time having come for the Faroese people to stand up and protect their heritage. An organisation called the *Føringafelag* was formed as a direct result of the meeting to fight for both the language and the self-sufficiency of the islands.

The young radicals were opposed by many of the wealthier landowners, who feared higher taxes to pay for local self-government. Indeed it was the opponents of Home Rule that formed the Faroes' first political party, the Union Party, to campaign for even closer links with Denmark. In response, Jóhannes Patursson, one of the young men behind the Boxing Day meeting, formed the Self-Rule Party to fight for gradual moves towards independence. The battle lines were drawn, but the conservatives still held the upper hand and after a centrist Social Democratic Party was formed in 1927, the radicals were kept out of power until World War II.

The conflagration that hit Europe had a sudden and dramatic effect on the Faroe Islands. Denmark quickly fell to Germany and Britain sent troops to the islands to prevent them also falling under Nazi control. Needless to say the British were more concerned about the strategically important North Atlantic shipping lanes than the welfare of the islanders, but the effect was the same: the changes came with remarkable speed.

A Faroese ship on its way to Aberdeen was intercepted by a British warship and ordered to lower the Danish flag and to fly the Faroese flag instead. The Danish governor of the islands protested but was overruled, and the BBC announced that all Faroese shipping would fly the islands' own flag from then on. The day of the announcement, April 25, has been the national flag day ever since. In practice, the Faroese enjoyed Home Rule in all but name during the war years and in return they braved the dangerous seas to the south to deliver much-needed fish to the British Isles. There was a high cost to pay in human lives but the economy prospered and the islands built up their own financial reserves for the first time.

By the end of the war the political plates had shifted. Despite a rearguard action by the conservative parties, the people voted narrowly in a referendum for independence from Denmark. The Danish Prime Minister agreed – at first – and it seemed that self-government was indeed on the way. A change of heart by the Danish government swiftly followed when it was felt in Copenhagen that Danish national honour was being challenged. So, far from greater independence, the Faroes suffered the indignity of having the Løgting dissolved by the King of Denmark and new elections ordered. The new Løgting agreed instead to a middle way of greater self-rule within the union with Denmark and the Faroese Home Rule Act was duly passed and came into effect on April 1 1948.

The Faroes has shifted from being a mere county of Denmark to a 'self-governing community within the Kingdom of Denmark', a status it holds to this day. But the battle goes on, though with none of the fervour of the 1940s. In 1948, a new political party was formed to insist that the referendum result be honoured and the islands be given full independence. In recent years that came tantalisingly close, but never close enough. The post-war settlement has survived, just, not least because it gives a substantial measure of self-rule to the islanders themselves. Having said that, the current compromise has some confusing inconsistencies.

The Løgting is now wholly democratic and the representative of Denmark in the islands has no vote in its proceedings. There is a Faroese prime minister, the *Løgmaður,* and a cabinet. Its powers cover taxation, customs, communications, education, sanitation and the post office. Faroese stamps are a great money-spinner for the islands. But while Faroese is the official language of domestic politics and national life, Danish must still be taught in all schools as a link to the motherland. Denmark controls the police, defence and foreign policy, and the currency. There is a Faroese currency, the Faroese króna but it is tied to the Danish currency and Faroese banknotes are printed and issued by the National Bank of Denmark. But trade, that historically contentious issue, has been left in the hands of the Faroes.

So it was that when Denmark joined the European Union the Faroes refused to go in with them, choosing to stay outside and preserve their fishing rights. If the Danes were ever to vote to join the Euro the position of the Faroes would prove an interesting side issue.

The last 20 years

The islands have benefited financially from the link with Denmark. They pay no direct taxes to Copenhagen but receive subsidies that amount to some 14% of their gross domestic product.

The continued existence of the 200-mile exclusion zone for fishing helped the Faroese economy prosper in the post-war years. For a while the population was enjoying the world's highest standard of living and the Faroese were spending up to ten times as much as their Danish counterparts. Road and tunnel building brought the islands' communities closer together but the cost per head of the population was high. The Faroese were living on borrowed time, and for that matter on borrowed money. It couldn't last.

The fishing industry had been cushioned by over-generous government subsidies during the good years. So when drastic falls in fish stocks in the North Atlantic, due to overfishing, hit the fishermen hard, the knock-on effects for the entire community were catastrophic. The Faroes had become a centre of expertise for high-tech, high-yield fishing equipment but now they had to pay the price of their success. The annual catch fell dramatically at the same time as fish prices were taking a tumble and as a result the whole economy was suddenly plunged into crisis.

The national bank was supporting massive debt and as people increasingly defaulted on their loans, the bank itself went under. The receivers were called in in October 1992 and the Faroese had no choice but to go cap in hand to Denmark to ask the government there to bail them out. It was a terrible humiliation that affected everyone on the islands. In return for financial support that eventually reached almost two billion Danish kroner, the Danish National Bank effectively took control of its Faroese equivalent. Not surprisingly the Danes demanded major reforms in return for their support. There was an emergency budget that produced lower public spending, higher taxes and cuts in wages for public employees. Unemployment rose to over 20% and the fishing industry was crippled, with half its boats and processing plants in receivership. Then to make matters worse the Faroese government discovered that an apparently generous offer to allow a Faroese takeover of the islands' second biggest bank from the Danish National Bank had a painful sting in the tail. Contrary to what they had been told, the bank was itself in serious debt, something the new owners only discovered 48 hours after taking it over. By October 1993 the islanders were back asking Copenhagen for more cash. The

Danish media attacked them ferociously as if they were spoiled and irresponsible children. Demands for an official enquiry into the bank issue were refused and things looked bleaker than ever until a Danish journalist revealed the extent of the scandal, with evidence of a high-level conspiracy effectively to bankrupt the Faroes completely. The revelations led to a compromise with a big reduction in the islands' debt and an interest-free loan from the shamed Danes.

The last few years of the 20th century were a period of recovery. Fish stocks stabilised and the catch increased once more. Some of the five thousand or so people who had left the islands during the slump started to return as the economy picked up considerably. But the political impact of the crisis was more long-lasting. For only the second time ever pro-independence parties won a majority in the Løgting with a programme designed to achieve full independence by the year 2000. Denmark agreed to negotiate and experts were asked to investigate how the Faroes might manage if they decided to go it alone. The experts predicted that a Faroese state would be viable and plans were laid for independence subject to a vote in favour in a referendum.

Then suddenly it all went wrong. The Faroese accused the Danes of bad faith in the negotiations. The Danish government insists the Faroese plans were unworkable, although there are suspicions that Copenhagen was afraid Greenland would follow the Faroes down the path to independence and decided instead to stop the process in its tracks. By the spring of 2001 Prime Minister Anfinn Kallsberg was forced to tell the Faroese people that he was now convinced Denmark had never intended to grant the islands their freedom. Could the Faroes achieve full nationhood by themselves? They concluded that they couldn't. The plans had relied on gradually reducing Danish subsidies over 12 years but that was not on offer any more, if indeed it ever had been. So the planned referendum for May 2001 was cancelled.

Interestingly, the elections in May 2002 produced a stalemate between the pro- and anti-independence parties suggesting that the groundswell in favour of a split with Denmark was not as powerful as Kallsberg had hoped. Since then, the islands have adopted a policy of gradually taking greater control of the school and health systems, with less dependence on Danish grants, along with attempts at economic diversification to protect the islands from future upheavals in the fishing industry. The discovery of oil deposits has excited a lot of optimism for the future, not least because Denmark signed away any rights to oil and mineral finds before the discovery was made. So far it seems the oil may be hard to extract and, while the first drilling started in 2001, nobody is anticipating a quick bonanza.

The Faroese have learned the hard way to temper their enthusiasm. But few could deny that a country that had one of the world's first parliaments more than a thousand years ago has shown admirable patience in its relations with its more powerful neighbours.

GOVERNMENT AND POLITICS

Since the Home Rule Act, passed on March 23 1948, the Faroe Islands have been a self-governing region of the Kingdom of Denmark. They have their own Prime Minister and government, parliament, flag, currency (albeit tied to that of Denmark), national airline – even football team. Unlike Denmark, the Faroes are not part of the European Union and all trade with EU countries is governed by specially negotiated treaties drawn up in consultation and co-operation with the Danish foreign ministry. The islands are represented in the Danish parliament, the *Folketing*, by two MPs. Although to all intents and purposes the islands are self-governing, Denmark is still responsible for policing, defence and justice. However, it is the intention of the Faroese administration to gradually take control of all the islands' affairs in preparation for the possibility of full independence some time in the future. Public opinion, however, remains divided on the issue of independence – not least because the generous subsidies which the Danes pour into the islands, funding everything from childcare to healthcare, would cease, leaving the Faroese totally dependent on their own resources for continued prosperity.

ECONOMY
Fishing
The Faroese economy is totally dependent on fishing and fish rearing and the islands operate a 200-mile exclusive fisheries zone offshore. Fisheries products, including farmed salmon, account for more than 95% of total exports and nearly half of the Faroese gross domestic product. Few other countries have such a degree of dependency on living marine resources, hence safeguarding the marine environment and ensuring its sustainable use are top priorities for the Faroese government. With around 190 fishing vessels working the waters of the North Atlantic, the fishing fleet is among the most modern afloat, comprising mainly coastal vessels and long-liners as well as a number of ocean-going trawlers. The islands operate a fisheries management system of fishing days, rather than quotas, which entitles vessels to fish for a set number of days per year irrespective of how much fish they catch. In recent years the Faroese fish-farming industry has undergone tremendous growth and today represents a significant component of the country's economic activity. The clean temperate waters around the islands are ideal for fish farming, particularly of Atlantic salmon, and most islands in the archipelago have now one or two fish farms in operation.

Whaling
Although many different species of whales occur in the waters around the Faroe Islands, the only whales the Faroese catch today are small pilot whales which are driven ashore into shallow bays and killed by a deep cut through the spinal cord: death is almost immediate. Pilot whales, so called in English because of their habit of following a leader or pilot and known as *grindhvalur* in Faroese, are actually a species of large dolphin and can be found across the North Atlantic from Canada to Norway. The whales are not on the endangered species list drawn up by the International Whaling Commission and experts estimate there are around 700,000 pilot whales in the North Atlantic. The Faroese catch around 900 whales each year in several drives. The

meat and blubber have long been a staple part of the national diet. Whales are shared among the participants in a whale drive and residents of the local district where they are landed.

Whaling began with the settlement of the Faroes in the 800s, though it wasn't until 1584 that records began to be kept recording the numbers killed and documenting strandings of pilot whale schools. When commercial whaling began in the second half of the 20th century it was blubber rather than meat that was the most sought-after product. The blubber was boiled down on site into oil which was then used for heating and the production of soaps and cosmetics. Then, in the 1970s and '80s, a market developed in Japan for whale meat. Whales were caught in the Faroes until 1984 (the last big whale caught in the islands was a fin whale winched ashore at the former whaling station, við Áir, on Streymoy) when protests were reaching a peak and environmental groups such as Greenpeace began flexing their muscles, calling for boycotts of seafood from whale-hunting nations. Public opinion in the Faroes is strongly in favour of whaling and most people would like to see a resumption. The government in Tórshavn is closely following the situation in neighbouring Iceland where scientific (minke) whaling was recommenced for the first time in 14 years in August 2003. If Iceland successfully resumes commercial whaling within the jurisdiction of the IWC in the future, calls will no doubt increase in the Faroes for a similar move.

PEOPLE AND CULTURE

According to the latest demographic figures available for the Faroes, 47,700 people live in the islands, 18,420 (about 40%) of them in the capital, Tórshavn, and 5,250 (11%) in Klaksvík, the country's second town on the island of Borðoy. The population of the other main islands is: Suðuroy 5,100 (10%); Sandoy 1,450 (3%); northern islands excluding Klaksvík 750 (1.5%); Eysturoy 10,500 (21.5%); Vágar 2,800 (6%); and Streymoy excluding Tórshavn 3,300 (7%). Population density in the Faroes is 34 people per km², considerably more than Iceland's 3 per km² though much less than Denmark's 124 per km². The Faroese are of Scandinavian origin, descendants of Vikings who came originally from southwestern Norway. It's estimated that around 25,000 Faroese now live in Denmark bringing the total number of speakers of Faroese to around 70,000. Although there are a number of Danes living in the islands, and small numbers of other nationalities, immigration to the Faroes is still relatively small. It is not common to see any other skin colour than white in the islands.

Language

Today, **Faroese** is the official language of the Faroe Islands used in schools, administration, the Church and the media. A Viking tongue, brought to the islands with the first settlers around AD800, it's a grammatically complicated language, composed of many case endings, genders and dialects, which not surprisingly few visitors take the trouble to learn. However, its history is a fascinating, and ultimately successful, struggle for survival against much more prestigious Danish, the national tongue of a Kingdom and Empire. Indeed,

Faroese is one of only two languages (both variants of Old Norse, the language spoken in Scandinavia during the Viking period) exported by the Vikings, which still exists today. Between the 13th and 18th centuries the Norse spoken in the Scottish Hebrides, the Isle of Man, Orkney and Shetland died out, with the result that Faroese and Icelandic are today the closest relatives to the original language of the Vikings.

Delve into the history of Faroese and you'll quickly come up with some quite remarkable facts: the first monolingual Faroese–Faroese dictionary was only published in 1998, the first Bible in Faroese didn't appear until 1961 and the language only won official status in the islands in 1948 with the introduction of the Home Rule Act. The reason for this rather late coming-of-age is quite simple: over the centuries Faroese, little more than a ragtag of dialects spoken by farmers and fishermen with no written form, always played second fiddle to **Danish**, the respected language of merchants and officials. In 1380, when Norway and its dependencies, which then included the Faroe Islands, became part of the Dano-Norwegian kingdom, the status of Danish as the official language of the crown was confirmed right across the new kingdom, including the far-flung Faroes, which few people in Denmark at the time had even heard of. It was a status that the Reformation only served to reinforce – Luther's aim was that the word of God be translated from Latin into the language of the people, which, in the view of the Danish Church, was most definitely Danish. For over 400 years during the period of Danish administration, Faroese stagnated; it remained little more than a collection of peasant dialects spoken by countryfolk amongst each other. Any communication with the authorities had to be carried out in Danish since no official could speak, or indeed had any intention of learning, Faroese. In fact, it wasn't until 1823 that the first Faroese text, the Gospel of St Matthew, was published in Faroese. Ironically, it was met with much derision by the islanders themselves and the experiment wasn't repeated for another 20 years. A similar problem was encountered in 1856 when the theologian, **V U Hammerschaimb**, chose to preach in Faroese rather than Danish, the official language of the Church; there was great indignation amongst the congregation who didn't deem their lowly tongue worthy of the great words of God. The abolition of the Danish trade monopoly the same year marked a turning point in the islands and in the fortunes of the Faroese language. People became more mobile, trade (and ultimately contact with the outside world) increased and in the 1870s the Faroese began sloop fishing, laying the first tentative steps towards economic growth and independence – national confidence and linguistic credibility naturally increased. Although compulsory schooling was introduced by the Copenhagen authorities in 1840, the language of instruction remained Danish and the range of subjects heavily Denmark-orientated. It was a common complaint amongst Faroese students that they learnt everything about the history of Denmark from the Stone Age to the present day yet nothing about their own country or traditions. In fact, oral Faroese only became an official subject in the curriculum in 1912, the written version of the language being introduced in 1920. As late as 1938 Danish remained the official language of education in the Faroe Islands. However, following World War II, the Home Rule Act of 1948, which made the islands a self-governing region of the Kingdom of Denmark, finally brought official recognition of the Faroese language, which, today, is the national language of the Faroe Islands. Danish, however, still has official status with Faroese in public affairs and all laws passed by the Faroese parliament are painstakingly translated into Danish. Yet, the battle is still not won. Faroese, a language spoken by around 48,000 people, is under constant pressure from Danish (many television programmes are broadcast in Danish without subtitles) and English with the result that many foreign words are seeping into the language and diluting what the Faroese claim is one of the purest languages in Europe thanks to centuries of (Danish imposed) isolation. In fact, until ten years ago, dictionaries between Faroese and any language other than Danish simply didn't exist; there is still, for example, no Faroese–English dictionary today.

For words, phrases and grammar, see *Appendix 1*, page 181.

Religion

Religion is important to the Faroese and 84% of the population belongs to the established national Church in the islands, the Evangelical–Lutheran *Føroya Kirkja*. There are 60 churches in the islands and three out of every four marriages are held in one. Around 10% of the islanders belong to the Christian Brethren (Plymouth Brethren).

Arts and culture

The arts scene in the Faroes is in its infancy. The lack of a written language for centuries combined with a subsistence lifestyle meant there was little time left for the finer things in life. Culture, as we know it, was essentially limited to the **chain dance**, which is still going strong today. The dancers hold hands to form a chain or ring which moves slowly to the left in a heavy rhythm marked by two double steps to the left and one to the right. This form of dancing began in France where it was known as the *branle simple* from where it spread across Europe, eventually reaching the Faroes, now the only place it still exists. The singing of the dancers is the only music and the texts used are mainly those of the *kvæði* – lengthy medieval ballads written in 6/4 time which tell of heroic deeds of the period. Although the ballads were never written down, they were passed orally from generation to generation and remained the sole linguistic form of Faroese until the mid-1800s. Chain dances are still held at special Faroese evenings in Tórshavn – details are included in the text.

It was in this manner, too, that the first Faroese stories were passed on, though once again they were not written down. Over the years a number of minor authors and poets came and went, but it was not until the early 20th century, with the acceptance of a standardised written language, that writing began to progress. However, it's the work of **William Heinesen**, born in Tórshavn in 1900, that really marks the beginning of the Faroese novel. Although regarded as one of the Faroes' greatest writers, Heinesen wrote in Danish, rather than Faroese, Danish considered the language of culture in his day. A similarly delayed start was also the case for the visual arts in the islands. Although several new artists are now coming to the fore, there is little tradition of painting or sculpture in the islands. The most renowned artist in the Faroes is undoubtedly **Sámal Joensen Mikines**, whose work is displayed in the National Art Gallery in Tórshavn. Drawing heavily on the unforgiving character of the Faroese landscape, his and his successors' work has produced some inspired interpretations of land, sea and sky. One of the latest stars to emerge is Tróndur Patursson, whose work with stained glass in particular has won him justifiable praise.

Practical Information

WHEN TO VISIT

Undoubtedly the best time to be in the Faroes is during the long days of **summer**. From May to the end of July, when the evenings are light and the weather is at its most stable, the islands show their best side: wild flowers grow amid the deep-green tussocky grass of the valley slopes, the waterfalls glisten against the patchwork of whites and blues of the northern sky and everywhere the air is heavy with the scent of freshly mown hay and full of the calls of thousands of birds. August and September, too, are delightful months to be in the islands, though by now the birds have stopped singing and the nights are starting to get shorter. The days, though, are still long and can be pleasantly warm – September, in particular, can be a great time to have the islands to yourself; most other tourists have left and you can hike without seeing a soul and experience the unsullied Faroese nature totally undisturbed. However, the weather now is on the change and the first of the winter storms is never far away. Although **autumn**, and especially **winter**, are not ideally suited to tourism in the Faroes, there is nevertheless a certain masochistic pleasure to be gained from being buffeted by winds and rain, the intensity of which you will probably never have experienced before. The downside, of course, is that daylight is scarce at this time of year, and in December and January, it's already starting to get dark around 14.00–14.30 – it's black by 14.30–15.00. Under a fresh fall of snow, the elemental beauty of the Faroese landscapes of mountain peaks and deep valleys is certainly breathtaking, but it's worth remembering that many attractions are closed or inaccessible during the long winter months. **Spring** brings a new lease of life to the islands, and daffodils and snowdrops are in full bloom in the Faroes way before they even start to peek out of the ground in Iceland, for example, barely an hour's flight to the north. March and April, in particular, are incredibly satisfying months to visit the country – not only can you appreciate the fresh leaves on the trees and the newly opened flowers, but the birds are starting to return, a sure sign that spring has arrived.

FAROESE HIGHLIGHTS – AND WEATHER

The Faroe Islands have three things in plenty: vast areas of unspoilt mountainous terrain perfect for hiking; vertical sea cliffs teeming with birdlife ideal for ornithologists; and picturesque villages of wooden houses topped with turf roofs waiting to be discovered. In fact, if there's a fourth thing the

WEATHER CONDITIONS

Faroese	Danish	English
skýfrítt	skyfrit	bright
smáskyggjað	let skyet	fair
skyggjað	skyet	cloudy
samdrigið	overskyet	overcast
skyggjað loft	vekslende skydække	variable clouds
tjúkt	lavt skydække	low clouds/hill fog
grátt	gråvejr	dull
támut	diset	misty/hazy
mjørki	tåget	fog/foggy
þollamjørki/mjørkaflókar	tågebanker	fogbanks
sól	sol/solskin	sun/sunny
sólglottar	solstrejf	sunny spells
turt	tørt	dry
sirm	finregn/støvregn	drizzle
regn	regn	rain
ælingur	byger	showers
hækkar	drejer	veering/backing
lækkar	drejer	veering/backing
hvirlur	vindstød	gusts
vátaslettingur	slud	sleet
heglingur	hagl	hail

Wind

Faroese	Danish	English	Beaufort wind scale	Wind m/sec
stilli/logn	stille	calm	0	0.0–0.2
fleyr	svag luftning	light air	1	0.3–1.5
lot	svag brise	light breeze	2	1.6–3.3
lítíð lot/gul	let brise	gentle breeze	3	3.4–5.4
andøvsgul	jævn brise	moderate breeze	4	5.5–7.9
frískur vindur/ stívt andøvsgul	frisk brise/ frisk vind	fresh breeze/ fresh wind	5	8.0–10.7
strúkur í vindi	kuling/hård vind	strong wind	6	10.8–13.8
hvassur vindur	stiv kuling	near gale	7	13.9–17.1
skrið	hård kuling	gale	8	17.2–20.7
stormur	storm	strong gale	9	20.8–24.4
hvassur stormur	stærk storm	storm	10	24.5–28.4
kolandi stormur	orkanagtig storm	violent storm	11	28.5–32.6
ódn	orkan	hurricane	12	32.7–36.9

Faroes are not short of either, it's **weather** – a factor which must always be calculated into a trip featuring any or all of the above. Don't forget that if the weather turns, as it often does, it's alarmingly easy to become stranded on one or other Faroe Island (it has happened to me on several occasions) with no choice but to batten down the hatches and sit it out.

If you have only a couple of days in the Faroes, it makes sense to concentrate on the capital, **Tórshavn**, and the immediate vicinity, perhaps adding in a visit to the medieval cathedral at **Kirkjubøur** or a boat trip across to **Nólsoy**. With a little more time, it's definitely worth seeing the spectacular bird cliffs at **Vestmanna**, a boat tour every visitor to the islands should try to make, and taking a trip anywhere by helicopter – most dramatically past the remote outpost of **Stóra Dímun**. An ideal week's holiday in the islands could include all the above plus a trip to **Mykines** to see the puffins and gannets or a visit to **Klaksvík** and a tour of the northern islands – either a hike out to one of the world's tallest vertical sea cliffs, **Enniberg** on Viðoy, or an unforgettable boat trip across stormy seas to the island of **Fugloy** where there are some wonderful coastlines to discover (returning by helicopter if you can), or a hike out to the lighthouse on northern **Kalsoy** for the best views anywhere in the country. With two weeks at your disposal it's well worth considering hiking, perhaps on **Vágar** or **Suðuroy** and touring the villages of **Streymoy** and **Eysturoy**, in particular **Saksun**, **Tjørnuvík** and **Gjógv**.

The statement that the Faroes can experience all four seasons in just one day may well have become a cliché over the years, yet it remains a fact that any visitor to the islands will become all too familiar with. A morning may start out beautifully sunny and warm, only for dark menacing clouds to roll in off the Atlantic within an hour or so, and by lunchtime it's pouring with rain. Then, slowly, the clouds disperse, there's a brilliant rainbow, and the sun comes out again by mid-afternoon – only for the wind to pick up by evening and almost knock you flat. Faroese weather is certainly very changeable and it pays to be one step ahead and have raingear with you at all times. You can best prepare any day out in the islands by looking at the weather forecasts you will find in the Faroese newspapers or on the website of the Danish Meteorological Institute which puts out regularly updated daily briefings for the Faroes at www.dmi.dk/dmi/index/faroerne.htm and a five-day forecast at www.dmi.dk/dmi/index/faroerne/femfaro.htm. Although the forecasts are in Faroese (newspapers) and in Danish (Met Institute), you should be able to work out whether you're going to be drenched, baked or swept unceremoniously into the sea by gale-force winds – a key factor in whether the helicopter will take to the air. Besides the words for weather (Faroese *veðrið*; Danish *vejr*), see box opposite for the key meteorological terms for deciphering a synopsis (Faroese *yvirlit*; Danish *oversigt*).

Daily (Mon–Fri) at around 08.45 from late May to early September there is also a weather forecast in English on Faroese national radio, Útvarp Føroya. The main frequencies are Tórshavn 89.9FM, Klaksvík 94.3FM, Suðuroy 97.5FM, Sandoy 88.5FM, Eysturoy 87.6FM, Vágar 87.9FM and across the country on 531kHz medium wave.

INFORMATION AND MAPS

The best source of information on the Faroes is the internet. The website of the **Faroese National Tourist Board** (www.visit-faroeislands.com and www.tourist.fo) should be your first port of call when trying to assemble information. The office, based in Tórshavn, also dispatches a wide variety of printed information about the islands if you write to them. Their address is Ferðaráð Føroya, Undir Bryggjubakka 17, PO Box 118, FO-110 Tórshavn. Their only office abroad is in Denmark: Færøernes Turistråd, Hovedvagtsgade 8, 2, DK-1103 København; tel: +45 33 14 83 83.

In other countries the **Danish Tourist Board** represents the Faroes and carries a certain amount of publicity material. Contact details are as follows:

Australia Level 4, 81 York St, Sydney NSW 2000; tel: 02 9262 5832
Canada Box 115, Station N, Toronto, ON M8V 3S4; tel: 416 823 9620
United Kingdom 55 Sloane St, London SW1X 9SR; tel: 020 7259 5959
United States 655 3rd Av, Suite 1810, New York, NY 10017; tel: 212 885 9700

In Ireland and New Zealand there is no Danish Tourist Board; however, the embassy and consulate respectively will have information. See page 28 for contact details.

Alternatively, should you wish for specific information relevant to Tórshavn or any of the other towns or islands, it's better to contact the individual tourist office or *kunningastova* concerned; see the individual entries in the text for details.

Maps

The best **map** of the Faroes is the *Føroyar Topografiskt Atlas 1:100 000* by the Danish Cartographical Institute, Kort & Matrikelstyrelsen. It is readily available in the bookshops in Tórshavn and costs around 120kr. For more detailed mapping, particularly for hiking purposes, you should get hold of the *Føroyar Topografiskt kort 1:20 000* by the same publisher which break the islands down into 37 individual sheets; they, once again, are readily available in Tórshavn and cost 65kr each.

TOUR OPERATORS

Although the Faroes are geared up for individual travel, with a full range of accommodation and transport options to ensure a trouble-free stay, there are a number of tour operators who also specialise in holidays to the islands. The main ones are listed below.

United Kingdom

Brightwater Holidays Tel: 01334 657155; email: info@brightwaterholidays.com; www.brightwaterholidays.com
Chiltern Trains Tel: 01844 353500; email: enquiries@chilterntrains.com; www.chilterntrains.com
Discover the World Tel: 01737 218801; email: sales@discovertheworld.co.uk; www.discovertheworld.co.uk

Donald Mackenzie Travel Tel: 0141 221 4333; email: travelshop@donaldmackenzie.com; www.donaldmackenzie.com
Explore Worldwide Tel: 01252 760000; email: info@exploreworldwide.com; www.exploreworldwide.com
Icelandair Tel: 0870 443 2372 (England and Wales); tel: 0845 758 1111 (Scotland); www.icelandair.co.uk
Island Holidays Tel: 01764 670107; email: enquiries@islandholidays.net; www.islandholidays.net
North West Frontiers Tel: 01854 612628; email: andy@nwfdrontiers.com; www.nwfrontiers.com
Scantours Tel: 020 7839 0927; email: scantoursuk@dial.pipex.com; www.scantours.co.uk
Scot Rail Tel: 0870 161 0161; email: scotrailshortbreaks@uk2.net; www.scotrail.co.uk
Scotsell Tel: 0141 558 0100; email: holidays@scotsell.com; www.scotsell.com
Smyril Line Tel: 01595 690845; email: office@smyril-line.fo; www.smyril-line.com

USA
5 Stars of Scandinavia Tel: +1 253 857 4852; email: info@5stars-of-scandinavia.com; www.5stars-of-scandinavia.com

Canada
Great Canadian Travel Company Tel: +1 204 949 0199; fax: +1 204 949 0188; email: north@gctc-mst.com; www.greatcanadiantravel.com

Australia
Bentours International Tel: +61 2 9241 1353; email: scandinavia@bentours.com.au; www.bentours.com.au

EMBASSIES, CONSULATES AND REPRESENTATION
Faroese Representation in the UK
In the United Kingdom, the Faroe Islands now proudly have their own mission whose aim is to further ties with its biggest neighbour. It was founded in September 2002 on the initiative of the Faroese government in collaboration with the Danish Ministry of Foreign Affairs. Before then the Faroese Representation had simply been part of the Danish Embassy in London. The move is part of the ongoing efforts by the Faroese government to take control of as much of the islands' affairs as is practically possible.

United Kingdom Sendistova Føroya, Representation of the Faroes, 55 Sloane St, London SW1X 9SR; tel: 020 7333 0227; email: faroes.representation.uk@tinganes.fo; web: www.faroeislands.org.uk

Although the Representation cannot issue visas for anyone living in the UK who may need one to visit the islands (not UK citizens – see below), it does provide general information about the country, particularly in the fields of trade and commerce.

Embassies and consulates

Elsewhere abroad, the Faroe Islands are represented by Denmark which has embassies and consulates around the world. European Union, US, Canadian, Australian and New Zealand nationals need only a valid passport to enter the Faroe Islands for up to three months. Some other nationalities require an entry visa for Denmark – consult your Danish embassy or consulate in your home country for further information and note that a Danish visa does not give the right to enter the Faroes unless specifically stated.

United Kingdom Royal Danish Embassy, 55 Sloane St, London SW1X 9SR; tel: 020 7333 0200; email: lonamb@um.dk; www.denmark.org.uk
United States Royal Danish Embassy, 3200 Whitehaven St, NW, Washington DC 20008–3683; tel: 202 234 4300; email: wasamb@um.dk; www.denmarkemb.org
Australia Royal Danish Consulate General in Sydney, Level 14, Gold Fields House, 1 Alfred St, Circular Quay, Sydney NSW 2000, tel: 02 9247 2224; email: dtcsydney@dtcsyd.org.au
Canada Royal Danish Embassy, 47 Clarence St, Suite 450, Ottawa, Ontario K1N 9K1; tel: 613 562 1811; email: ottamb@um.dk; www.danish-embassy-canada.com
Ireland Royal Danish Embassy, 121–22 St Stephen's Green, Dublin 2; tel: 01 475 6404; email: embassy@denmark.ie; www.denmark.ie
New Zealand Royal Danish Consulate General in Wellington, Level 7, Forsyth Barr House, 45 Johnston St, PO Box 10–874, Wellington 6063; tel: 04 471 0520; email: consulate@brc.co.nz

GETTING THERE AND AWAY
By air

The quickest and easiest way to reach the Faroe Islands is by air. Since November 2004 services to the islands have been operated by the national airline, **Atlantic Airways** (tel: +298 34 10 10; fax: +298 34 10 01; email: booking@atlantic.fo; web: www.atlantic.fo).

From the United Kingdom

The most useful routes from the UK are Aberdeen–Faroes (all year, twice weekly; 1 hour) and London Stansted–Faroes (late March to late October twice weekly; 2 hours). The international airline code for Atlantic Airways is RC; the airport codes are FAE (Faroes); ABZ (Aberdeen) and STN (London Stansted).

When the London service is not running, connections can be made via Aberdeen from airports across the UK and Ireland as follows:

from Belfast International (Eastern Airways); Birmingham (British Airways); Bristol (Eastern Airways); Dublin (Ryanair); Glasgow (British Airways); Humberside (Eastern Airways); Leeds Bradford (Eastern Airways); London Heathrow (bmi and British Airways); London Gatwick (British Airways); London Luton (easyJet); Manchester (bmi and British Airways); Newcastle (Eastern Airways); Norwich (bmi and Eastern Airways); Nottingham East Midlands (Eastern Airways); Orkney (British Airways); Shetland (British Airways); Southampton (Eastern Airways); Teesside (Eastern Airways); Wick (Eastern Airways). Useful websites are:

bmi www.flybmi.com
British Airways www.ba.com
Eastern Airways www.easternairways.com
easyJet www.easyjet.com/en
Ryanair www.ryanair.com

If you're connecting at Aberdeen from a regional airport, you'll need to buy two separate tickets – one to Aberdeen, and a second one with Atlantic on to the Faroes.

From mainland Europe

Another option, and one which suits travellers coming from mainland Europe, is to travel **via Denmark**. Atlantic flies Copenhagen–Faroes all year, two or three times daily late October to late March, rising to three to four daily during the summer; 2 hours) and Billund–Faroes all year (two weekly from late October to late March, rising to daily during the summer; 2 hours).

Connections in Copenhagen (and more restrictively through Billund) are available with the Danish airline, Maersk (tel: 45 70 10 74 74; email: reservation@maersk-air.dk; web: www.maersk-air.com; airline code DM) from many cities in Europe (including London Gatwick and Manchester in the UK). Maersk also sell onward connections to the Faroes with Atlantic on a codeshare basis, ie: with a DM flight number.

Several other airlines fly to Copenhagen from across Europe. The most useful operators are British Airways (www.ba.com); easyJet (www.easyjet.com); Lufthansa (www.lufthansa.com); and SAS Scandinavian Airlines (www.scandinavian.net). The relevant airport codes are CPH (Copenhagen) and BLL (Billund).

If you're travelling to the Faroes **from Norway**, it's probably more convenient to take the direct Atlantic Airways flight from Oslo Gardemoen (OSL) which operates from late June to mid-August.

From the United States and Canada

The best way to reach the Faroes **from the USA** is to travel via Reykjavík with Icelandair (www.icelandair.com; airline code FI) or via Copenhagen with SAS (www.scandinavian.net; airline code SK). Remember though that you'll need to change airports in Iceland (Icelandair flights arrive at the main international airport, Keflavík, and onward Atlantic Airways flights to the Faroes (1 hour) leave from Reykjavík city airport; both airports are linked by transfer bus). The airport codes are KEF (Keflavík) and RKV (Reykjavík city). Icelandair currently fly from Baltimore, Boston, Minneapolis, New York (JFK) and Orlando to Keflavík. **From Canada**, pick up a flight to one of Icelandair's east-coast gateways and transfer there for Iceland and then on to the Faroes. SAS fly from New York (Newark), Chicago and Seattle to Copenhagen.

From the rest of the world

Getting to the Faroes from the rest of the world naturally involves first reaching either London or Copenhagen, from where connections are available as described above. It's worth remembering, though, that many online travel websites, such as Expedia, do not sell Atlantic Airways tickets. The best place to buy an Atlantic ticket is directly with the airline on their website, www.atlantic.fo.

Fares to the islands have fallen dramatically over recent years and there are now occasional special offers available on the Atlantic website which can bring the cost down further – make them your first port of call when shopping around for the best deal. Atlantic are keen to build up their London Stansted route and may have special fares on it (at the time of writing, for example, they were offering a single ticket STN–FAE for £69 before tax). Regular Atlantic fares are roughly as follows: STN–FAE £278 return; ABZ–FAE from £190 return; CPH–STN from 2,378 Danish kroner; BLL–FAE from 2,413 Danish kroner. Although Atlantic don't have an office in the United Kingdom, it's possible to buy tickets through Icelandair in London: 3rd Floor, 172 Tottenham Court Road, London W1T 7LY; tel: 0870 443 2372; fax: 020 7387 5711.

By sea

If you prefer not to fly, it's also possible to travel to the Faroes by sea: the Faroese-owned **Smyril Line** (J Broncksgøta 37, PO Box 370, FO-110 Tórshavn; tel: +298 34 59 00; fax: +298 34 59 50; email: office@smyril-line.fo; web: www.smyril-line.com) connects the islands with **Lerwick** in Shetland, **Hanstholm** in Denmark and **Bergen** in Norway all year round, extending up to **Seyðisfjörður** on the east coast of Iceland in summer (May to mid-September).

Timetabling is complicated but essentially from mid-September to late April, the *Norröna* sails a weekly route as indicated in the box opposite. Connections are available in Lerwick from the rest of the UK by taking the overnight ferry from Aberdeen to Shetland: winter northbound Aberdeen Sat 17.00, arrive Lerwick Sun 07.00 connecting on Sun 13.00 to Tórshavn or, alternatively, on Thu with a longer connection time in Lerwick (arrive 07.00 from Aberdeen, leave again 22.00 for Tórshavn); summer northbound Aberdeen Mon 18.00, arrive Lerwick Tue 08.00, connecting on Wed 02.00 for Tórshavn.

For the 2003 summer season, Smyril Line introduced a new superferry on their circuit of the North Atlantic. The new *Norröna* is the last word in luxury: shopping arcade, bars, nightclub, sauna and solarium, swimming pool and fitness centre are all on board. Weighing in at a whopping 36,000 tons and measuring 164m in length and 30m wide, she can carry nearly 1,500 passengers

SMYRIL LINE TIMETABLE: NORRÖNA

Smyril Line's timetabling is complicated, but essentially the *Norröna* sails a weekly route as follows, depending on the time of year. All times given are departure times, unless stated.

Mid September–April

Departure	Day	Time
Hanstholm	Sat	15.00
Lerwick	Sun	13.00
Tórshavn	Mon	10.00
Bergen	Wed	11.00
Lerwick	Wed	24.00
Tórshavn	Thu	22.00
Lerwick	Fri	13.00
Hanstholm (*arr*)	Sat	11.00

May–mid September

Hanstholm	Sat	20.00
Tórshavn	Mon	08.30
Lerwick	Mon	22.30
Bergen	Tue	15.00
Lerwick	Wed	02.00
Tórshavn	Wed	18.00
Seyðisfjörður	Thu	12.00
Tórshavn	Fri	08.30
Lerwick	Fri	21.30
Hanstholm (*arr*)	Sat	16.00

and 800 cars with a service speed of 21 knots. The new ship is a far cry from the previous *Norröna*, which was long overdue for retirement – however, the sheer size of the new vessel (complete with new terminal building in the tiny Tórshavn harbour) has created problems. Manoeuvring her into the harbour when she's being buffeted by strong cross winds is no mean feat. Although there can be no doubt that sailing the North Atlantic to the Faroes in the wake of the Vikings is a wonderfully romantic notion, it's really only recommended for those who want to take a vehicle with them on holiday – and for those with a cast-iron stomach. Although the *Norröna* is stabilised, being caught far out at sea with nothing to break the swells and towering waves sweeping in unopposed from the coast of North America is certainly not to everyone's liking.

Fares

Fares are ludicrously high in high season (low-season fares, essentially May to early June and mid-August to September, are in brackets). A return ticket from Lerwick to the Faroes in high season in a couchette is £144 (£104) rising to £448 (£336) for a two-berth cabin; a car in high season is £112 (£84). Remember, though, that these are fares from Shetland and you will need to add on a further £219 per passenger in a two-berth cabin or £59 for a reclining seat for the return journey from Aberdeen to Shetland – these are the high-season prices. Annoyingly, because these routes are operated by different companies, it is not possible to sell one through-ticket for Aberdeen–Lerwick–Tórshavn, although bookings can be made at the Smyril Line office in Lerwick for each leg of the journey.

A number of **discounts** are available between Shetland and the Faroes: children under 6 years of age travel free; those aged 6–15 receive a 50% discount; senior citizens are entitled to 25% off the standard fares, whereas students under 26 get 25% discount on couchette fares against presentation of valid identification.

Although it's possible to book tickets on the Smyril Line website, the company also has representatives around the world (there's a full listing on the website) who will also sell tickets to individuals. The main ones are:

Smyril Line Shetland The Gutters' Hut, North Ness Business Park, Lerwick ZE1 0LZ; tel: 01595 690845; fax: 01595 692287; email: office@smyril-line.co.uk; www.smyril-line.com

Smyril Line Danmark Trafikhavnsgade 7, DK-7730 Hanstholm, Denmark; tel: +45 96 55 03 60; fax: +45 96 55 03 61; email: office@smyril-line.dk

USA 5 Stars of Scandinavia, 13104 Thomas Rd KPN, Gig Harbor, Washington DC 98329; 2914 Yelm Hwy SE # 27, Olympia, Washington DC 98501; tel: +1 360 923 0125; + 1 360 923 0488; email: info@5stars-of-scandinavia.com; www.5-stars-of-scandinavia.com

Canada Great Canadian Travel Company, 273 Donald St, Winnipeg, Manitoba; tel: +1 204 949 0199; fax: +1 204 949 0188; email: north@gctc-mst.com; www.greatcanadiantravel.com

Australia Bentours International, Suite 3, Level 7, 189 Kent St, Sydney NSW 2000; tel: +61 2 9241 1353; fax: +61 2 921 1574; email: scandinavia@bentours.com.au; www.bentours.com.au

HEALTH AND SAFETY

The health risks while travelling in the Faroe Islands are minimal and health care is of an excellent standard. Language is rarely a problem and health workers are generally proficient in English. However, should you encounter any communication problems, the local tourist office should be able to point you in the direction of a doctor or dentist who does speak English. Under Faroese law, a national of any country is entitled to emergency health care in the case of an accident; it is the responsibility of the individual doctor treating you to decide just what 'emergency care' consists of. If, however, you suffer from a medical condition requiring regular treatment or medication, this is not free and you will have to pay for all treatment received. It is necessary to present your passport at the hospital to receive any form of emergency care. It goes without saying that you should have comprehensive travel insurance.

As far as safety is concerned, the main risks are the Faroese landscapes – vertical sea cliffs that drop into the sea from a height of up to 900m should obviously be approached with great care. It's also important to remember that when you're out in the countryside the weather can change at any moment and hiking conditions can very quickly become hazardous; however, with common sense, it's unlikely you'll encounter serious danger. In relation to crime, the Faroes are one of the safest parts of the world you will ever visit: police figures put the yearly number of break-ins and cases of theft at barely 500 for the entire country.

Women and gay travellers

Women travelling alone are unlikely to encounter any problems. Faroese males are generally well mannered and far too shy to create trouble. On Friday and Saturday nights in Tórshavn, when the beer starts to flow, it's obviously sensible to keep your wits about you, but, once again, you're unlikely to become the target of abusive behaviour. Gay travellers will have to forego the pleasures of gay bars and clubs whilst in the Faroes – quite simply, there is no gay scene whatsoever. Attitudes towards homosexuality are generally tolerant, though older people's views are often tempered by their religious beliefs. The sight of a same-sex couple walking hand in hand through a remote Faroese village is likely to cause quite a stir so it's probably best to keep outward shows of affection for private.

WHAT TO TAKE

The first thing to pack when planning a trip to the Faroes is a decent **waterproof jacket**. If you're considering hiking, a good pair of **sturdy waterproof boots and trousers** are essential – you will doubtless find yourself on marshy ground at some point on your wanderings, even if it doesn't rain (unlikely) during your stay. Don't be tempted to bring an umbrella as they are no use whatsoever in the Faroes – it will only be blown inside out by the strong winds. A **waterproof cover for your rucksack** is also a wise thing to pack in your luggage. As crazy as it may sound for a summer holiday, it's also a good idea to take a pair of **gloves** and even a **woolly hat** with you because even in the middle of July up on the mountains it can be chilly when the wind blows. In order to hear the English-language weather forecast broadcast during the summer months by Faroese radio, a **small portable radio** can also be useful. Also consider taking a **torch** with you if you're camping and an **alarm clock** is handy for early-morning buses and ferries. If you're planning on taking photographs during your stay, you'll save money by buying your **films** at home (or at the airport when you leave) rather than in the Faroes, where they are generally more expensive and not always easy to find outside the main villages.

As far as electricity is concerned, the Faroese supply is 220V and all plugs are the northern European two-pin standard (the same as throughout the rest of Scandinavia), for which **adaptors** are readily available at major airports.

MONEY AND COSTS

There are two **currencies** in the Faroe Islands, both of which have equal value: the **Faroese króna** and the **Danish krone**. Although you'll find both Faroese

HINTS ON PHOTOGRAPHY
Nick Garbutt and John Jones

All sorts of photographic opportunities present themselves in the islands, from holiday snaps to that close-up encounter with a puffin. For the best results, give some thought to the following tips.

As a general rule, if it doesn't look good through the viewfinder, it will never look good as a picture. Don't take photographs for the sake of taking them; be patient and wait until the image looks right.

Photographing **people** is never easy and more often than not it requires a fair share of luck. If you want to take a portrait shot of a stranger, it is always best to ask first. Focus on the eyes of your subject since they are the most powerful ingredient of any portrait, and be prepared for the unexpected.

There is no mystique to good **wildlife** photography. The secret is getting into the right place at the right time and then knowing what to do when you are there. Look for striking poses, aspects of behaviour and distinctive features. Try not only to take pictures of the species itself, but also to illustrate it within the context of its environment. Alternatively, focus in close on a characteristic which can be emphasised.

- Photographically, the eyes are the most important part of an animal – focus on these, make sure they are sharp and try to ensure they contain a highlight.
- Look at the surroundings – there is nothing worse than a distracting twig or highlighted leaf lurking in the background. Getting this right is often the difference between a mediocre and a memorable image.
- A powerful flashgun adds the option of punching in extra light to

and Danish notes in circulation, only Danish coins are used. Notes come in denominations of 1,000kr, 500kr, 200kr, 100kr and 50kr; coins in 20kr, 10kr, 5kr, 2kr and 1kr. Occasionally you may also come across 50 and 25 øre coins, ie: half and one quarter of one krone. Since Denmark is not yet part of the eurozone, the European Union's single-currency area, it is not possible to spend euro in the Faroes. If Denmark does eventually join the euro, it's still unclear whether the European single currency will become legal tender in the islands since the Faroes are not part of the European Union yet are part of the Kingdom of Denmark. In October 2004, exchange rates for the Danish krone were roughly £1 = 10.24 Danish kroner, US$1 = 6 Danish kroner and €1 = 7.44 Danish kroner.

The best way to get money in the Faroes is by using a debit card which has a Cirrus facility on it. This makes it possible to withdraw money from cashpoints much as you would do at home. Although there is a small charge levied by banks for this purpose, it is generally less than you would pay in bank commissions when exchanging travellers' cheques – the other main way of accessing cash in the islands. The use of credit cards such as Visa and transform an otherwise dreary picture. Artificial light is no substitute for natural light, though, so use it judiciously.

- Getting close to the subject correspondingly reduces the depth of field. At camera-to-subject distances of less than a metre, apertures between f16 and f32 are necessary to ensure adequate depth of field. This means using flash to provide enough light. If possible, use one or two small flashguns to illuminate the subject from the side.

Landscapes are forever changing, even on a daily basis. Good landscape photography is all about good light and capturing mood. Generally the first and last two hours of daylight are best, or when peculiar climatic conditions add drama or emphasise distinctive features. Never place the horizon in the centre – in your mind's eye divide the frame into thirds and either exaggerate the land or the sky.

Film

If you're using conventional film (as against a digital camera), select the right film for your needs. Film speed (ISO number) indicates the sensitivity of the film to light. The lower the number, the less sensitive the film, but the better quality the final image. For general print film, ISO 100 or 200 fit the bill perfectly. If you are using transparencies for home use or for lectures, then again ISO 100 or 200 film is fine. However, if you want to get your work published, the superior quality of ISO 25 to 100 film is best.

- Try to keep your film cool. Never leave it in direct sunlight.
- Don't allow fast film (ISO 800 and above) to pass through X-ray machines.
- Under weak light conditions use a faster film (ISO 200 or 400).

Mastercard is widespread and provides another way of paying for goods and also, of course, for withdrawing cash on credit. The advantage of credit and debit cards over travellers' cheques naturally is that you are not bound to banking hours and can essentially draw money whenever you choose from a hole in the wall. **Banks** in Tórshavn are generally open Monday–Friday 09.00–16.00, with longer hours on Thursday until 18.00.

Costs and budgeting

Costs in the Faroe Islands are roughly in line with those you'll find in other countries in northern Europe. Accommodation, eating out and domestic travel, although not especially cheap, are on the whole good value. There are, though, two notable exceptions to the above statement. Alcohol is likely to be a third more expensive than you're used to paying at home (in a restaurant a bottle of wine costs around 200kr, whereas a half-litre of beer in a bar is about 50kr); and travel by helicopter is an absolute bargain – 215kr, for example, is all it costs to fly from Tórshavn out to Mykines.

Although tipping and bargaining are not expected in the Faroes, you may wish to round a restaurant bill up to the nearest large number, for example 126kr becomes 130kr, as a small sign of your appreciation.

When it comes to budgeting for a trip you should be able to get by on around 300–350kr per day if you're staying in a youth hostel, self-catering and not making too many trips around; 450–650kr if you want to stay in a guesthouse (sharing a room with one other person), eat out in a restaurant every so often and go for a couple of beers; and upwards of 700kr per day per person for (shared) hotel accommodation, sightseeing trips and eating out with alcohol.

GETTING AROUND THE ISLANDS

Travel around the Faroe Islands is a doddle. All 17 inhabited islands are connected by bus, ferry or helicopter – and in a couple of instances by all three – operated by Strandfaraskip Landsins (Yviri við Strond 4, PO Box 88, FO-110 Tórshavn; tel: 34 30 00) and Atlantic Airways (tel: 34 10 60; web: www.atlantic.fo) respectively. Details of all public transport (bus and ferry) are kept up to date at www.ssl.fo, where you'll find timetables and fares. For information on the helicopter service check out Atlantic Airways' website and select *Tyrlan* – the Faroese word for helicopter, at the top of the homepage.

The **helicopter** service is incredibly good value – short hops between islands can cost as little as 85kr and the single fare from the most northerly islands to the other end of the country is a mere 360kr; government subsidies are responsible. Fares on buses and ferries are equally low and services are dependable; most ferry routes cost 35kr one way, whereas it's 75kr for the Tórshavn–Drelsnes run – the equivalent prices for a car (where carried) are 90kr and 130kr. The following are examples of through-ticket prices (bus and ferry if required) from Tórshavn: Mykines 160kr; Tjørnuvík 60kr; Dalur 85kr; Gjógv 50kr; Airport 100kr; Klaksvík 95kr; Trøllanes 160kr; Fugloy 140kr. If you're spending any length of time in the Faroes and intend to travel extensively, it makes sense to buy an SL visitor travel card which allows unlimited use of all buses and ferries in the country. The card is valid for either four or seven days and costs 600 or 900kr respectively (children aged 7–13 years are entitled to a 50% reduction). It can be bought on arrival at the airport in Vágar from the tourist information desk in the terminal or alternatively in Tórshavn from the Farstøðin bus terminal at the harbour. You'll often find that if your journey involves changing from bus to ferry or vice versa departures are timed to correspond perfectly making travel a dream.

Bus services on the main routes are frequent, though out of the summer months some routes are suspended. **Ferries** operate on the following routes: Tórshavn–Drelsnes (Suðuroy); Tórshavn–Nólsoy; Gamlarætt–Skopun (Sandoy); Gamlarætt–Hestur; Sandur (Sandoy)–Skúgvoy; Sørvágur (Vágar)–Mykines; Leirvík–Klaksvík; Klaksvík–Syðradalur (Kalsoy) and Hvannasund (Viðoy)–Svínoy and Fugloy. Of the ferries, only the services to

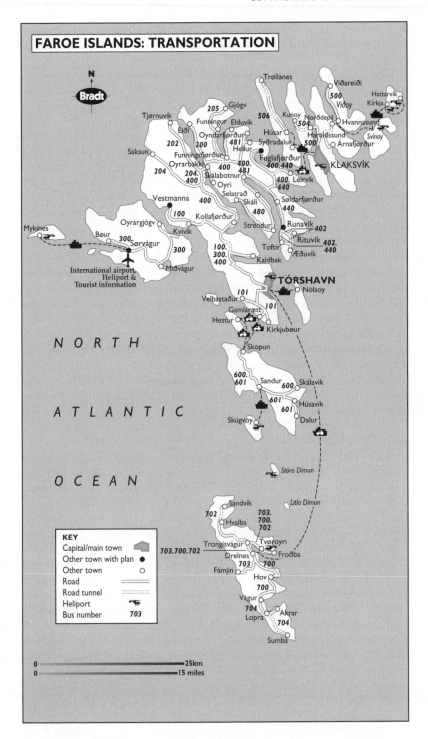

Suðuroy and Sandur take vehicles. It's not possible to book a space for a car on a ferry; you simply turn up at the quay in good time and the chances are you'll get on board.

Getting around by **car** has become much easier in recent years thanks to a plethora of tunnels which have been bored through the islands, reducing the need to navigate twisting mountain roads. Nearly all roads are sealed and wide enough to allow two lanes of traffic. Tunnels, however, are often single-lane with passing places; priority is always in one direction making it the responsibility of drivers coming in the opposite direction to pull in and stop until they can safely drive on against the direction of priority. An undersea tunnel now connects the islands of Vágar and Streymoy in the west of the country and work has begun on a second submarine connection between Eysturoy and Borðoy in the north; when this second tunnel is complete, it will then be possible to drive all the way from the Faroes' northernmost village, Viðareiði, all the way to the airport on Vágar – a journey which until recently would have required a morning and afternoon to complete. The Faroese drive on the right and use the traffic signs for international standards. The speed limit is 80km/h (60km/h for caravans) on country roads and 50km/h in built-up areas. Seatbelts are compulsory and headlights must also be used at all times, even during daylight hours. One of the hazards of driving in the Faroes is sheep – most of which seem to have an innate death wish compelling them to leap out onto the road as you approach. Should you accidentally hit a sheep you should call the police on tel: 35 14 48 and you will probably be liable to pay the owner compensation for the loss of an animal; in short, slow down and take it easy. For details of **car hire** in the Faroes, see page 53 in the *Tórshavn* chapter.

ACCOMMODATION

Outside Tórshavn finding somewhere to stay in the Faroes can be tricky since many of the villages simply don't have anywhere. We've listed all accommodation options in the text; however, it's always worth checking with the local tourist office who will know the very latest situation. In the capital, things are not nearly so bleak and there's a choice between three **hotels**, a number of **guesthouses** where you often have access to a kitchen to prepare your own meals, a **youth hostel** and a number of private homes offering **bed and breakfast** accommodation. Prices are roughly in line with what you would expect to pay in any other northern European country. The best value for money are **guesthouses** which allow you to cut costs by self-catering. There's also a limited number of **youth hostels** (web: www.farhostel.fo) and **campsites** dotted around the islands though most are only open during the summer months. Since there is no common or public land in Faroes (unlike in the other Scandinavian countries where an *Allemansrätt* or 'Everyman's Right' provides free land access to all), camping is only permitted in designated areas. It is not allowed to camp in a caravan on the roadside nor is it permitted to camp in car parks, in lay-bys or at viewpoints.

Previous page The southern coastline of Mykines (JP)

Above Gannet: the largest bird found in the Faroes (TC)

Right Wild thyme can be found throughout the islands (DP)

Below Fulmars nest in large numbers on cliff faces (TC)

EATING AND DRINKING

Similarly, the greatest choice of eating and drinking establishments can be found in Tórshavn where you will find everything from Burger King to sumptuous smorgasbord spreads of every Faroese and Nordic delicacy you care to imagine, generally served in the hotels. In the villages, though, it can often be difficult, if not impossible, to find somewhere to eat and you may well find yourself backtracking to the nearest main village to get your fill. Whilst out in the sticks, you can always rely on filling stations to hold a small selection of sandwiches and to serve up hotdog-style sausages with mustard (always very good and not nearly as hideous as you may think) and sometimes chips. If the worst comes to the worst, look for a supermarket and go self-catering; there's generally some kind of food store in all but the smallest of villages. On board the larger ferries (operating on the routes Tórshavn–Drelsnes, Gamlarætt–Skopun and Lerivík–Klaksvík), there are cafeterias serving snacks and coffee.

Faroese **breakfast**, as served in the hotels in Tórshavn, and less extravagantly elsewhere in the country, is a Scandinavian-style cold table sagging under the weight of hams, cheeses, herring, cereals, yoghurts, fruit and sometimes Danish pastries. It's a help-yourself affair and you're permitted to take as much as you like and visit the table as many times as you like, though it's somewhat frowned upon to stuff your pockets and take things with you when you leave. There are also limitless supplies of coffee and generally a rather substandard fruit drink, usually orange. The main meal of the day in the Faroe Islands is **lunch**, which, in Tórshavn at least, throws up a variety of options. Once again, most restaurants serve an extremely good value help- yourself buffet where you can eat your fill for around 65kr. A soft drink is usually included. None of these buffets is particularly traditional and the emphasis is more on pizzas, pasta, salads or indeed Chinese-style food in certain establishments. Lunchtime in the Faroes is any time between about 11.00 and 14.00, though most people tend to eat around noon or 13.00. If you're looking to save money whilst in the Faroes, switch your main meal of the day to lunchtime and you'll save a packet – have a snack in the evening instead, bought from the supermarket or bakery, and you'll make your money go much further. **Dinner** can be expensive for what you get – meals are often heavily meat (less so fish) orientated with an accompaniment of (more often than not) overcooked vegetables and masses of that Faroese staple – the potato. Sadly, due to the lack of fresh vegetables in the islands, many eateries serve cubed veggies straight out of a can. Frustratingly for a country so influenced by the sea, it can be hard to find fresh fish on the menu. You should count on around 200–250kr for an upmarket two-course restaurant dinner, though, of course, you can eat in the pizzerias and ethnic restaurants of Tórshavn for around half of that. Whilst in the Faroes, it's worth searching out and sampling some of the islands' **traditional foods**. A particular favourite is wind-dried sheep's meat, *skerpikjøt*, prepared around Christmas time and then nibbled throughout the year; virtually every home in the islands has its own *hjallur* or meat-drying outhouse. Puffin breast is also popular, and when served with a blueberry sauce, verges on the divine. Pilot whale meat and blubber is occasionally also available on the menu (particularly at a Faroese evening or on the Faroese smorgasbord served up during the summer at Hotel Hafnia in Tórshavn) though is somewhat of an acquired taste. Look out too for roast lamb and boiled wind-dried fish, *ræstur fiskur* – two other delicacies. Popular fish dishes (should you be able to find them on the menu) include haddock, halibut, plaice and salmon. What will push the bill up is alcohol; a bottle of wine is roughly around 200kr, a draught beer usually starts at 40kr. It's much cheaper to do your drinking at home – which is what many of the Faroese also do. Due to a strong temperance movement (and religious objections), alcohol has only been (relatively) freely available in the islands since 1992. Before then the Faroes practised a system of public prohibition and every bottle of the hard stuff (including wine) had to be shipped in from Denmark and was doled out in rations. Mercifully, the Faroes have now entered the modern age and alcohol is more readily available – albeit restricted by some bizarre legislation. Forget any notion of nipping into the nearest supermarket to buy a bottle of wine for dinner because alcohol is not available in the shops. The only place to buy any form of alcohol, be it strong beer, wine or spirits, is the sexily named **Rúsdrekkasølin Landsins** (literally 'the country's alcohol sale'), a state-run monolith responsible for all-things alcoholic. Opening times are limited (listed in the text) and you'll find only six of these liquor stores in the entire country; they're located in Klaksvík (Borðoy); Miðvágur (Vágar); Saltangará (Eysturoy); Skálavík (Sandoy); Tórshavn (Streymoy) and Tvøroyri (Suðuroy). In short, if you're heading out into the wilds, stock up before you leave town or you'll be left with the pathetically weak fizzy beverage sold in supermarkets, *ljóst pilsnar*, purporting to be beer yet with an alcohol content of barely 2.8%.

PUBLIC HOLIDAYS

Despite the restricted sale of alcohol throughout the islands, there's certainly no shortage of the stuff during **Ólavsøka** (literally 'the wake of St Olav'), the principal public holiday and national festival, held on July 28 and 29. People from across the country flood into Tórshavn for the festivities held in honour of the islands' patron saint, the Norwegian king, **Olav**, who fell in battle at Stiklestad in Norway on July 29 1030. At this time, the Faroes were governed by Norway and all disputes were settled there. Hence, it was natural for **Sigmundur Brestisson**, one of the great characters of Faroese medieval history and hero of the *Færeyinga Saga*, to call for the king's help to overthrow his heathen rival, **Tróndur í Gøtu**, who was frustrating efforts to introduce Christianity to the islands. Although Sigmundur failed to see off Tróndur, and was eventually slaughtered whilst fleeing from him, King Olav's help has been commemorated ever since in the Faroes, which adopted the day of his death as their national day. Events kick off on the afternoon of the 28th with a procession through Tórshavn headed by men on horseback proudly bearing the Faroese flag. They head for the grassy area in front of the parliament where crowds assemble to hear speeches from the country's leading politicians. Next off it's the final of the summer boat races, where the year's winners will be decided in a competition to row across the harbour. A series of sporting events, public meetings and concerts follow amid much drinking and merrymaking. Often nursing severe hangovers, festival-goers are a little more restrained on the 29th, a day marked by a ceremonial procession from the parliament to the cathedral where a service is held. On returning to the parliament, a choir sings and the prime minister holds his opening speech which marks the beginning of the new parliamentary session. The other public holidays are:

January 1	New Year's Day
March/April	Easter: Maundy Thursday, Good Friday, Easter Sunday, Easter Monday
April 25	Flag Day (in celebration of the announcement on the BBC on this day in 1940 calling on all Faroese shipping to fly the national flag, Merkið, instead of that of occupied Denmark)
May	Common Prayers' Day
May	Ascension Day
May	Whit Sunday, Whit Monday
June 5	Constitution Day
December 24, 25, 26	Christmas
December 31	New Year's Eve

SHOPPING

Absolutely the best thing to buy in the Faroes is a traditional woollen **sweater,** which are all locally knitted in the islands. Prices vary according to design and fashion, but you can pick up a plain white jumper, popular with local fishermen, for around 500–600kr. For something a little more contemporary, you'll need to pay something in the region of 700–1,100kr, though, of course, you're then moving away from the traditional to the fashionable. Companies such as Sirri (with an outlet in Tórshavn), Töting in Syðrugøta on Eysturoy, and Snældan at Strendur, also on Eysturoy, are the main manufacturers and between them they produce a range of products ranging from knee-length coats made entirely of wool, to mittens. However, it's a much better idea to nosy around the Heimavirki stores dotted around the islands (the best one is in Klaksvík) where you'll find a whole array of sweaters hand-knitted by local women who then receive the profits of their labours; these homemade jumpers cost around 650kr and are some of the warmest you'll come across. There's also something tremendously satisfying about buying one of these sweaters; not only do you know that it was made just around the corner from where you bought it but also you're putting money directly into the local economy. There are details of the Heimavirki shops and about the knitting mills themselves in the relevant sections of the guide text.

Another popular souvenir from the Faroes is a **stuffed puffin** or other bird, usually a gull of some kind, which you can buy for 400–500kr. The *kunningarstovan* in Tórshavn generally keep a couple in stock and as you travel around the country you may see one or two for sale in bookstores or gift shops here and there. However, the best place to pick up a stuffed bird is on Nólsoy where Jens-Kjeld Jensen (see page 80) sells nothing but. If you're lucky he might also have a couple of gannets for sale that he's collected from his taxidermic wanderings on Mykines. Before buying, it's probably a good idea to check any restrictions your home country may have on importing stuffed birds. Puffins for example are a protected species in the United Kingdom.

Since the Faroese began issuing their own **stamps** in 1975, they have become a much sought-after collector's item for their rarity. Particularly popular are designs which feature images of the Faroe Islands themselves but also the country's birds and animals. Stamp collectors will want to visit Traðagøta 38 in Tórshavn (tel: 34 62 00; email; filateli@postur.fo; web: www.stamps.fo) where the Faroese Philatelic Organisation is based. Stamps can also be bought on the net at the above address.

For such a small nation with a limited pool of talent, Faroese contemporary music is surprisingly good. CDs can make an excellent souvenir of any stay in the islands and whilst browsing through record stores (the best one in the country can be found upstairs in the SMS shopping centre in Tórshavn) be sure to listen to the two Faroese artists to make the big time abroad: Guðrun Sólja Jacobsen, a sort of home-grown Björk, and the truly wonderful and gifted Teitur, whose albums *Poetry and Aeroplanes* (sung in English) and *Sólin og regnið* (in Faroese) are a good showcase of his songwriting and performance talents; his style is a mix of REM and David Gray. Also worth a listen are the more traditional CDs of Faroese folk songs and chain dancing – though perhaps not to everyone's taste. Count on around 160kr for a CD. For information about tax-free shopping in the Faroes see *Customs and tax-free goods*, page 43.

ARTS AND ENTERTAINMENT

Unfortunately for visitors, much of the arts and entertainment available in the islands is in Faroese only. Cinema films, however, are one notable exception since they are always shown in their original language (often English); there are cinemas in Tórshavn and Klaksvík. Another is the excellent *Listastevna Føroya* or Faroese Arts Festival (tel: 31 79 00; email: oddva@nlh.fo; web: www.listastevnan.com) which is generally held during the first half of August. Always an eclectic collection of different genres, the festival generally features folk music, opera, poetry, dance and art. Performers and artists come from across the world to take part in the event which is slowly gaining justified international recognition (Britain's Fay Weldon and Norwegian Sámi musician, Mari Boine, were just two of the participants in 2003). Tickets are available at the Nordic House and at the tourist information office in Tórshavn. Indeed, the **Nordic House** (see page 68) is one of the best sources of culture in the islands and often has exhibitions of contemporary Nordic and Faroese art. As for art galleries and museums, they are pretty much confined to Tórshavn and are all detailed in the text. If you're a veritable culture vulture you are bound to leave the Faroes with your appetite barely whetted. In a small country with a population of 48,000, there simply aren't enough people to create a buzzing arts and entertainment scene. If you are heading out into the sticks during your stay in the islands, make sure you get your fill of everything the Faroese capital has to offer before moving on – and take a couple of good books and a perhaps a radio with you.

CUSTOMS AND TAX-FREE GOODS

Import restrictions governing alcohol are strict and allowances are minute. The following goods can be imported into the Faroes **tax- and duty-free** by anyone over the age of 18: one litre of spirits between 22% and 60%, two litres of beer with an alcohol content no higher than 5.8%, plus one litre of fortified wine and one litre of table wine, or two litres of table wine. You should avoid bringing non-recyclable containers into the islands. Travellers over the age of 15 may also bring in 200 cigarettes or 100 cigarillos or 50 cigars or 250g tobacco. Perfume (maximum 50g), toilet water (maximum 25cl) and three kilos of confectionery are also permitted. Special import restrictions apply to fishing gear for salmon and sea trout. Anyone intending to use such equipment in the islands must present a certificate from veterinary officials in the country of origin certifying that it has been disinfected immediately before departure to the Faroe Islands. This measure is aimed at preventing Faroese inland waters from becoming infected with diseases carried by fish outside the islands.

The good news about shopping in the Faroes is that most goods can be bought tax-free (books and home-made sweaters are two notable exceptions – their prices do not include tax anyway). The minimum purchase per store to qualify for a tax-free refund is 300kr – a sliding scale then applies with the amount of tax back increasing in line with the amount you spend though it is usually around 15–19% of the total. You then fill in the refund cheque you receive in-store with your name and address. On leaving the Faroes, you must show your purchases (do not pack them away in your hold luggage if leaving by plane) together with your passport to customs officials who will then stamp the tax-free cheque. All you then have to do is to take your cheque to either the Flogfelag Føroya travel agency or the tourist information desk at the airport or to the information desk on board the *Norröna* to receive your refund in Danish kroner. If you have several cheques to cash collected from various stores, you will receive the total sum of all of them. (More information on Faroese tax-free shopping is available on tel: 34 00 40; email: taxfree@ff.fo; web: www.ff.fo.) Remember, too, that if you're travelling to Denmark with Faroese notes it can be difficult to spend them in shops there – quite simply because many Danes don't realise that the Faroese currency is in fact legal tender throughout the Kingdom of Denmark and has the same value as its Danish equivalent. It's a better idea to play safe and ask for Danish notes instead of Faroese.

MEDIA, COMMUNICATIONS AND TIME
Radio

It's unlikely you'll have much to do with **Faroese national radio**, Útvarp Føroya, other than tuning in for the English-language weather forecast which is broadcast at 08.45 (Mon–Fri) from late May to early September within the breakfast programme, *Góðan morgun Føroyar* (Good Morning Faroes).

Broadcasting a mix of music and speech, this is the main station in the islands and the only one that can be heard right across the country; when reception is poor on FM, you can always fall back on their booming medium-wave signal on 531kHz AM which is aimed at reaching all shipping in Faroese waters. Although there are a couple of other FM stations which broadcast out of Tórshavn (the music station Rás 2 and Lindin, a religious broadcaster transmitting solely in Faroese) they're unlikely to be of much interest to visitors. A much better idea is to tune to the **BBC** whose medium-wave signals coming up across the sea from the north of Scotland can be clearly heard on a car radio (the body of the car seems to work as a signal booster), and occasionally, also on a regular hand-held radio. The stations and frequencies to aim for are: BBC Radio 5 Live on 693kHz medium wave (the strongest of all the BBC medium-wave signals audible in the Faroes); BBC Radio Scotland on 810kHz medium wave and BBC Radio 4 on 198khz long wave. If you don't mind the interference and crackle you may also be able to pick up MFR, the commercial station in Inverness, broadcasting on 1107AM.

Television

Faroese television, Sjónvarp Føroya, is a remarkable organisation – the mere fact that the Faroese population is so small and that over 50 transmitters and transformers are needed to get the signal out to even the most remote village makes it a wonder that the station exists at all. SvF, the only station based in the islands broadcasting in Faroese and founded in 1984, transmits about 40 hours a week, and like most public-service broadcasters its programmes cover a range of news, documentaries, entertainment, culture, sport and drama. Its news programme, however, is not on air every day due to staffing levels – only 35 people work here full time. The company produces about one in five of all its transmissions and translates into Faroese about the same percentage of foreign programmes. Whilst you're in the Faroes, do try to catch the inordinately popular Friday evening Bingo draw – it's a classic of its kind. Having seen it, despite whatever you may think about your own national television stations, you'll certainly have experienced cutting-edge TV!

Telephones

Public telephones are all of the cardphone variety. Annoyingly, they are not usually found in the streets in the main towns, but more often in hotel lobbies, banks or some other public building. On the remoter islands you may come across a telephone in a village – but you certainly shouldn't count on it. Phonecards can be bought from Faroese Telecom offices in Tórshavn and Klaksvík – stock up before you head out into the sticks if you're planning on phoning home.

Post office and internet

Post offices can be found right across the islands, and in the larger towns and villages are open every day Monday–Friday. However, on the more remote

TELEPHONE CODES FROM AND TO THE FAROES

The international dialling code to make a call abroad from the Faroes is 00. International country codes are therefore as follows:

Australia	00 61
Ireland	00 353
New Zealand	00 64
United Kingdom	00 44
US and Canada	00 1

When ringing from abroad, the country code for the Faroe Islands is +298. There are no local codes within the islands and all numbers consist of six digits, for example, tel: xx xx xx.

islands, you will find that they may only be open for a couple of hours a day and closed on certain days, often Tuesday and Thursday.

Internet cafés have yet to reach the Faroes – instead, look for terminals in hotel lobbies or in libraries across the country. Booking is not generally necessary and if you ask the librarians they will generally let you use a terminal free of charge. Library opening hours vary but are listed in the text: the main ones (with internet terminals) are in Fuglafjørður, Klaksvík and Tórshavn. There are also several terminals at the Nordic House in Tórshavn.

Time

Time in the Faroe Islands is always the same as in Britain and Ireland – ie: GMT during the winter months and GMT + 1 during the summer. There is, however, always one hour's time difference between the Faroes and Denmark; when it is, for example, noon in Tórshavn (London and Dublin), it is 13.00 in Copenhagen. During the winter (November–March) when the islands return to GMT they then also share the same time as Iceland, which operates on GMT all year round. Daylight saving applies from the end of October to the end of March when clocks are put back by one hour. The dates for putting the clocks forward and back are the same as in the rest of Europe.

INTERACTING WITH LOCAL PEOPLE

The Faroese, like many of the other Nordic nationals, can on the surface seem rather reserved. It is certainly true that the Faroese aren't the easiest of people to get to know, and are often thought of by foreigners as being distant. On the whole they are straight-talking, saying what they mean with a minimum of words and fuss. Many visitors interpret this as a lack of interest in conversation or even downright rudeness, but both are unlikely to be the case. In short, overt expressions of emotions and raucous conversations punctuated with wild gesticulations are not the name of the game in the Faroes – indeed, when talking, some men are very wary of even taking their hands out of their pockets. However, when the weekend comes liberal quantities of beer help people throw off their inhibitions and you may find that even the most monosyllabic fisherman can talk (and drink) you under the table. On meeting a Faroese man or woman for the first time, it is customary to shake hands – though unlike in some other countries it is not usual to shake hands again on leaving, or when you meet again, even if it is several days later. It is not the done thing to kiss on meeting – that is something the Faroese avoid at all costs. Nudity is also something the Faroese find difficult to deal with; despite signs in shower rooms in public swimming pools instructing bathers to shower without a swimming costume before entering the pool on hygiene grounds, you will often see people showering, albeit rather guiltily, with their swimwear on. If you play by the rules, you should never wear swimwear in a sauna either – also for hygiene reasons – although this rule, too, is often flouted.

Red-necked phalaropes

Part Two

The Guide

Tórshavn

Surprisingly for a place bearing such an imposing name, **Tórshavn** (literally Thor's Harbour, named after the Norse god of war) is built around one of the worst natural harbours in the entire country, dangerously exposed to the gales and accompanying heavy swells of the North Atlantic.

In the face of climatic adversity, this strategic settlement, today the islands' capital and home to two out of five Faroe Islanders, grew up around the rocky promontory, **Tinganes**, still the seat of government today and the heart of the old town. It was here, around AD900, that the *ting* or Viking parliament first began meeting every summer to chew over matters of national importance, doing so uninterrupted until 1816, but it's the nearby bishopric of **Kirkjubøur**, founded around 1100 on the southwestern shore of Streymoy that provides the key to understanding Tórshavn's location and strategic importance. Since there were no secure harbours along this stretch of coastline, the bay on the more protected eastern shore, where the *ting* was held, soon became the preferred landing place. An annual market was also held here to coincide with the assembly, developing in the Middle Ages – with the introduction of the Trade Monopoly in 1579 – into a permanent trading place with warehouses for the importing and exporting of goods. Although Tórshavn's superior location was confirmed, population growth was slow due to restrictive land ownership laws that made farming difficult; by the beginning of the 17th century, barely 100 people lived in the settlement. In 1673 there was a further setback when a devastating fire raged across Tinganes, destroying all but two of the warehouses there. Over the ensuing centuries growth gradually increased, helped in large part by reform of land ownership rights, and by 1900 Tórshavn's population had soared to 15,000, tripling in just a hundred years. Today Tórshavn has finally come of age, blossoming into a self-confident, bustling medium-sized town with a population of around 18,000 people and all the trappings of a national, if diminutive, capital: government offices, parliament and foreign consulates are all here.

For orientation, take the **harbour** as your point of reference: from here, Tórshavn stretches in three directions; west up the steep hillsides behind the town centre that act as the capital's backdrop as well as both north and south curving around the waterfront. However, it is the all-important harbour,

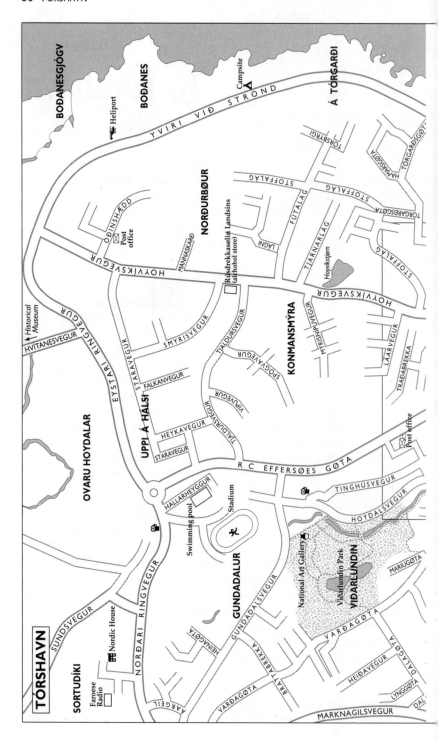

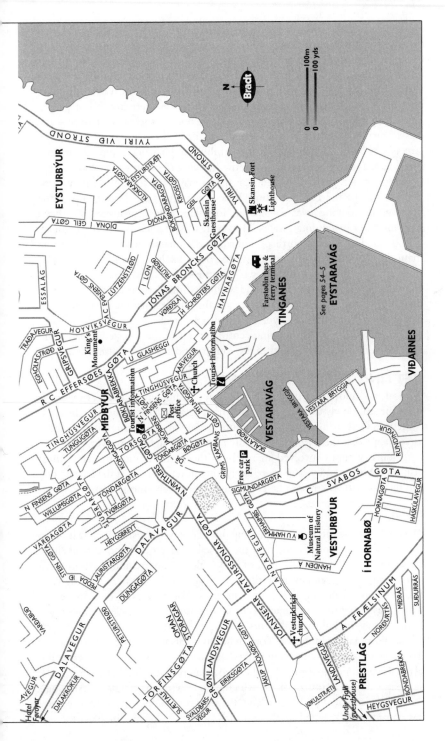

through which the country maintains contact with the rest of the world, that remains the town's focal point and is arguably the most attractive part of town. Here a long row of converted warehouses with façades ranging in colour from a rich yellow ochre to bright reds and blues, reflect in the crystal-clear waters of the harbour bursting with small wooden fishing vessels; during the long summer days, the couple of cafés on the waterfront here are full of people enjoying a cup of coffee, watching the boats bob on the Atlantic swell – the classic picture-postcard view of Tórshavn. From here a warren of narrow streets and lanes leads up and over the hill onto Tinganes, winding past tiny black-tarred houses with white window frames and green turfed roofs to the grander former merchants' houses that today are home to the various departments of the Faroese Home Rule government on the very tip of the promontory looking over to Skansin fort which once protected Tórshavn harbour from marauding pirates. However, it is in and around the compact grid of modern streets north of Tinganes, dominated by the pedestrianised main drag, **Niels Finsens gøta**, where you're likely to spend most of your time. It's here that most of the town's facilities are located: shops, restaurants and the post office are all to be found within a central area measuring no more than 1km^2 or so – Tórshavn is, after all, the smallest national capital in the world. From the centre of town, Tinghúsvegur streaks north, past the Faroese parliament, to the SMS shopping centre and on to the forested Viðarlundin park, one of the few plantations in the country and a favourite place for a stroll.

GETTING THERE AND AWAY

Without a shadow of a doubt, the most appealing approach to Tórshavn is from the sea; slowly turning the corner into Eystaravág bay, watching the town come into view, banking more and more steeply up the surrounding hillsides as you approach the harbour, is a truly remarkable sight. However, given the long journey times involved in reaching the Faroe Islands by ferry, most visitors opt to fly and you're more likely, therefore, to arrive at the Faroes' one and only airport, 47km west of Tórshavn on the neighbouring island of Vágar.

By air

Although there is often talk of building one, Tórshavn doesn't actually have an airport, just a heliport; annoyingly the capital's fog-prone location is likely to forever rule out any fanciful idea of relocating the international airport from its current location, not even on the same island as Tórshavn. Accordingly, all flights to and from the Faroes operate from Vágar **airport** (tel: 35 33 00) which has a slightly better track record when it comes to inclement weather. Following every flight arrival, a **bus** (#300; 100kr; 55min) leaves from in front of the terminal building for Tórshavn. Buses also leave the bus station in Tórshavn to connect with every flight departure, roughly two hours before the plane leaves; times are printed in the *Ferðaætlan* timetable (20kr) or simply ask at the bus station or tourist office, which both also sell the timetable. Although the airport is located on Vágar island, the new road tunnel across to Streymoy has considerably speeded up the journey. Before its opening in 2002, the trip involved taking a ferry across Vestmannasund sound in order to reach Streymoy and Tórshavn.

By ferry

Taking the ferry to Tórshavn certainly avoids the hassle of arriving on an altogether different island to that of your destination, but it does involve a lengthy journey across some of northern Europe's most unpredictable waters. The *Norröna* ferry and the various cargo ships that carry passengers to the Faroes all use the main eastern harbour, Eystaravág. The *Norröna* ties up right alongside the Farstøðin **bus and ferry terminal** (tel: 34 30 30), whereas the cargo ships use the berths a little further out, at the harbour entrance. From the terminal it's a five-minute walk northwest along Havnargøta to reach the town centre.

GETTING AROUND

One of the best things about Tórshavn is its wonderfully compact size. Nowhere is too far to reach on foot, and in this town of narrow streets and alleyways, you're frankly better off without a car. Although there is a limited **city bus** service (tel: 31 51 60), you're unlikely to find it very useful since its primary purpose is to link the town with far-flung housing areas on the outskirts. Known as *Bussleiðin*, these red-and-white town buses don't serve the Farstøðin terminal, but instead pick up and drop off in central Tórshavn, most usefully along Niels Winthers gøta. In general, services operate every 30 minutes from 07.00 to 17.00, though during evenings and at weekends departures are skeletal, down to around one an hour. Individual tickets bought on the bus cost 10kr, though a strip of 10, known as a *10-túrakort*, goes for 80kr. Of the four routes, predictably called Leið 1, 2, 3 and 4 (*leið* means route), only routes 2 and 3 are likely to be of use to you since they run out to the National Museum in Hoyvík saving a lengthy walk. The village of Kollafjørður is also served by these buses; look for route 4.

Taxis can be handy if the weather is bad or if you don't feel like hiking up the hill to the youth hostel or Hotel Føroyar; reckon on 70–80kr from the town centre and tipping is not expected. You can generally find taxis hanging around outside the Farstøðin terminal or at the ranks at the bottom and top ends of Niels Finsens gøta. Otherwise you can call **Auto** on tel: 31 12 34 or **Bil** on tel: 31 14 44, the two main operators.

Long-distance buses are blue in colour and usually emblazoned with the word *Bygdaleiðir* (tel: 34 30 00 and 34 30 30; www.ssl.fo), indicating their readiness to depart for even the most remote *bygd* or settlement. These buses leave from the Farstøðin terminal and travel via various suburbs of Tórshavn en route for their final destination; the network is extensive and reliable. If you're planning on travelling around the islands under your own steam, you may want to consider hiring a car which will cost around 500kr per day. The best **car rental** bets are: Avis at 1–3 Staravegur (tel: 31 35 35; email: avis@post.olivant.fo); Hertz at Hoydalsvegur 17 (tel: 34 00 36 and 21 35 46; email: hertz@ff.fo) and Bilútleigan at Argjaboðagøta 5 in the district of Argir

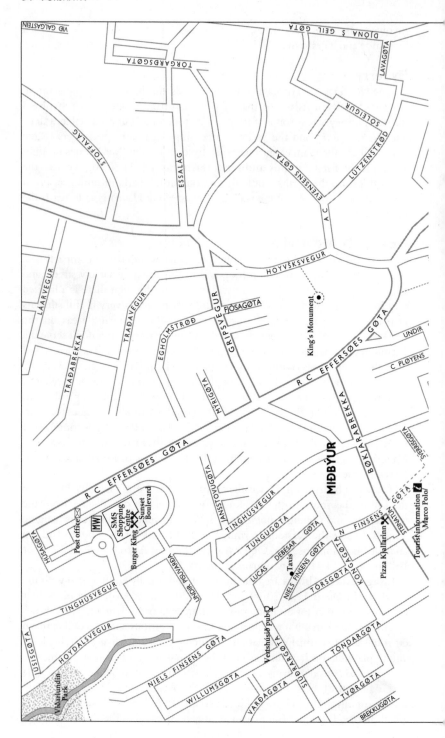

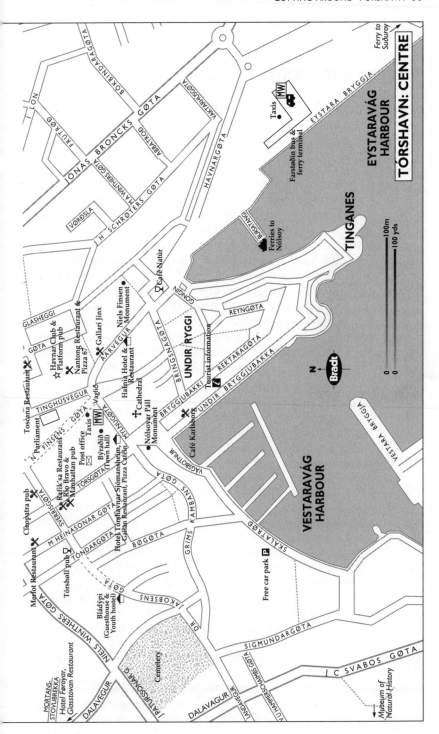

TÓRSHAVN: CENTRE

Ferry to Suðuroy

EYSTARAVÁG HARBOUR

EYSTARA BRYGGJA

Taxis

Farstoðin bus & ferry terminal

Ferries to Nólsoy

TINGANES

100m
100 yds
0
0

REYNGØTA

UNDIR RYGGI

Tourist information

UNDIR BRYGGJUBAKKA

REKTARAGØTA

N

BRYGGJUBAKKI

GONGIN

VESTARA BRYGGJA

Café Natúr

Niels Finsen Monument

Gallarí Jinx

Café Karlsborg

Hánni Hotel & Restaurant

Cathedral

Nólsoyar Páll Monument

VESTARAVÁG HARBOUR

VÁGSBOTNUR

SKÁLATRØÐ

Free car park

KAMBANS GØTA

GRIMS GØTA

BØGØTA

VAGLIÐ

Býráðið (Town hall)

Post office

Taxis

MW

TINGHÚSVEGUR

Parliament

FINSENS GØTA

TORSGØTA

MYLNUGØTA

Hotel Tórshavn Sjómansheim, Gællan Restaurant, Pizza Cafée

Rafik'sa Restaurant

Rio Bravo & Manhattan pub

Cleopatra pub

TONDARGØTA

Tórshøll pub

M HEINASONAR GØTA

Mørkot Restaurant

Bládýpi (Guesthouse & Youth hostel)

JAKOBSENS GØTA

ÍPALÚRSSONAR G

Cemetery

DR

DALAVEGUR

DALAVAGUR

SIGMUNDARGØTA

J C SVABOS GØTA

Museum of Natural History

NIELS WINTHERS GØTA

MORTANS STOVUBREKKA

Hotel Føroyar, Glasstovan Restaurant

Toscana Restaurant

Havnar Club & Platform pub

Nantong Restaurant & Pizza 67

AARVEGUR

GLASHEGGI

GØTA

VØRÐSLA

I H SCHRØTERS GØTA

MA WINTHERS GØTA

JÓNAS BRONCKS GØTA

ABBATORÐ

BÓKBINDARAGØTA

FRÚTRØÐ

LON

HAVNARGØTA

VAKTARHUSGØTA

BRINGSNAGØTA

Bradt

just outside Tórshavn (tel: 31 78 65; email: carrent@post.olivant.fo). The only free unlimited car park in town is at Skálatrøð overlooking Vestaravág harbour.

TOURIST AND WEATHER INFORMATION

Tórshavn has two tourist offices, both in the town centre. The **Kunningarstovan** (May–Sep Mon–Fri 07.00–17.30, Tue–Thu from 08.00, Sat 09.00–14.00; rest of the year Mon–Fri 09.00–17.30, Sat 10.00–14.00; tel: 31 57 88; email: torsinfo@post.olivant.fo; www.visittorshavn.fo) at Niels Finsens gøta 13 is the place to head for if you need information on the capital and surrounding attractions. The friendly staff here also have a list of bed and breakfast accommodation (see below) but it's also a good place to pick up Faroe souvenirs such as playing cards, badges, posters and stickers. Every morning the staff post the latest weather forecast in the tourist office window – always worth a look when passing. From May to early September an English-language weather forecast is also broadcast by Faroese national radio, Útvarp Føroya, on weekdays at around 08.45. The frequency for the Tórshavn area is 89.9FM. For full details on deciphering Faroese and Danish weather terminology found in the newspapers and on the net, see page 24.

The second tourist office, **Ferðaráð Føroya** (Mon–Fri 08.00–16.00; tel: 31 60 55; email: tourist@tourist.fo; www.visit-faroeislands.com), actually the Faroese National Tourist Board located down by the harbour at Undir Bryggjubakka 17, is the outlet for information about the rest of the islands. They also have a limited amount of gifts for sale, such as posters of the islands.

WHERE TO STAY

Due to Tórshavn's modest size, the town is not awash with accommodation options, although in recent years things have dramatically improved. Outside the budget category, your choice is essentially between an upmarket hotel charging typical northern European prices for very average double rooms, or much simpler guesthouse accommodation (where breakfast is not always included in the room rate) for around half the price.

Should you opt for a hotel, you will be treated to a lavish eat-as-much-as-you-can buffet breakfast featuring everything from herring to Danish pastries. Since Tórshavn really has only two upmarket hotels to speak of, your decision over which one to plump for should be based on whether you wish to be in the town centre or not. If you choose to stay at the Hotel Føroyar for its magnificent views (see reviews below), bear in mind that it is a very steep 20–30-minute walk from the town centre – a distance that seems all the further when the wind and rain are blowing you back down the hill!

Prices quoted here are per room unless otherwise stated. Single hotel rooms are not good value; they generally cost barely 200kr less than a double; guesthouse singles offer better value for money, at around two-thirds the price of a double. It is always a good idea to book in advance since accommodation is quite limited. If you require somewhere to stay during the national festivities of Ólavsøka in late July you'd be wise to book at least six months in advance or you will most probably find everything has already been taken.

Top end

Hotel Føroyar við Oyggjarvegin; tel: 31 75 00; email: hf@hotelforoyar.com; www.hotelforoyar.com. Although the rooms at this hilltop hotel have few frills, each does boast an unsurpassed view out over the whole of Tórshavn. All in all, this modern hotel, justifiably popular with tour groups, is undoubtedly the best in the country. Free internet access in reception; 1,095kr including breakfast.

Hotel Hafnia Áarvegur 4–10; tel: 31 32 33; email: hafnia@hafnia.fo; www.hafnia.fo. Crying out for a makeover, this dingy hotel beats its rival, Hotel Føroyar, in terms of downtown location, but its rooms feel cramped and far too '70s for comfort; 1,150kr with breakfast.

Hotel Tórshavnar Sjómansheim Tórsgøta 4; tel: 35 00 00; email: hotel@hotel.fo; www.hotel.fo. With grey carpets, pink walls and cheap furnishings, style is not high on the agenda at this centrally located converted seaman's hostel. However, they do have 9 doubles with sea views, which help distract the eye; 915kr including breakfast.

Moderate

Bládýpi Dr Jacobsens gøta 14–16; tel: 31 19 51; email: bladypi@bladypi.fo; www.bladypi.fo. Two adjoining buildings make up this popular guesthouse in the town centre. The best doubles, all modern and bright with wooden floors and minimalist Nordic design, are found in the same building as reception (3 have private facilities). The other older guesthouse rooms, although adequate, are less good value and located in the original street-side building. Cooking facilities are available; 430kr.

Skansin Jekaragøta 8; tel: 31 22 42; fax: 31 06 57. Run by Magna Restorff, who doesn't speak English, the rooms at this seafront guesthouse, although sharing facilities, are pleasant and simple. Bright and airy though with no frills. A guest kitchen is available; 540kr including breakfast.

Undir Fjalli Vesturgøta 15; tel: 32 05 27; email: info@undirfjalli.com; www.undirfjalli.com. Open late Jun to mid-Aug. Located in 2 blocks of student accommodation, the rooms here are what you'd expect: small, unluxurious though perfectly adequate. All have private facilities and a kitchen is available; 490kr.

Budget

Bládýpi Dr Jacobsens gøta 14–16; tel: 31 19 51; email: bladypi@bladypi.fo; www.bladypi.fo. Dormitory beds are available at this guesthouse on the ground floor of the main building. Although the facilities are more cramped than at the official youth hostel, it does benefit from a more central location; 120kr per person.

Campsite Yviri við Strond; tel: 31 57 99 or 32 07 39; email: torsinfo@post.olivant.fo; www.visittorshavn.fo. Open mid-May to mid-Sep for both tents and caravans; 50kr per person.

Youth Hostel við Oyggjarvegin; tel: 34 59 00 and 31 75 00; email: office@smyril-line.fo; www.farhostel.fo and www.smyril-line.fo. Comfortable, modern and well-kitted out, this superbly located youth hostel on a hilltop overlooking the capital has the same views as its expensive hotel neighbour but at a fraction of the cost. Bookings are necessary in summer as this is one of the first places to fill up – particularly when the *Norröna* is in; 145kr per person.

In addition, a large number of private rooms are available on a **bed and break-fast** basis with local families. Contact the tourist office at Niels Finsens gøta 13 (tel: 31 57 88; email: torsinfo@post.olivant.fo; www.visittorshavn.fo) for their latest list. A double room costs 430kr, a single is 360kr.

WHERE TO EAT

If you're arriving in Tórshavn from one of the other remoter Faroe Islands, the wealth of eating possibilities in the capital will make you quite dizzy: if you're coming directly from anywhere else grit your teeth and bear it. Mercifully though, the range of eateries in Tórshavn has mushroomed beyond even the locals' wildest dreams in recent years; barely ten years ago it was virtually impossible to find anything worth consuming that wasn't the greasy-spoon fare served up by the array of fast-food outlets at the bottom of the range or the expense account five-course hotel dinners at the other. Today Tórshavn boasts an impressive range of restaurants for its size, offering everything from Thai and Chinese to traditional Faroese – even Burger King is in residence. A word of advice: there can be a surfeit of heavy meat dishes on Faroese menus, seemingly because, when the Faroese go out to dine they're looking for something different, a change from the fish dishes they regularly eat at home. With this in mind, it may be wise not to rush straight for a steak because the chances are it'll be on pretty much every menu you come across in the islands. Why not opt for something a little less mainstream if you spot it – you can always fall back on steaks when out in the sticks.

There are some particularly good value Monday-to-Friday eat-as-much-as-you-can **lunch deals** on offer in most of the mid-range places aimed at office workers nipping out for a bite to eat. Join them, eating at lunchtime, and you'll save plenty of cash into the bargain. In short, make the most of the possibilities the capital has to offer if you're moving on into the countryside beyond. It is not necessary to book a table during the week; however, it can be wise to do so on Friday and Saturday nights, and absolutely necessary during Ólavsøka.

Top end

Glasstovan inside Hotel Føroyar, við Oyggjarvegin; tel: 31 75 00. Undoubtedly the restaurant with the best views in town, overlooking the entire capital from its hilltop location. However, although the food here is amongst the best in the country, it can sometimes be overcooked. A three-course affair is 295kr, 495kr with a bottle of wine thrown in. Specialises in seafood, for example grilled tournedos of monkfish with vegetable soufflé (198kr) or ovenbaked salmon with sautéed vegetables (192kr). Puffin breast with a raspberry chilli sauce is also on the menu (205kr). Bottles of beer from 30kr; draught beer from 40kr; bottles of wine from 195kr. Certainly the place to come to impress.

Hafnia inside Hotel Hafnia, Áarvegur 4–10; tel: 31 32 33. This place is widely regarded as serving the best food in the Faroes. It specialises in Scandinavian-style buffets where you help yourself to anything as many times as you like. The lunch buffet here (noon–14.00) is especially good value at 98kr for its mix of meat and fish dishes. In summer there is often a fish buffet on Tue and Thu evening (215kr). The adventurous may wish to sample the summer-only 'Faroese Symphony' buffet (110kr), which includes dried fish, blubber, whale meat and dried lamb. Alternatively go à la carte: saddle of lamb (195kr) or pepper steak in cognac sauce with vegetables (180kr) are especially tasty.

Marco Polo Sverissgøta 12; tel: 31 34 30. This place is trying hard to be in the same league as the hotel restaurants but isn't quite there yet. Nevertheless, there are some things worth seeking out: the three-course set menu for 275kr is not bad value. Otherwise you're looking at steaks for 165kr, fillet of lamb (195kr) or haddock in filo pastry at 185kr. Don't rule out the lunch buffet here (noon–14.00), often a fish or meat treat, for just 69kr.

Merlot Magnus Heinasonargøta 20; tel: 31 11 21. Chichi cuisine at prices to match. Delicious food but definitely somewhere to watch the kroner. A limited fish menu including pan-fried monkfish with sautéed onions and spinach (198kr), steaks (from 178kr), venison (228kr) and lamb fillet (198kr).

Rio Bravo Tórsgøta 11; tel: 31 97 67. Upstairs from Rafik'sa, this upmarket restaurant has similar fare to Marco Polo, and frankly there isn't much to choose between them. However, this place does have puffin breast (198kr) if you're looking for something more traditionally Faroese. Also salmon in puff pastry (175kr) and fillet of lamb in dill sauce (180kr).

Toscana Nólsoyar Páls gøta 13; tel: 31 11 09. The newest Italian restaurant in town serving pasta and spaghetti dishes for around 120kr, fish for 165kr and steaks (195kr). Although the décor inside is quite chichi, the quality of the food receives mixed reports.

Moderate

Café Natúr Áarvegur 7; tel: 31 26 25. Serving snacks until 21.00, for example pitta filled with chicken (55kr) or chicken tortillas (also 55kr), soup (35kr). *Café au lait* here is 20kr. Also has a wide range of beer (see below). Open Mon–Thu 11.00–midnight, Fri & Sat 11.00–04.00, Sun 14.00–midnight.

Gallan Tórsgøta 4, inside the Hotel Tórshavnar Sjómansheim; tel: 35 00 00. Alcohol-free restaurant with good views over the harbour serving decent helpings of fish and chips (69kr), deep-fried chicken (65kr) and various beef concoctions (125kr). Open daily 11.30–14.00, Thu–Sun 17.30–21.00.

Gallarí Jinx Áarvegur 3; tel: 31 71 01. Modern, stylish Eurocafé replete with art for sale on the walls. Excellent selection of speciality coffees (around 20kr), cakes (30kr), salads (60kr) and sandwiches (from 55kr). Also has breakfast from 09.00 to 11.00 including cornflakes (18kr), croissant (18kr), coffee (16kr) and Sat brunch featuring the works (89kr). Open Mon–Thu 09.00–midnight, Fri & Sat 09.00–01.00, Sun 14.00–midnight. Licensed.

Nantong Tinghúsvegur 8; tel: 31 86 98. This second-floor Chinese restaurant has finally got its act together and is now serving some pretty decent stuff. Best value at lunchtime when the eat-as-much-as-you-can buffet (11.30–14.00) is just 69kr. Otherwise starters from 65kr, the usual mains from 135kr. Beer here is 45kr, a bottle of red wine 175kr. Open Tue–Fri 11.30–14.30 and 17.00–midnight. Closed Mon.

Pizza Caféin Tórsgøta 4, inside the Hotel Tórshavnar Sjómansheim; tel: 35 00 00. The best pizzas and pasta in the entire country. Excellent value at lunchtime when a pizza, salad and bread costs just 49kr. Otherwise pizzas are 65–85kr, calzone (80kr), tortellini alla panna (69kr) – all genuinely tasty and authentic. Open daily noon–21.45. No alcohol served. Also takeaway service.

Pizza 67 Tinghúsvegur 8; tel: 35 67 67. The Faroese outlet of this Icelandic pizza chain that dishes up all your favourite pizzas and pasta, including the unusual and delicious Crazy Bananas pizza for around 80kr. Open noon–23.30.

Rafik'sa Tórsgøta 11. This cheap and cheerful place really knows how to draw the crowds at lunchtime (11.30–14.00) who come here to fill up on the (not overly authentic) Thai buffet for 65kr. Also pizzas for 90kr and kebabs from 65kr. A beer here is 50kr.

Budget

Burger King Inside the SMS shopping centre, RC Effersøes gøta 31. The usual array of burgers and fries (Whopper Meal is 57kr) proudly served up by Faroese teenagers using impeccable English. Most easily accessed by the main shopping centre entrance off Tinghúsvegur.

Café Karlsborg Undir Bryggjubakka. A cosy café overlooking the harbour with a couple of outdoor chairs and tables in summer, serving soup (28kr), baked potatoes (40kr) and filled pittas (45kr); coffee here is 10kr. Open 11.00–18.00.

Pizza Kjallarinn Niels Finsens gøta 21; tel: 35 33 53. Takeaway pizzas for either 65kr or 75kr depending on size.

Sunset Boulevard Inside the SMS shopping centre, RC Effersøes gøta 31 adjacent to Burger King. No-nonsense American-style salads and sandwiches (35–60kr) are served up at this fast-food eatery. Bear in mind though that the Faroes are not famed for their imported fresh vegetables and salads, hence, the range of ingredients can be limited.

ENTERTAINMENT AND NIGHTLIFE

For a town of its size, Tórshavn supports a surprisingly large number of pubs and clubs. Although not as frenetic as the legendary night scene in Reykjavík in Iceland, the Faroese capital can certainly hold its own. The busiest nights out are always Friday and Saturday, though that doesn't mean to say that if you go out for a midweek drink you'll be sitting alone. Chances are there'll always be someone to keep you company since fresh faces always attract attention and interest; the drinking scene in Tórshavn is extremely friendly. Clubs in the Faroes are not the sophisticated affairs you might be used to at home; emphasis is pretty much on getting drunk as quickly as possible and having a wild time.

In addition to a visit to the cinema (two screens), Tórshavn is also one of the best places in the islands to catch a traditional Faroese evening which combines a buffet of local delicacies with a chance to perfect your footwork in the ancient Faroese chain dance.

Pubs and clubs

Café Natúr Áarvegur 7; tel: 31 26 25. Open Mon–Thu 11.00–midnight, Fri & Sat 11.00–04.00, Sun 14.00–midnight. More bar than café, this is one of the most popular places to come for a drink; Gull and Black Sheep are 50kr, the weaker Pilsner and Classic, 40kr. The upstairs seating area opens only when it gets busy. Although the surroundings are great – wooden floors and a maritime feel – it can get a bit raucous and drunken in here as the evening progresses.

Cleopatra Niels Finsens gøta 11. A good bet for a mid-evening drink. The clientele is generally more restrained than at Café Natúr and hence it can be a good place to come for a drink and a chat. Open Mon–Thu & Sun 17.00–midnight, Fri & Sat 17.00–04.00.

Havnar Club Tinghúsvegur 4–11; tel: 31 15 52. Rough and ready, upfront club that attracts a cross-section of Tórshavn society. Not renowned for its restrained behaviour – hold on to your hat and lose any preconception that the Faroese don't know how to party.

Manhattan Sverrisgøtan 15; tel: 31 96 96. Open Mon & Fri noon–23.00, Sat 14.00–02.00, Sun 17.00–23.00. Located behind the Rio Bravo restaurant, this identikit pub looks as if it's been imported from a British theme park; wooden wall-panelling and dartboards failing to add authenticity. However, it's a popular place for a drink, particularly later in the evening. The only beers served here are non-Faroese.

Platform Tinghúsvegur 8; tel: 31 63 63; www.platform.fo. Your best bet for a night's clubbing in Tórshavn. Attracting a crowd of 20- to 30-somethings, there's '60s music on Friday nights, '80s on Saturdays. A bottle of beer here is just 20kr. Open Fri & Sat 23.00–04.00.

Tórshøll Sverrisgøta 22; tel: 31 15 65. A graceless drinkers' den that's fun if you want to get under the skin of Tórshavn. Plenty of local colour.

Vertshúsið Niels Finsens gøta 34; tel: 31 48 48. Open Mon–Thu & Sun 14.00–midnight, Fri & Sat 14.00–04.00. Definitely the best bar in Tórshavn. This buzzing place stretching over three floors is stylishly decked out in sculptures by Faroese artist Tróndur Patursson. The ground floor is divided into two main bars – one painted a deep marine-blue with female busts draped on the walls, the other an exotic red adorned with muscly male torsos – buy your drink, and choose your room. Although this is definitely the place to come to meet Tórshavn's trendy young things, sadly, it only serves Restorff beer since it's owned by the eponymous brewery, headed by the former British consul!

Cinema and Faroese evenings

Havnar Bio Tinghúsvegur 8; tel: 31 19 56; www.bio.fo. The only cinema on Streymoy and one of the few in the entire islands, it's well worth catching a film if you can. Details of screenings are posted up outside the cinema. Foreign-language films are never dubbed and are generally shown with Danish subtitles.

Faroese evenings Sjónleikarhúsið, Niels Finsens gøta 32. Tue only (20.00) from mid-Jun to mid-Aug. A wonderful way to get to grips with Faroese culture by combining a buffet of traditional foods such as sausages, dried fish, whale meat, blubber, salmon, prawns, lamb and various breads, with an opportunity to share the floor with professional dancers as they explain the various steps of the Faroese chain dance. There is sometimes also a reading of old poems and a dramatisation of Viking history from the sagas. Book at the Kunningarstovan; minimum 20 people; 300kr each including the buffet.

LISTINGS

Airline Atlantic Airways, at the airport; tel: 34 10 00; www.atlantic.fo

Alcohol store Rúsdrekkasøla Landsins, Høyvíksvegur 51 (entrance is at the rear); tel:

31 42 77; www.rusan.fo. Open Mon–Fri 10.00–17.30, Thu until 19.00

Banks Føroya Banki, Niels Finsens gøta 15; tel: 31 13 50, also in the SMS shopping centre; Føroya Sparikassi, Tinghúsvegur 49; tel: 34 83 80

Bookshops Hjalmar Jacobsens Bókahandi, Niels Finsens gøta 14; tel: 31 15 84; www.bokhandil.fo; Bókasølan í SMS, inside the SMS shopping centre; tel: 31 95 75; www.bokasolan.fo

Consulates Finland, Hoyvíksvegur 74; tel: 31 46 50; France, Bringsnagøta 21; tel: 31 17 44; Norway, Yviri vid Strond 4; tel: 31 12 60; Germany, Staravegur 5; tel: 28 47 67; Sweden, Bøgøta 16; tel: 35 17 10; UK, Niels Finsens gøta 6; tel: 35 99 77

Emergencies Tel: 112

Ferry Jonas Broncks gøta 37; tel: 34 59 50; email: office@smyril-line.fo; www.smyril-line.fo

Internet Teledepilin, Niels Finsens gøta 10 (Mon–Fri 09.00–17.00, Thu & Fri until 18.00, Sat 10.00–14.00); Býarbókasavnið town library, Niels Finsens gøta 7 (Mon–Fri 10.00–18.00, Sat until 13.00); Nordic House, Norðari Ringvegur (Mon–Sat 10.00–18.00, Sun 14.00–18.00)

Laundry Ruba vaskeri og renseri, Magnus Heinsoonar gøta 15; tel: 31 63 01

Library Býarbókasavnið town library, Niels Finsens gøta 7 (Mon–Fri 10.00–18.00, Sat until 13.00); Føroya Landsbókasavn national library, JC Svaboes gøta 16; tel: 31 16 26 (mid-Jun to mid-Aug Mon–Fri 13.00–17.00, rest of the year Mon–Wed 10.00–20.00, Thu & Fri 10.00–17.00

Pharmacy Tjaldurs Apotek, in the SMS shopping centre; tel: 34 11 00 (Mon–Fri 09.00–17.30, Sat 10.00–14.00, Sun 14.30–15.00)

Police Jonas Broncks gøta 17; tel: 35 14 48

Post office Posthúsbrekka, off Niels Finsens gøta; tel: 31 10 10 (Mon–Fri 10.00–16.00, Thu until 18.00); also in the SMS shopping centre; tel: 31 56 54 (Mon–Wed & Fri 10.00–16.00, Fri until 18.00)

Sauna and swimming pool Svimjihøllin, Hoydalsvegur 21; tel: 31 56 13 (late June to early Aug Mon, Tue, Thu & Fri 06.45–20.00, Wed until 10.00; rest of the year Mon–Fri 06.45–09.00, also Mon, Tue, Thu & Fri 15.00–18.00, Sat 09.00–17.00; all year Sat 09.00–17.00, Sun 08.00–10.00 and 14.00–17.00)

Travel agent Faroe Travel, Sverrisgøta 20; tel: 31 26 00 (Mon–Fri 08.00–17.30, Sat 09.00–noon)

WHAT TO SEE AND DO

Although the centre of Tórshavn doesn't take more than a long morning or afternoon to explore, you'd be wise to allow the capital two or three days if you want to take in some of the more cultural offerings such as museums, the Nordic House and galleries. What follows below is an account of the town's attractions working inland from the areas around Tinganes and Skansin fort, which can be sampled in any order you choose:

The Old Town: Undir Ryggi and Havnar kirkja

If Tórshavn has an old town, it is the delightful confusion of narrow winding lanes and passageways known as Undir Ryggi that spill south from **Bringsnagøta**, a street which cuts west to east across the Tinganes promontory between Bryggjubakki and Áarvegur. Here neat 19th-century wooden houses, their black-tarred walls punctuated by white-framed window frames, nestle eave to eave under roofs of springy grass. Mercifully, these homes were spared the devastation wrought by the fire of 1673 which swept through Tinganes destroying everything in its path. Take time to amble around these alleyways in summer and you're more than likely to find children playing undisturbed in their tiny gardens and chickens wandering freely scratching for food – in fact a snapshot of Tórshavn life that has barely changed over several hundred years; as late as the 1950s there were still some 3,500 hens and chickens registered in the town! Houses here were built purposely small and low, not simply because they were correspondingly easier to keep warm, but also because wood was a scarce commodity. Indeed, it was in Bringsnagøta that the Faroese storyteller, William Heinesen, once lived and scenes from this tightly woven web of lanes and alleyways, where grinding poverty was such a prominent feature of life, pop up repeatedly in so much of his work. Although there's no set path to take when wandering around this area, sooner or later you're bound to come across **Gongin**, once Tórshavn's main street, today a charming narrow lane of picturesque restored houses and small stores dating from the 1800s, many sporting the typical Faroese turf roof and black-tarred walls.

Sitting squat in the middle of the churchyard on the northern side of Bringsnagøta is **Havnar kirkja** (Mon–Fri 16.30–18.00), the church that effectively functions as Tórshavn's **cathedral**. The term 'cathedral', however, is something of a misnomer since this unassuming wooden church is by no means the structure of soaring stone buttresses and giant steeples you may be expecting and has only functioned as the Faroes' cathedral since 1990. In fact the first known church in Tórshavn, built in 1609, didn't even occupy this spot, but was instead located further out on the Tinganes peninsula. At the time it was the largest in the country seating around 150 people, although Tórshavn's population was barely 100. It was this first church with its choir, nave and porch that served as a model for the traditional Faroese timber church which proliferated after 1816. In 1788, it was replaced by today's unadorned white-painted timber structure topped by a grey-slate roof. Major rebuilding in 1865 added an extension to the east and heightened the belltower to make room for a clock. Though demure on the outside, the church interior is altogether more vivid, consisting of garish orange-coloured pews, white walls and blue ceiling panels dotted with gold stars and an altarpiece totally dominated by the early 19th-century painting of the burial of Christ by Daniel Conrad Blunck. Also worth a quick look are the model ships hanging from the roof; one is a model of the *Norske Løve* of the Danish East Indies Company which foundered in a storm in Lambavík off Eysturoy in 1707. Tradition has it that several members of the crew made the model, donating it to the church in thanks for their rescue. Look out too for the church silver, which includes an altar crucifix from 1713 and a leatherbound service book with silver ornamentation which was given to the church by the crew of another ship, the *Justitia*, in 1686.

Tinganes

Marked at its northern edge by the wooden dwellings of Undir Ryggi, Tinganes is the tooth-shaped point of land that reaches out southwards into the waters of Tórshavn harbour, separating the commercial harbour of Eystaravág from the shipyards and marinas of its westerly neighbour, Vestaravág. Today this flat rocky outcrop is dominated by a gaggle of hulking maroon-coloured turf-roofed structures that, quite unassumingly, are home to the Faroese Home Rule government. Forget any notion of security guards armed to the teeth posted outside the seat of national power; instead visitors are free to meander at will amongst these coarsely hewn former warehouses, now home to various ministries, and ponder the admirably low-key approach the Faroese take to government. Although little remains on Tinganes to indicate its medieval importance largely due to the great fire of 1673 and several ensuing blazes including one in 1950, the remaining structures still give the impression of the trading station that once operated here. Indeed, the most significant building on Tinganes is the **Skansapakkhúsið**, a former storage building, that was erected in 1749 furthest out on the promontory on the site of an earlier small fort. In its original form, the building consisted of little more than a single timber storey atop a basement of stones glued together by mortar made from burnt sea shells, a structure typical of much of Tinganes. The addition of several floors and various extensions has given the building its present multi-storey form, grand enough today to house the offices of the prime minister. Whilst you're here, it's worth winding your way behind the building to reach the flagpole close to the very tip of the promontory; it's close to here that a **Viking sundial** or sun rose, as it's called in Faroese, is engraved into the rock. Although little is known about its origins, it's thought the sundial is linked to the worship of the god Thor which took place here until the acceptance of Christianity in the islands around AD1000. You'll find the sundial roughly halfway between the flagpole and the right- hand corner of Skansapakkhúsið when standing with the building behind you; it's about the same size as a large dinner plate.

Tagged on to the side of Skansapakkhúsið, **Salurin, Vektarbúðin, Sjóbúðin**, along with **Bakkapakkhúsið** opposite, are essentially more of the same – wooden structures balanced on a base of stone and mortar, which today house the administrative offices of the Prime Minister and his deputy. The only two buildings to survive the 1673 fire stand on the other side of a low stone wall from here; the **Leigubúðin** once functioned as the Royal Rent Collection Store where the king's revenue, paid in kind, was stored, as did the **Munkastovan** (Monk's Dwelling) opposite, attached to the Bakkapakkhúsið. The unusual structure of this low thick-set turf-roofed building is noteworthy, not only because it is different to the other timber structures on Tinganes, but also because its chunky cavity stone walls are reminiscent of the building style at nearby medieval Kirkjubøur, reliable proof that this building dates from the early Middle Ages and is therefore the oldest building in Tórshavn. Diagonally opposite the Munkastovan, the bizarrely named **Portugálið** (literally Portugal, though the word is a Faroese corruption of the

French *corps de garde*), erected in 1762, superseded a jail or guardhouse with cells in its basement and today still contains an inscription of the crowned monogram of King Christian V in its right wall, the date 1693 and the name of the feudal overlord of the day, Frederik von Gabel, whose family originated from Hamburg. Immediately behind here is one of Tórshavn's most impressive constructions, the **Reyngarður** vicarage built in 1630 in Danish style with four wings around a central courtyard. The west wing has been recently restored and is a fine example of Danish half-timbered design.

Skansin fort

Across the water from Tinganes, at the seaward end of Havnargøta, Skansin fort once marked the entrance to Tórshavn harbour. Dominated by a red-and-white-painted lighthouse, this small fortress was built around 1580, most probably on the orders of the great Faroese adventurer, Magnus Heinason. Construction of a fort to protect the trading centre of Tórshavn was deemed necessary in the face of the steadily increasing number of seaborne attacks across the North Atlantic. Indeed, shortly after Skansin's completion, news reached Tórshavn of a devastating attack on the town of Hvalba in Suðuroy by Turkish pirates in 1629. The original fortification didn't last long before falling victim to the French plundering of Tórshavn in 1677; they destroyed the fort when their final demand for 100 oxen, 200 sheep, 500 pairs of gloves, 1,200 pairs of stockings and 60 nightshirts couldn't be met by the people of Tórshavn within the 12-hour deadline. Skansin was rebuilt a century later only to suffer a similar attack, this time by the British in 1808 during the Napoleonic Wars; two Faroese boat crews were dispatched by the fort commander out into the harbour – where the English Brig, *Clio*, had laid anchor – to enquire what the vessel required, only to return as shields as the British mercilessly attacked the fort, without the demand for either stockings or nightshirts. Finally rebuilt into its present star shape to accommodate an artillery battery and a permanent Danish garrison of around 40 soldiers, the fort later saw the British return as it served as the Royal Navy headquarters when they occupied the Faroes during World War II. Indeed, the two guns which face out to sea from behind the fort were used here to defend the islands against German attack. Four older brass cannons from the time of the Danish Trade Monopoly can also be seen. Although there's not much more to Skansin today, it does offer some quite exceptional views out over the sea to neighbouring Nólsoy, back towards the extremities of Eysturoy and naturally of Tórshavn and Tinganes itself.

Around Niels Finsens gøta

Tórshavn's main shopping street is named after the islands' one and only Nobel Prize winner, Doctor Niels R Finsen (1860–1904), who became only the third scientist to win the prize for medicine. Widely regarded as the man who founded and developed the use of radiotherapy to treat skin diseases, he was awarded the prize in 1903, an event which is commemorated by a plaque close to the southern end of the street, near the junction of Áarvegur and undir Glaðsheyggi. Take the steps leading to Laðabrekka just to the left of Café

Natúr when walking towards the harbour and continue up past the white gates of the residence of Denmark's representative in the Faroes. The exact spot for the memorial was chosen because, as a child, Finsen had carved his initials NRF in the rock which now bears the plaque. However, Niels Finsens gøta is not without sculptures and statues; the small square, **Vaglið**, at its southern end formed by the junction of Niels Finsens gøta, Tinghúsvegur, Mylnugøta and Áarvegur, boasts several: a bust of the Faroese poet and politician, RC Effersøe, the bronze sculpture 'Man and Wife' by Janus Kamban and a portrait of two workers by Fridtjof Joensen. Incidentally, the statue in stainless steel of dancing children a little further along Niels Finsens gøta was originally intended to be the centrepiece of a fountain. However, passers-by became so tired of being drenched by spurts of horizontal water whipped up by the unpredictable Faroese wind that the tap was finally turned off.

On the opposite side of Vaglið square, at the junction of Niels Finsens gøta and Mylnugøta, you'll find one of old Tórshavn's best-preserved turf-roofed wooden buildings which now houses the H N Jacobsen bookshop, without a doubt the best store for books and stationery in town. Well concealed under a row of maple trees, this three-winged structure from 1860, set in front of a well-tended garden, once served as Tórshavn's secondary school, before opening as a bookstore in 1918. Take a step inside and feel the old wooden floorboards creak and twist as you peruse the books for sale.

There could hardly be a greater contrast between the delicate timber façade of the bookshop and the sturdy grey-basalt slabs used to construct the **Býraðið** opposite which today houses the offices of Tórshavn district council. Built in 1894, this rather oppressive block-like building served as a district school before conversion into a town hall in 1955. Thankfully, the impressive sculpture, *Traðarmaðurin* ('Crofter') by Hans Pauli Olsen, of a naked man bearing a fantastically heavy rock, in front of this ugly edifice, enlivens an otherwise gloomy corner.

Løgting: the Faroese parliament

Despite its dominant position at the southern end of Niels Finsens gøta overlooking Vaglið Square, the Løgting (www.logting.fo), one of the smallest parliament buildings in the world, looks more like a suburban family home than the nation's principal debating chamber. Nevertheless, the Faroese parliament has been meeting in this modest timber building since its erection in 1856, although it has undergone several renovations over the years, most recently in 2000 when major restoration work was undertaken to improve the cramped working conditions of the parliamentarians inside and to recreate the building's original pale-grey exterior walls and slate roof. The ground floor is devoted to the chamber, cramped in the extreme and more akin to a town council meeting room in most other countries, whereas the first floor is given over to administration. Every year in July the grassy lawn in front of the small flight of stone steps leading up to the parliament is where Faroe Islanders from across the country gather to listen to the speeches that mark the beginning of the national Ólavsøka festivities.

Kongaminni: the King's monument

From the parliament it's a short dog-leg walk up Tinghúsvegur, right towards undir Glaðsheyggi, right again into R C Effersøes gøta and finally left into Hoyvíksvegur to reach one of the finest viewpoints in Tórshavn: the King's monument. This basalt obelisk was erected in 1882 to commemorate the visit of Danish King Christian IX to the Faroe Islands eight years before. From the monument there are arresting views out over the whole of the Faroese capital and the island of Nólsoy; indeed, it's hard to find another place to take equally good close-up aerial shots of the town.

SMS shopping centre and Viðarlundin Park

Back on Tinghúsvegur, you'll soon cross the busy Bøkjarabrekka heading north out of town for the biggest shopping centre in the Faroes, **SMS** (tel: 31 30 41; www.sms.fo). Occupying what appears from a distance like a series of vast upside-down V-shaped warehouses, this is where the Faroese come to indulge in serious retail therapy, though its relative small scale and lack of big-city sophistication has earned it the nickname, SOS, amongst many visitors. Nonetheless, this is definitely the place to come if you're self-catering since it's also home to the country's largest **supermarket**, Miklagarður (tel: 31 30 11) selling everything from whale meat to chewing gum. Benetton, Body Shop and Burger King are also here, alongside a bank, post office, bookshop, record store and various other purely Faroese stores. Whilst you're here make sure to see the superb multi-coloured glasswork that adorns the central spiral staircase, courtesy of local artist, Tróndur Patursson.

If the array of delights inside the shopping centre has left you out of breath, you may wish to recuperate amid the delightful surroundings of **Viðarlundin Park**, barely a five-minute stroll from the main exit across Tinghúsvegur and then right into Hoydalsvegur which leads directly to the park walls. More tree plantation than park, this is the place to come to get your arboreal fix before heading off into the treeless expanses of the rest of the country. Although efforts began in the 1880s to try to create a wooded park in Tórshavn, they met with little success and most of the specimens present today are barely 100 years old. Storm-force winds tearing in from the Atlantic regularly uproot the plantation's trees and bushes in the park making maintenance a year-round task. On a positive note, the presence of the small forest here has attracted several species of birds rarely found in the Faroes including blackbirds, redwings and collared doves. Countless paths criss-cross the park and it's not difficult to find your own shady glade to relax and enjoy the crisp clean air. Following the small stream which runs through Viðarlundin up through the hilly terrain will bring you to two small ponds, noisy with ducks and geese. Here, at the highest point in the park, a monument bears memory to the Faroese sailors who lost their lives during World War II.

Listasavn Føroya: the National Art Gallery

Housed in what appears at first sight to be a series of top-secret military bunkers hidden among the trees of Viðarlundin, the Listasavn Føroya,

Gundadalsvegur 9 (tel: 31 35 79; www.art.fo; open Jun–Aug Mon–Fri 11.00–17.00; rest of the year Tue–Fri 14.00–17.00; all year Sat & Sun 14.00–18.00; 30kr), is the Faroes' premier art exhibition. Dedicated to continually changing displays of work by local artists and sculptors, this really is the place to come to get to grips with one of the least-well-known arts scenes in Europe. Although Faroese art is still, relatively, in its infancy it's easy to pick out the recurrent themes that determine much of the art this small Nordic nation produces: landscapes, turf-roofed village houses and, above all, the many moods of the sea, are all dominant. Indeed, all the big names are here: Sámal Joensen-Mikines, Janus Kamban and Zacharias Heinesen are usually on display at one time or another.

The gallery, a delightfully light and airy building whose floor is composed of curiously shaped wooden blocks, is divided into a handful of small rooms and corridors, making browsing painless and straightforward. Downstairs a much larger exhibition hall is often used for fashion shows or lectures.

Although the gallery's exhibitions change, the old favourites are generally always on display: the *Mykinesmaður* ('Man from Mykines') by S J Mikines, from 1934, depicting the enigmatic face of an old man with an unkempt grey beard wearing a pointed black hat is classic Faroese art; so too is his *Grindadráp* from 1960, a mêlée of deep reds, maroons and purples to portray the alfresco slicing up of a pod of pilot whales. As the first Faroese painter, Mikines specialised in peaceful, idyllic village portraits as well as the soaring cliff-faces and crashing surf that characterise the Faroe Islands. His work has been an example to all those who have followed after him. Another favourite is Zacharias Heinesen, who is best known for his cubist landscapes; his *Vár* from 1987 portrays a Faroese village in spring, bound by the whites, blues and greens of land merging into sky. The sculptures by Janus Kamban are also demanding of your attention: his engaging series of men's heads and his maternal *Ewe with Lamb* are certainly worthy of greater exposure. Before leaving, make sure you have a look, too, at the postcards the gallery sells for an idea of some of the other works that may not be on display when you visit.

It's also worth noting that this museum is sometimes also known as **Listaskálin**, but, this term really only refers to the building that houses the Faroese National Gallery, not the exhibitions themselves.

Norðurlandahúsið: the Nordic House

A ten-minute walk northwest from the art gallery along Gundadalsvegur then right along the Norðari Ringvegur, passing Faroese national radio, Útvarp Føroya, on the way, brings you to a building that since its inauguration in 1983, has become a Faroese institution: the Norðurlandahúsið (tel: 31 79 00; www.nlh.fo; open Mon–Sat 10.00–18.00, Sun 14.00–18.00; admission free). As its name suggests, the Nordic House is the Faroes' link with the rest of the Nordic countries; indeed, it was one of the aims of the Nordic Council, on whose instigation the building was constructed, that it should help develop cultural links with the rest of the Nordic region through art exhibitions, film shows and lectures. However, over the years the Nordic House has grown into a fully fledged concert hall-cum-theatre-cum-cinema showcasing the many facets of Faroese culture; the concert hall alone, measuring an impressive 500m², can comfortably seat up to 400 people. The true Nordic nature of the project is encapsulated in its construction: the floor tiles are Norwegian, the furniture Finnish, the timber walls Swedish, the glass Danish and the roof is Icelandic. Indeed, the very design of the house was carefully chosen to fit in with the Faroese landscape; no surprise then that the pebble-dashed monster that is Faroese national radio next door looks all the more ghastly next to its sleek and stylish neighbour.

Since the Nordic House is regularly used as a venue for seminars, exhibitions, music festivals, theatre productions and film shows, there's likely to be something of interest going on when you visit. If nothing appeals, there's always a chance to read one of the Nordic-language newspapers which are kept here (the Faroese and Danish ones are particularly useful for weather forecasts – see page 24 for weather terminology) or sample the tasty soup (25kr), sandwiches (35kr) or cakes (25kr) over a cup of coffee (20kr) in the excellent café whilst enjoying the views over Tórshavn and the curious sheep sculptures, Seyðafylgi, made of galvanised iron by Bernhard Lipsøe just beyond the floor-to-ceiling windows here, which help to make the Nordic House such a light, airy and altogether agreeable place to while away an hour or two. Internet access is also available (15kr per 15 minutes, or 40kr per hour; contact reception to get logged on).

Other museums
Føroya Fornminnissavn: Historical Museum
No visit to Tórshavn is complete without taking in the best museum in the country, the Historical Museum, (tel: 31 07 00; www.natmus.fo; bus #2 and 3; open mid-May to mid-Sep Mon–Fri 10.00–17.00, Sat 14.00–17.00; all year Sun 14.00–17.00; 30kr), located at Brekkutún 6 in the town of Hoyvík on the northeastern outskirts of the capital. Housed in a new two-storey building looking out over the Atlantic, this is the place to come to really understand how the Faroes and the Faroese have developed over the centuries. After paying your modest entrance fee, forsake the ground-floor exhibitions and head straight away down the staircase to your right for an eyeful of the museum's pièce de résistance: the medieval **Kirkjubøstólarnir** pew-ends. In a dark room lit only by soft overhead lighting, these ornately carved bench-ends, all 16 dating from the early 1400s, are truly breathtaking in their elemental beauty; intricate carvings of the 12 apostles, including St Peter holding the key to heaven and John the Baptist with a poisoned chalice, readily discernible. Justifiably regarded as the Faroes' greatest national treasure and in a quite remarkable state of preservation, they each adorned the pews of the medieval episcopal residence in Kirkjubøur (today's parish church). During extensive renovation work during the mid-19th century, all woodwork in the church was replaced and dispatched to the Museum of National Antiquities in Denmark. For over 100 years, the pew-ends remained a bone of contention between Tórshavn and Copenhagen, with frequent

requests by the Faroese for this invaluable piece of their heritage to be returned to the islands, ignored. However, spurred on by the success of their Icelandic neighbours in ensuring the return of several strategic medieval Icelandic manuscripts held by the Danes, the Faroese persisted and finally signed an agreement in the summer of 1999 with the Danish government for the return of around 400 antiquities and documents, including the Kirkjubøurstólarnir, in July 2002.

Sadly, the other exhibits elsewhere downstairs can only pale into insignificance in comparison: a *tíggjumannafar*, a boat with a ten-man crew, from Nólsoy used for trading journeys whose rowlock bindings are made from pilot-whale skin; and the *áttamannafar*, whose eight-man crew used the vessel for whale hunting and springtime fishing, are the least dull of the five rowing boats on display down here.

Back on the ground floor, it's best to skip the mind-numbing array of predictable how-we-used-to-live paraphernalia, featuring such highlights as patterned women's knitted jumpers and ornamental jewellery, in favour of the altogether more engaging sections on the **Viking age**. Especially noteworthy is the glorious jumble of archaeological finds recovered in the mid-'80s from four 10th-century houses in Leirvík on Eysturoy, including wooden nails, counting sticks and knife handles. During similar excavation in the '50s at Yviri í Trøð in Tjørnuvík, also on Eysturoy, fragments of a skull were found when 12 graves were unearthed – also on display.

Before leaving, have a look too at the section devoted to the history of the **Faroese flag**, a subject close to the heart of all Faroese. The current flag, a red and blue cross on a white background, was designed by students at the University of Copenhagen in 1919, keen that their own country should also have a Nordic-style flag as a symbol of nationhood to replace the ram and oystercatcher emblems which had been in use until then. With the support of the Faroese people, the new flag, the Merkið, first flew in the islands in June 1919 in Fámjin on Suðuroy where it can still be seen on display in the village church. The museum example is the flag first made in Copenhagen as a 'table flag' as it's known in Faroese, a kind of prototype.

Hoyvíksgarður: Open-air Museum

An operating farm from the Middle Ages until the 1960s, the Open-air Museum, Hoyvíksgarður, barely a stone's throw across Hvítanesvegur from the Historical Museum, is worth a look for an insight into Faroese farming traditions through the centuries. Hoyvík was originally a settlement of just two farmhouses and associated outhouses; the farm has been divided and reunited several times over during its existence. The museum site is composed of several small barns and storage huts gathered around the main farmhouse, a solid timber construction from 1803 designed to withstand the worst of the Atlantic storms that sweep in from **Hoyvík Bay**, the farm's location. Inside, the low ceiling and solid timber walls create a snug atmosphere for the array of rooms that lead off the main living room. Close to the farmhouse, there are a number of slatted outhouses, where mutton was left to dry in the fresh air;

worthy of a quick peek. In the opposite direction, a path heads off through the farm down to Hoyvík Bay ending at a series of landing places; take care to stick to the paths and not to walk on the grass.

Náttúrugripasavn: Museum of Natural History

Although the Museum of Natural History at V U Hammerschaimbs gøta 13 (tel: 35 23 00; www.ngs.fo; open Jun–Aug Mon–Fri 11.00–16.00, Sat 15.00–17.00; all year Sun 15.00–17.00; 20kr;), the tongue-twisting Náttúrugripasavn in Faroese, can't hope to compete with the Historical Museum in terms of content, it is nevertheless worth a visit for its eye-opening exhibits on Faroese **whaling**. Run by the ebullient marine biologist, Dorethe Bloch, this place contains all the information you ever wanted to know about whales and whaling; the only problem is it's not in English. Still, with a little perseverance and help from the staff, it's possible to get an insight into the Faroese obsession with pilot whales. Start with the skeleton and model of a pilot whale, suspended from the museum ceiling, to get an idea of the size of these creatures, roughly around a couple of metres in length, which populate the waters off the Faroes. Alongside, proudly exhibited on the walls of the museum, is a series of photographs of a whale hunt together with the various implements used to kill the whales. The Faroese language is awash with whaling terms, not least for the vast array of tools used for the job, some of which you can see here: everything from a *grindaknívur*, a specially designed knife that has become a popular gift to Faroese boys on their confirmation and a potent symbol of the transition to manhood, to the *sóknarongul*, a no-messing blunt gaff. Although many visitors to the Faroe Islands want to witness a *grindadráp* or whale hunt, most leave disappointed since they occur infrequently and with little warning. The museum holds unbroken statistics dating back to 1709 on the frequency and location of the kills; it seems Miðvágur, close to the airport on Vágar, is a popular place for the whales to come ashore.

To be honest though, given the lack of translations of the exhibits, it's the models, skeletons and assorted other stuffed bits-and-bobs around the museum that are most likely to impress: the 15m-long skull and jawbone of a sperm whale from 1987, a now-extinct great auk and a squid, caught alive by a local fishing boat, whose tentacles museum staff are only too keen to point out, measure a whopping five metres in length. Have a fleeting look, too, at the display of fish found in Faroese waters, if only to be able to identify anything which might later appear on your dinner plate.

Adjoining the museum there's a small **botanical garden** containing most species of flora found in the Faroe Islands which might be worth a quick look – if it's not raining.

Western Tórshavn: Vesturkirkja church

From the Museum of Natural History it's an easy ten-minute walk back down V U Hammerschaimbs gøta and left into Landavegur to one of the most striking landmarks in Tórshavn, the Vesturkirkja church. Its soaring copper tower, built in the form of a pyramid, can be seen across the capital and caused much controversy on completion in 1975. The church has restricted opening hours (Jun–Aug, Mon–Sat 15.00–17.00; rest of the year Tue, Thu and Fri 16.00–17.30, Wed 10.00–noon) although it's generally possible to visit at other times by making an appointment; ask at the Kunningarstovan in Niels Finsens gøta. The unadorned interior is dominated by a 30m-high vertical column of white stone behind the altar which reaches up into the pyramidal tower, high above the grey-slate flooring.

Around Vestaravág harbour

Retracing your steps east along Landavegur brings you to Tórshavn's old walled **graveyard**, a grassy muddle of ancient moss-covered headstones and gnarled trees twisted into curious shapes by the ferocious winds. Although burials now take place in the much larger churchyard on Velbastaðvegur in the southwestern reaches of the town, it's this smaller affair, straight out of a *Scooby-Doo* episode, that is the more atmospheric. From here **Gríms Kambans gøta** leads downhill towards **Vestaravág harbour** passing some of Tórshavn's most elegant dwellings: a lovely place to stroll, with its huddled wooden houses and twisting corners; this street evokes much of the atmosphere of 19th-century Tórshavn. It's worth studying some of the houses closely, not least the one towards the western end of the street at No 26 – a weathered creamy orange and red structure dating from 1902 with an elaborate carved roof in Norwegian style. Look out too for the turf-roofed wooden house, Smiðjan í Litluvík, at the corner with Skálatrøð. A stylish gallery used by the town's artists to exhibit their work, its opening times vary according to the exhibition, so ask at the Kunningarstovan for details. Continue along Gríms Kambans gøta and you'll eventually come to the area known as Vágsbotnur, literally the end of the bay, which marks the corner of the Vestaravág harbour with the beginnings of Undir Ryggi and Tinganes. It's here that you'll find a monument to **Nólsoy Páll** (see *Nólsoy*, page 81) who is remembered in the islands as the man who fought for the lifting of the Danish Trade Monopoly.

Around Tórshavn

Even if you're only staying for a short time, it's a good idea to get out of Tórshavn and see some of the surrounding attractions. Indeed, it's only on leaving the Faroese capital and venturing into some of the smaller villages and islands that you'll fully appreciate Tórshavn's charms; life in this pint-sized town may be enviably sedate, but the place is a veritable metropolis when compared with some of the remoter villages and islands which are all totally dependent on the capital for their economic well-being. Whilst all roads may lead to Rome, in the Faroe Islands it's Tórshavn that acts as the focal point for all buses and ferries. Travelling on the islands' superb network of public transport therefore makes day trips an absolute doddle and a refreshing contrast to the big smoke.

The one place everybody who comes to the Faroe Islands wants to see is barely half an hour outside Tórshavn: **Kirkjubøur**. Easily the most significant settlement during the Middle Ages, the wonderfully preserved medieval **cathedral** here stands as a monument to the leading role this tiny hamlet, once the site of the bishop's see, played throughout Faroese history. However, it's also a possibility to combine a trip to Kirkjubøur with a one-way hike up over the barren moorlands of southern Streymoy that helps to make a visit here such an alluring option; you can then hop on the bus and be whisked back into Tórshavn. There's more religious history at hand in the village of **Kaldbak**, barely a 30-minute bus ride north of Tórshavn on the shores of the eponymous fjord, where the handsome **wooden church** complete with turf roof, one of many dotted around the Faroes, dates from 1835.

Equally appealing, though for totally different reasons, is a short boat trip out to **Nólsoy**, the island with the flat-topped mountain immediately off Tórshavn, which helps make views out across the harbour so striking. The huddle of narrow streets that make up the tiny village couldn't be more different to the capital: not only are there no cars here but also life goes on seemingly as it has for decades. Wander through the village and you'll doubtless see seabirds being plucked ready for the pot and old men sitting gossiping at the harbourside watching the comings and goings of the fishing boats. Nólsoy is also the place to come to go hiking: an easily negotiable path leads out across the springy heathland, skirting the foot of the Eggjarklettur

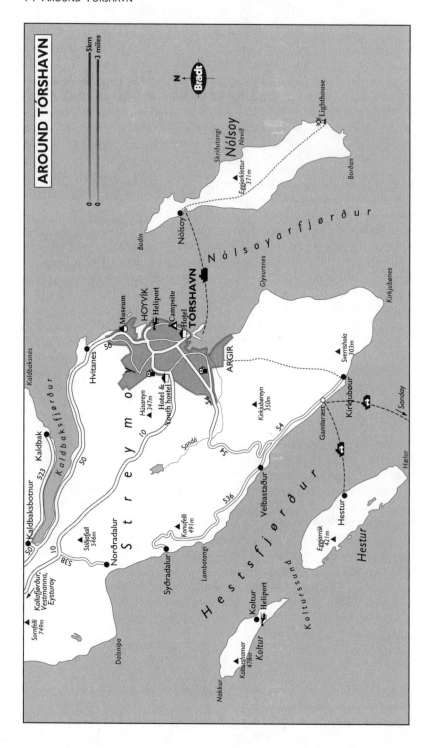

AROUND TÓRSHAVN

0 5km
0 3 miles

N

Bradt

Nólsoy

Skriðutangi
Neviò

Eggjarklettur
371m

Borðan

Lighthouse

Bøðin

Nólsoy

Nólsoyarfjørður

Glyvursnes

Kirkjubøanes

Kaldbaksnes

Kaldbaksfjørður

Kaldbak
523

Kaldbaksbotnur

50

Hvítanes

50
10

Streymoy

Museum
HOYVÍK
Heliport
Campsite
Hotel
TÓRSHAVN

Húsareyn
347m
Hotel &
youth hostel

Sandá

54

ARGIR

Sverrishola
303m

Kirkjubøreyn
350m

54

Kirkjubøur

Sandoy

Gamlarætt

Staðafjall
546m

Norðradalur

50
10

538

Syðradalur

Kanufelli
491m

536

Lambatangi

Velbastaður

Hestsfjørður

Hestur

Eggjarrók
421m

Hestur

Hælur

Kollafjørður,
Vestmanna,
Eysturoy

Sornfelli
749m

Dalsnípa

Koltursund

Koltur
Heliport

Koltur

Kolbushamar
478m

Nakkur

peak, to the old lighthouse station on the island's southern tip, from where there are dramatic views out over the Atlantic swells to Sandoy.

If after a stay in Tórshavn you're looking to get totally out into the wilds and take in some awesome mountain scenery along the way, you're in luck. Off Streymoy's southwestern coast, the little-visited islands of **Hestur**, and better still **Koltur**, home to just one solitary farm, are within easy reach. A ferry runs out to Hestur from the harbour at Gamlarætt, just north of Kirkjubøur and connected to Tórshavn by bus, making a total journey time of around 90 minutes. However, it's Koltur that is the real draw. Accessible only by helicopter, the working sheep farm here offers simple accommodation and an insight into what it's like to live on one of the most isolated of all the Faroe Islands. Koltur also boasts one of the most beautiful and unusually shaped mountains in the country, the sugar-loaf Kolturshamar that can be seen for miles around; if you're looking for a quintessentially Faroese experience, it's right here.

KIRKJUBØUR

Curiously for such a historically significant site, Kirkjubøur (web: www.patursson.com) owes its existence to two seemingly incidental things: driftwood and seaweed. Thanks to the tidal currents, the preponderance of driftwood that washes up on the shore here, matched nowhere else in the country, coupled with copious amounts of seaweed, proved invaluable for the settlement's development. In a denuded country where trees simply don't grow, driftwood was a much-prized and sought-after commodity, not simply for construction of houses but also for kindling. Seaweed, on the other hand, was used as fertiliser on the barren land to aid the cultivation of crops. In fact, it's widely believed this enabled Irish hermits, probably the area's first inhabitants, to eke out a simple existence here around AD800, brief accounts of which can be found in the work *De mensura orbis terrae* by the Irish monk, Dicuil.

However, their stay in the Faroes was short-lived and, as the arrival of Norwegian Vikings in their longboats became steadily more frequent, the Irish fled. It wasn't until several centuries later, around 1020, with the islands firmly under Viking control, that Kirkjubøur began to flourish. It was on the instigation of a wealthy woman known as Gæsa, daughter of the local farmer Tórhallur the Rich who then owned half of Streymoy, that a church was first built here. With the arrival of Gudmundur, the first bishop in the Faroes around 1100, the tiny settlement's strategic role in Faroese religious life was not only assured, but was also strengthened as the Church, from its base here at Kirkjubøur, asserted its dominance by seizing land across the country. According to tradition, Gudmundur confiscated large parts of Gæsa's land as punishment for her breaking the Church's strict fasting rules.

Today, in addition to the overgrown and somewhat uninspiring remains of what's thought to be a church and graveyard to the east, up beyond the main site, the farmstead of Kirkjubøur effectively consists of three main elements: the farmhouse itself, **Roykstovan**; the present parish church, **Ólavskirkjan**, benefiting from a superb location right on the shoreline; and the reason for all the fuss: the magnificent medieval **Magnus Cathedral**, the effective seat of power over several centuries.

Getting there and away

Bus #101 runs seven times daily (less frequently on Sat and Sun) from the Farstøðin in Tórshavn to Kirkjubøur via the harbour at Gamlarætt. A single ticket costs just 20kr. Returning to Tórshavn from Kirkjubøur requires calling ahead (tel: 34 30 30) and letting the bus company know that you're intending to travel. If you're hiking (see below), you may want to time your walk to coincide with return bus times to Tórshavn. Following a lengthy break in services after 10.40 (daily), the first afternoon bus currently leaves at 14.25. There's then roughly one bus every 60 to 90 minutes until the last one at 18.55.

Other practicalities

Since there is no overnight accommodation available at Kirkjubøur, it's best not to get stuck here. Other than a small **café** which sells refreshments and snacks during the summer months, there are no facilities here, so if you're planning a day trip it might be a good idea to bring everything you need with you.

What to see
Magnus Cathedral

It's for the impressive Magnus Cathedral (Múrurin in Faroese, literally 'The Walls') that Kirkjubøur is justifiably best known. This whopping Gothic structure measuring 27m long and 11m wide was built around 1300 from rock and stone quarried from nearby hillsides at the behest of the Faroese bishop, **Erlendur** (1269–1308) and served as the Faroe Islands' cathedral until the Reformation in 1538. However, it was probably never completed and today looks pretty much as it did on the day building ground to a halt 700 years ago – roofless. It seems the bishop overestimated the capacity of the islanders to construct such a vast monument to their new God (Christianity had come to the Faroes barely 300 years earlier); in fact, depending on which story you believe, building stopped due to a bloody uprising against the bishop's extortionate taxes, or as a symbol of the poverty wrought by the Black Death in the mid-1300s. According to new research, it is possible that a roof may actually have been built.

Today the cathedral's stone walls, over 1.5m thick, still stand at their full height of 9m, quite a remarkable achievement given the inclement nature of Faroese weather. Whereas the long southern wall is decorated by five steeply arched windows and two smaller openings, the opposite wall has just one access point leading into the sacristy where the remains of a staircase are still visible. Although a roof once covered this part of the cathedral, an avalanche in 1772 brought it crashing to the ground destroying the staircase, which it's believed led up into a tower; barely one or two steps now remain. Carved into the interior walls, six of the original 12 Maltese crosses are still in place, whilst on the external eastern wall a stone plaque portraying Christ on the cross with the Virgin Mary and Mary Magdalene at his side bears a weather-beaten inscription in Latin denoting the fact that the cathedral is dedicated to St Magnus and St Thorlak. According to the plaque there is also, bizarrely, a secret cavity in the wall behind containing a number of ancient relics. In 1905 the plaque was indeed removed to reveal seven religious artefacts including a silk ribbon supposedly from the habit of the Virgin Mary and pieces of bone from bishop Thorlak and Magnus Erlendsson, the Earl of Orkney who was canonised in 1135.

Following heated debate about how best to preserve the crumbling remains of Magnus Cathedral, it was decided to cover the outer walls with metal to give the stone chance to dry out. Sadly, therefore, whilst this building work is in progress, it's officially no longer allowed to enter the cathedral. Although ugly scaffolding is omnipresent a visit here is still incredibly worthwhile; it's only by getting close up to the cathedral that you can comprehend the sheer scale of this unfinished venture. In fact, there are now controversial plans to finally complete the cathedral and cover it with a steel roof as protection against the worst of the weather.

Roykstovan farmhouse

Dating from the 11th century and formerly used as the bishop's residence, the turf-roofed **Roykstovan** (May–Aug, Mon–Sat 09.00–17.30, Sun 14.00–17.30; 30kr; at other times ask at the farmhouse) is the oldest inhabited wooden house in Europe. The Faroese name, literally meaning 'smoke room', refers to the ancient practice of lighting a fire in a specially constructed room with a hole in the roof, which allows the smoke to escape. Built of coarsely hewn timber logs smeared in black tar, the farmhouse sits atop a basement of sturdy stone walls, in parts more than 2m thick. According to tradition, the farmhouse is of Norwegian origin and first stood in the Sognefjord before being dismantled, its logs numbered and floated across the sea to the Faroes. Today, the Patursson family, who have occupied the building for centuries and can trace their ancestors back over 17 generations to the time of the Reformation, still live here. Naturally, their home is not open to visitors but the oldest part of the building, the **Stokkastovan**, built from driftwood around the same time as the cathedral, as well as the more interesting Roykstovan itself, are open to visitors. Entrance is via the stone staircase directly opposite the cathedral; put your entrance fee in the box provided. Once inside take the narrow staircase up into the Roykstovan which occupies the central portion of the farmhouse. Formerly a living, working and dining area all rolled into one, this long rectangular room was where the fire was set; indeed, the blackened roof timbers are now thickly impregnated with smoke from the turf fires that once burned in here. To escape the inclement weather outdoors, the entire family would gather here to comb wool, sew and make everything they needed to keep the house in good order. It was also here that they told stories and danced the Faroese chain dance around the fire, naturally for enjoyment's sake, but also as an effective way of keeping warm. Today, though, the room is smoke free and a window covers the hole in the roof above where the fires once burned. Alongside various traditional household implements that were once used in the room (the fanciful wooden carvings are sadly 20th-century imitation), there's a bust of the Norwegian king, Sverri, who, as the illegitimate son of King Sigurd, was brought up by Kirkjubøur's bishops away from the prying public eye. The cramped room, located right up under the eaves off the Roykstovan, is where the bishops once worked.

Ólavskirkjan church

The whitewashed parish church at Kirkjubøur, dedicated to St Olav, is the oldest still in use in the Faroe Islands. Originally built sometime during the 12th century, most probably around 1111, it served as a cathedral throughout the medieval period, but has since been extensively rebuilt and renovated, most notably in 1874 (to save it from falling into the sea) and 1966. The restoration work, though, was heavy handed and it was from this church that the ornate Kirkjubøurstólarnir **pew-ends** (see *Tórshavn*, page 69), which once graced the interior, were spirited away to the Danish National Museum in distant Copenhagen. Thankfully, the exquisitely well-preserved carved Madonna, dating from the 13th century, remained in the islands and is today on display in the Historical Museum in Tórshavn. Despite the rebuilding, one interesting feature of the church walls remains: the bricked-up hole in the northern wall, which until leprosy died out in the mid-18th century, was used by lepers, who were not allowed into the church, to listen to the service; be prepared to hunt around a bit to locate it. Unusually for a Faroese church, this one is never locked, making it not only an easy worthwhile visit, but also a welcome haven should the heavens open. Inside the 1.5m-thick walls, you'll find a solemn white-painted interior containing pews of natural wood; the only colour is that of the striking impressionist painting behind the altar by Sámal Joensen-Mikines of a religious scene depicting a rowing boat. During excavation work in the 1950s a bishop's staff with a gilded head was discovered in a grave under the floor of the crypt; an uninspiring replica is on display in a glass case near the altar, whereas the original is under the safekeeping of the Historical Museum.

Hiking to Kirkjubøur from Tórshavn

The easy 7km hike to Kirkjubøur takes about two hours and climbs up to around 230m. From Vestaravág harbour head west along J C Svabøes gøta out towards the hospital. Beyond here the road changes its name to Velbastaðvegur, passing the new cemetery and a small industrial estate, home to Föroya Bjór. Take the next left, við Sandá, to a farm and the start of the footpath to Kirkjubøur. Go through the gate which marks the end of the homefield and start climbing the hill – turn around and you'll have a fantastic view over Tórshavn and all of Nólsoy. Soon you'll start to see cairns marking two different paths – left to Kirkjubøur and right to Velbastaður. Take the much better trodden left path and after a short while you'll come across two small lakes where there's a profusion of kittiwakes during the summer months. Still following the cairns you'll next find a chair built of rocks; oddly for such a remote location, open-air public meetings have been held here since the late 1800s with flags fluttering, national speeches and patriotic songs filling the air. A superb panorama of Hestur, Koltur and Sandoy will come into view beyond here followed by a steady descent towards the tiny offshore islet, Kirkjubøholmur, which was once part of the main village and attached to the mainland; ruins of a couple of houses can still be seen on the island from Kirkjubøur's heyday during the 15th and 16th centuries when up to 50 dwellings stood here and the place counted 200 and 5,000 sheep. The last stretch of the path descends steeply before it turns into a wider track which then leads down into the farming settlement of Kirkjubøur.

NÓLSOY

A day trip to the island of Nólsoy is one of the most enjoyable things to do whilst visiting Tórshavn. Not only do you get a superb view of the Faroese capital from the water as the tiny ferry which sails to the island steadily chugs out of the harbour, but it's also a chance to explore the floating humpbacked finger of land that you'll have become distantly familiar with whilst in Tórshavn since it's an integral part of the view out to sea from all over town. Nólsoy also has the advantage of being just about the right size to tackle in a day: between ferries there's enough time to explore the village, visit the Faroes' most famous taxidermist to buy a stuffed puffin or two as well as hike out through unspoilt nature to the stunningly located lighthouse on the island's southern tip. However, should you choose to stay overnight, there's also a chance to visit the largest colony of storm petrels anywhere in the world.

Getting there and away

Although sailing time from Tórshavn to Nólsoy is just 20 minutes, ferry departure times vary from day to day. In addition to three daily sailings, there are extra trips on most days of the week, with ferries most frequent on Monday, Wednesday and Friday. The last return back to Tórshavn leaves at 18.25 every day except Friday, when it goes an hour later.

Where to stay and eat

Simple but comfortable accommodation with shared facilities is available at the **Kaffistovan** (tel: 32 71 75 or 32 70 25; fax: 32 71 76; 350kr including breakfast, a single is 200kr); the largest room here has a balcony overlooking the harbour. When it comes to eating and drinking Hervør will also rustle up something fishy for you if you ask in advance for around 100kr including dessert and coffee, though light snacks and drinks are available all day; you might also be able to buy a stuffed puffin here should the urge take you, in case you're unable to locate taxidermist Jens. Bear in mind though that neither Hervør nor her husband Edmund, who was born and bred on the island, speak English.

Other practicalities

There are two **food stores** in the village, one up behind the Kaffistovan, the other down by the harbour, as well as a **post office** (Mon–Fri 12.30–13.30).

Nólsoy village

Even though it's so readily accessible from Tórshavn, Nólsoy village makes a striking comparison with the capital. It's a wonderfully sedate, traditional and slow-moving sort of place where life is concentrated on the tiny harbour immediately below the couple of gently sloping streets that climb the hillside upon which the village perches. On leaving the ferry dock on the quayside, you enter Nólsoy under an archway made by the jawbones of a sperm whale, whilst being observed by the old men who gather on the couple of benches alongside to chew the fat and eye up the island's visitors. It's here too that you'll find a **memorial stone** to Ove Joensen, the local man who rowed single-handedly in the summer of 1986 to the Little Mermaid statue in Copenhagen to raise money for the construction of a swimming pool on the island. After several previously unsuccessful attempts (bad weather forced him to turn back), Ove reached the Danish capital in just 41 days after an arduous journey via the Shetland Islands and the Limfjord in Jutland. Tragically, just three months after his epic voyage and at the age of just 39, Ove slipped on deck and fell to his death in the icy November waters off the southern tip of Eysturoy whilst on his way back to Nólsoy following a day's fishing; it's thought alcohol may have been to blame for the accident. His grave can be visited in the village churchyard to the south of the main village; above the poignant inscription 'the fjord is rowed', the headstone bears a black and white photograph of the man and his rowing boat, the *Dana Victoria*. The entire island now celebrates Ove's heroic achievements on the anniversary of his arrival in Copenhagen in early August with the *Ovastevnan* – a sort of island games consisting of various sporting challenges held in the school playground, which attracts competitors from across the country; money raised goes towards the swimming pool project which is well under way. Ove's boat is still proudly kept on the island and is available for viewing in one of the boatsheds down by the harbour; gain instant respect for his feat by asking Edmund or Hervør at the Kaffistovan café (it's the second house behind the jawbone) to be shown around. Although there are no specific sights in Nólsoy other than the *Dana Victoria*, most people come here to visit Jens-Kjeld Jensen, Faroese taxidermist extraordinaire; everything from rabbits to gannets, you name it, he's got it stuffed. Every year Jens heads off to Mykines with his nets to catch birds for his collection, parts of which are for sale; reckon on around 350kr for a puffin. Jens's house, a yellow building on the northwestern side of the village, is the last on the road that climbs up left out of the village past the village school. Between June and late September Jens also leads night-time excursions (tel: 32 70 64 or book at the Kunningarstovan in Tórshavn or the Kaffistovan in Nólsoy) to the world's largest **storm petrel colony** on Nólsoy's east coast. Tours leave the village one hour before sunset for the 60-minute walk to the colony at Skriðutangi point below the island's main peak,

BUSINESS AS USUAL: NÓLSOY PÁLL AND THE TRADE MONOPOLY

Without a doubt, Nólsoy's most famous son is also one of the Faroes' greatest heroes: **Poul Poulsen** or **Nólsoy Páll** as he's popularly known. Born on the island in 1766, Páll grew up during the needy years of the Danish Trade Monopoly, which forbade the Faroese to own ships and trade with foreign countries. However, the young Páll was quick to benefit from the opportunities available in Tórshavn, where he learnt boat building and navigation, administration and book-keeping. Following the American War of Independence (1775–83), when the Faroes served as a strategic base for smuggled goods across the Atlantic, Páll made his first journey overseas to America at the age of 20 to work as a ship's master. It was following his later service on board ships operating between the Faroes and Denmark that he decided to challenge the unjust Monopoly. With the aid of friends, he rebuilt the wreck of the *Royndin Fríða*, which had stranded off Hvalba in Suðuroy, and set off on several trading trips to Copenhagen and Bergen; in 1805 he returned to the Faroes from Norway with much-needed smallpox vaccine, traded against Faroese coal. Páll's ship, the *Good Endeavour* in English, was the first trading vessel to be Faroese owned and operated since Viking times and hence marked a significant turning point in the commercial stranglehold the Danes had over the Faroes. However, facing opposition not only from the Danish authorities in Copenhagen but also from the Faroese petty bourgeoisie whose wealth depended on the Monopoly's continued existence, Páll took his complaint of unfair trading to Crown Prince Fredrik in 1807 who agreed that changes were indeed necessary. Although Denmark's fatalistic involvement in the Napoleonic Wars against England put paid to any agreement reached, it's widely believed that Páll's battle against Danish supremacy marked the beginning of the end of the Trade Monopoly which was finally lifted in 1856. Tragically, it was an achievement Páll never lived to see; in the winter of 1809, at the age of 42, his ship went down whilst transporting a cargo of corn to the famine-stricken Faroe Islands, a pawn in the war between Denmark and England, with all hands lost.

Eggjarklettur (372m). The trips offer a unique chance to see these nocturnal birds lunge through the night sky at truly remarkable speeds as they search for food, as well as a number of other species including fulmars and puffins. Incidentally, Nólsoy's main **puffin colony** is just down the coast from Skriðutangi, beyond the next headland, Nevið, at the cliff-face known as Urðin – though it's not a trip you should make in the dark. Accommodation is provided at the Kaffistovan in the village; the cost of the tour with a made-up bed is 350kr, or, in your own sleeping bag on a mattress it's 300kr.

Hiking to the lighthouse at Borðan

The walking path to the lighthouse on Nólsoy's southern tip, Borðan (6km each way; allow four to five hours there and back), begins just south of the main village beyond the island's narrowest point – literally a few metres across – to the left of which lie rounded basalt rocks thrown up by winter storms; to the right is the harbour. During easterly gales the greater part of the village can be drenched with spray and it's not uncommon for the enormous Atlantic rollers to crash right over the island at this narrow isthmus. Follow the road up past the graveyard through an area known as Korndalur where you may spot several 14th-century stone ruins by the roadside. Still in the homefield, these remains are the *Prinsessutoftir*, said to be the home of the pregnant daughter of a Scottish king, who fell out with her father and fled to Nólsoy after he refused to accept her choice of husband, none other than the man who had fathered her still-unborn child. Once beyond the homefield boundary the made road turns into a path following traces of an old water pipe and eventually reaching a small reservoir. From here cairns mark the steep climb up the lower reaches of the **Eggjaklettur** peak (371m). The path soon levels out and from hereon it's an easy, if somewhat soggy walk in parts, along a wide grassy plateau known as **Langabrekka**. There are some truly spectacular views from this part of Nólsoy, both up towards the northern islands as well as south towards Sandoy and – at one point – even the sugar-loaf mountain of Kolturshamar on Koltur can also be spotted. At times the cairns can be hard to pick out and it may be easier to use the two transmitters which will soon come into sight to help guide you towards the southern shore. Once beyond the small lake, Halavatn, it's a steady descent towards the main **lighthouse**, Nólsoyar Viti. At the time of its construction in 1893, the lighthouse boasted one of the largest lenses in the world at nearly three metres in height and four tons in weight. The two longhouses beside the lighthouse were built by the British during World War II to act as a decoy and mislead the Germans. Today, they're used solely for accommodating maintenance workers who come here every so often to keep the lighthouse in order. Unbelievably, three families with a total of ten children once lived at this remote outpost; there was even a school here which alternated classes with its equivalent in Nólsoy village. From the lighthouse a path leads down to the landing stage, Stallurin, where all goods in and out of Borðan had to be loaded and unloaded; if you choose to walk down to the landing stage, whose Faroese name 'the stall' was coined since boats here can lie side by side like horses in a stable, it will add another 800m each way to the hike. The smaller lighthouse you can see in the distance to the southwest is a much less impressive affair and not really worth the extra effort in reaching; it's this light that can be seen from Tórshavn not that of Nólsoyar Viti. Instead sit and enjoy the views from its much bigger brother whose light can be seen from up to 20 miles at sea. The route back to Nólsoy village simply involves retracing your steps.

HESTUR

Separated from southwestern Streymoy by the choppy waters of **Hestfjørður** fjord, the 6km² island of Hestur is home to just 50 people, most of whom live in the cluster of old houses grouped around the new harbour midway along the sheltered east coast. The steep hillsides which bank up behind the village are indicative of the terrain of much of the rest of the island; the peaks of **Eggjarrók** and **Múlin**, both 421m, dominate the northern and western parts of Hestur and render much of the coast inaccessible. In fact, the uninterrupted sheer cliff-faces of the west coast are a haven for many species of bird, particularly guillemot, and, until it became extinct in the 1800s, the great auk was also found here in considerable numbers. From the two peaks, the land gently falls away to the south towards an area of boggy farmland known as **Hælur**, just north of the lighthouse which guards the island's southernmost point, Skútin. It's on this relatively flat tract of land, dotted by several trout-rich lakes including the poetically named **Fagradalsvatn** (literally 'lake of the beautiful valley') that most of the island's farming takes place, since the land around the village of Hestur itself is too steep.

Getting there and away
A trip to Hestur requires careful planning since there's only one ferry a day over to the island departing at 08.45 from Gamlarætt on Streymoy; sailing time is just 15 minutes. The return boat leaves Hestur at 17.35, sailing first via Skopun on Sandoy before turning round and heading back for Gamlarætt. Handily, this routing makes it possible to combine a visit to Hestur with onward travel to the southern islands.

Other practicalities
Should you stay overnight on Hestur, there's also an early departure directly to Gamlarætt at 07.05 (Mon–Fri). Although there's no accommodation on Hestur, it is possible to **camp** near the lakes at Hælur though you should bring all provisions with you since there are no facilities on the island. There is, however, a small **grocer's store** in the village and a **post office**. Curiously for such a small place, Hestur also has a **swimming pool** to which every inhabitant has a key; it's in the modern-looking building up behind the school though it's not open to the public.

The island
Although some fishing boats still put out from Hestur, the island has suffered severe depopulation over the years as men have moved to Tórshavn to work on larger ocean-going vessels and earn considerably more money. However, in an attempt to stem the outflow of people, a new harbour and breakwater have been built to make it possible to fillet and freeze fish on the island, thus providing employment for the islanders.

Peacefully uneventful, Hestur is the place to come if you want to get away from it all; unlike Nólsoy, with a population five times that of tiny Hestur, this is a place to experience the Faroes at their most remote without trekking up to the distant north of the country. Rather than taking in sights, the island's charms are to be found more in a stroll up and down the one and only road that runs the length of the east coast, petering out past the Hvannagjógv cleft at the lighthouse, or a hike up to the high land known as **Heyggjur**. Although there are no marked walking paths on the island, it is possible, with local advice, to reach the flat-topped Eggjarrók and Múlin peaks, where some really quite stunning views unfold. Up here you're well above the hills that divide Kirkjubøur from Tórshavn over on Streymoy and you have picture-perfect vistas of neighbouring Koltur, barely a couple of kilometres away across Kolturssund sound.

KOLTUR

Dwarfed by its much bigger northerly neighbour, Koltur, measuring in at just 2km², may be the third-smallest of all the Faroe Islands (ahead only of Stóra and Lítla Dímun), but it is certainly one of the most beautiful. More than half of this long and skinny island is made up of **Kolturshamar**, the ice-cream-cone-shaped peak soaring to a height of 478m, that bears down ominously on the solitary farm here, today the only human habitation on the isle.

Getting there and away

Although there is a small harbour on Koltur it is no longer served by ferry traffic and the only way to get here is to take the Atlantic Airways helicopter. Indeed, a flight here skimming the vertical cliff-faces that make up Koltur's western coast, and clipping the top of Kolturshamar, is a truly breathtaking experience, as much a part of a trip here as a stay on the island itself. Bear in mind, though, that the helicopter can be subject to delays and cancellation in bad weather, so it's a good idea to allow several days' leeway between a visit here and an international flight home. Services operate to Koltur from several places in the country including both Tórshavn and the airport on Vágar three times a week (Sun, Wed and Fri).

The island

During Koltur's heyday in the 1900s, a couple of dozen people lived here working four dairy farms. Quite unbelievably for such a remote outpost, the islanders even had their own teacher who shuttled back and forth from Hestur to instruct the handful of children who once lived here. It was around this time that one of the Faroes' most tragic true stories, later used by the poet R C Effersøe as the basis for his play, *Magnus*, was played out. Having fallen in love with a girl from Hestur, local boy Magnus would swim on the ebb tide from the island's southernmost point, Kolturstangi, across to the Hestsbøði promontory on Hestur to meet his sweetheart, returning several hours later on the flood tide which would sweep him back home. However, the girl's disapproving father finally snapped and waited for Magnus at Hestsbøði with an axe threatening to kill him if he came ashore. Magnus was never seen again after turning back for Koltur and swimming against the strong tidal current which rushes through Kolturssund sound between the two islands.

Although, latterly, just two farming families shared the narrow isthmus of fertile land at the foot of the mountain (albeit without speaking to each other following a bitter row), they deserted the island after succumbing to the bright lights of Tórshavn. Life on Koltur has always been tough, not least in winter when the shortage of fuel forced people to make the often hazardous journey through open water to Skopun in Sandoy to cut turf. Indeed, during the worst of the ferocious winter gales which sweep in unopposed off the Atlantic, the low-lying southern end of the island between Kolturshamar and the smaller hill, Fjallið, was regularly inundated by the huge waves that can crash right over tiny Koltur. Needless to say, Koltur stood abandoned for several years until new life was finally breathed back into this most inscrutable isle in the mid-1990s. The current farmer, Bjørn Patursson, with his wife and daughter, fell for its charms and moved here to resume the long farming tradition tending sheep and Scottish Highland cattle.

Where to stay and eat

Bjørn now runs occasional farmstay visits (tel: 32 81 90; fax: 32 81 91; email: bjorn@post.olivant.fo; web: www.puffin.fo/koltur; 430kr) to Koltur offering a unique insight into island farming life and an opportunity to accompany him fowling; the island is a favourite haunt of various species of seabirds. A trip to Koltur is one of the most rewarding things to do in the Faroes; quite simply because you can't leave until the helicopter next comes to collect you several days hence, forcing you take stock of your surroundings and to appreciate and show respect for the forces of nature. Ask at the tourist office in Tórshavn about the possibility of staying on the farm because Bjørn only takes limited numbers of visitors. There are no facilities on Koltur other than the farm so it's imperative to bring everything with you that you might need, taking into account the possibility of being stranded for several extra days.

North to Kaldbak

Slicing deep into the southern portion of Streymoy, **Kaldbaksfjørður** fjord and its one principal village **Kaldbak** are within easy striking distance of Tórshavn, making a short but pleasant excursion if time is limited. The head of the fjord, 11km to the northwest of the capital, is known as **Kaldbaksbotnur** and is today the location for several fish farms producing salmon, trout and mussels. It's from here that Route 523 swings off to the right to follow the inlet's northern shore, passing several waterfalls cascading down the precipitous hillsides that tower above the steely waters, all the way to Kaldbak, a further 4km away at the mouth of the fjord. The route to reach this unspoilt village, home to around 200 people, may be circuitous but it has at least helped spare the place the fate that befell the farmstead of Sund on the opposite shore. There, the historic old smallholding, reputed to be one of the most beautifully located in the entire country, was levelled to make way for an industrial development that never saw the light of day.

Getting there and away

Kaldbak is best visited as a short day trip from Tórshavn since there is no accommodation here. City bus #4 (journey time around 30min) runs here from the Farstøðin terminal in the capital five times daily (three daily Sat and

Sun) though the most useful departures are likely to be at 11.20 and 16.15 (Mon–Fri); the morning bus gives you around three hours in Kaldbak before returning at just before 15.00, whereas the afternoon service leaves you an hour before leaving for Tórshavn around 18.00, not a tremendous amount of time but enough to see the church.

Kaldbak

As pleasant as Kaldbak may be, the real reason to come here is not to see the village itself, but to visit one of the oldest timber churches in the country. Enjoying a superb location right on the fjordside inside an immaculate dry-stone wall, the black-tarred walls, white window frames and turf roof of this church were constructed in 1835, making it one of only ten such structures in the country and undoubtedly one of the easiest to reach from Tórshavn. What makes this church stand out from the others is the unusual carving that decorates the screen dividing the choir from the nave. It appears the craftsmen who carved this particular screen ditched the stylised patterns they'd been given of the much-favoured tree of life, which adorns several others elsewhere in the country, and actually created their own designs and patterns, including a number of violins. Ask any local person to be let into the church and they'll point you in the direction of the warden who has the key.

Although there's little else to see or do in Kaldbak, before leaving make sure to glance across the fjord to the southern shore and pinpoint the waterfall virtually opposite Kaldbak; this point is known as **Kallanes**, literally 'Calling point' and it's from here that people would shout across the fjord to get messages to the villagers, hence saving a lengthy journey around the head of the fjord.

Above Fámjin in Suðuroy offers superb hiking opportunities (JP)
Below Tórshavn harbour looking west towards Vesturkirkjan church (LP)

Above Traditional turf-roofed houses in Mykines village (JP)

Right Roykstovan farmhouse and Ólavskirkjan church, Kirkjubøur, Streymoy (LP)

Streymoy and the Western Islands

The largest and longest of the Faroe Islands, measuring around 50km from Tjørnuvík in the north to Kirkjubønes in the south, Streymoy is named after the strong current, *streymur* in Faroese (*oy* is simply a shortened form of *oyggj* meaning 'island'), which rips up both the west and east coasts at speeds of up to 20 knots per hour, stopping any vessel in its path. Located at the heart of the country and sheltered to a large extent from the elements by its neighbours, Vágar to the west and Eysturoy to the east, this was the first of the islands to be settled. Geographically, Streymoy can be divided neatly into two portions, the deep waters of **Kaldbaksfjørður** fjord (see page 85) acting as a natural barrier. Emerging north of the fjord from the Kollfjarðartunnilin tunnel, which links the relatively low-lying southern area of the island around Tórshavn with the more rugged central and northern sections, an altogether different landscape unfolds. This part of Streymoy is essentially a land of deep valleys and craggy peaks; in fact, the western and northern coasts are almost perpendicular bird cliffs. Several of the mountains in the far northwest of the island are well over 700m high: **Melin** (764m) and **Kopsenni** (790m) both dominate the landscape for miles around. Although Streymoy is home to around 20,000 people, only one person in five lives outside Tórshavn, making large parts of the island virtually empty. Indeed, large parts of the western side of the island are totally uninhabited; villages tend to be concentrated on the flatter, more fertile eastern side of the island, which forms an almost straight line between Tjørnuvík and Kollafjørður.

Now linked to its bigger brother to the east by a tunnel under the choppy waters of Vestmannasund sound, **Vágar** is an altogether less dramatic island than Streymoy, though that's not to say it's without charm. In fact, what makes this island particularly appealing is the abundance of excellent walking paths which criss-cross the relatively flat centre of the island dominated by the lake, **Fjallavatn**. Vágar's other much larger lake, known as both **Leitisvatn** and **Sørvágsvatn** depending on who you're talking to, is one of the Faroes' most unusual natural features. Shaped like a twisting snake, this sizeable body of water is bound along its length by two equal hillsides yet by just the merest sliver of land at its seaward side, over which the impressive Bøsdalafossur waterfall cascades into the Atlantic below.

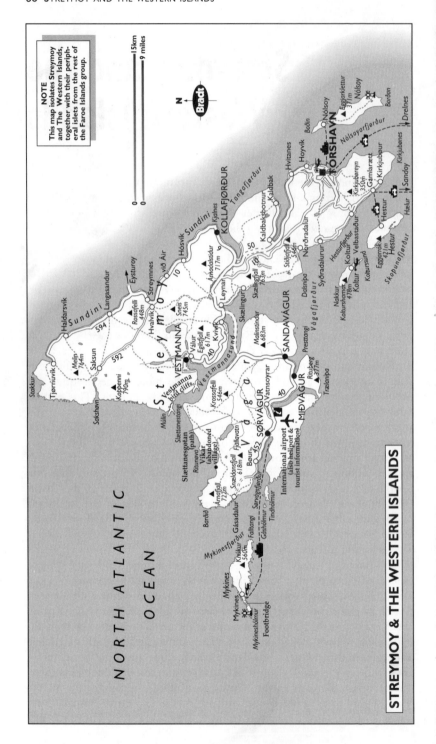

STREYMOY & THE WESTERN ISLANDS

NOTE
This map isolates Streymoy and The Western Islands, together with their peripheral islets from the rest of the Faroe Islands group.

Beyond Vágar, **Mykines** is the most remote of all the Faroe Islands and certainly the most beautiful. Shaped like a favourite old cap with the Faroes' most westerly extremity, **Mykineshólmur** islet, as its peak, this enigmatic island can often be cut off for days during bad weather. Indeed, it's the tremendous erosive power of the Atlantic that has sculpted the island's highly indented coastline, gnawed into countless craggy inlets over the centuries. From behind the turf-roofed houses that make up the solitary village here, the land rises steeply in ever-changing shades of green through the tussocky outfield of Djúpidalur valley up to the heights of Knúkur peak (560m) with its sweeping views. However, it's for its rich birdlife that Mykines has deservedly become a traveller's favourite; if you haven't yet seen a puffin, the chances are you will here because hundreds of them nest in burrows in the cliff-tops either side of the deep Hólmgjógv cleft which divides Mykines from Mykineshólmur.

WHERE TO GO

Like much of the rest of the Faroe Islands, **Streymoy** is blessed with a network of good roads which links even the most remote village with the capital in around an hour or so. Heading north from Tórshavn, **Kollafjørður** is the first stop, where the traditional timber church, dating from 1837, is immediately visible by the roadside. Although there's little else to see in the village, Kollafjørður is also the starting point for an enjoyable coast-to-coast hike up over the curiously named Sátan peak (621m) to the village of **Leynar** on Streymoy's western shore. Rounding the head of the fjord, the road now clings to the shores of Sundini, the narrow sound separating Streymoy from Eysturoy, en route for the former whaling station at **við Áir**, today a fish research centre, and the charming village of **Hvalvík**, home to another timber church, and a parting of the ways. From here, Route 592 heads northwest through the lonely Saksunardalur valley, to its namesake, **Saksun**, one of the most worthwhile destinations in the country. Stunningly set in a natural circular amphitheatre high above a tidal lagoon, this remote outpost is home to a fascinating museum recounting farming traditions over the centuries; there's also a pleasant walk to be had down to the lagoon and out to the open sea. Back in Hvalvík, the main road continues north to the Faroes' only octagonal church, a most unusual sight, in **Haldarsvík**, before arriving in gloriously pastoral **Tjørnuvík**, a village as typically Faroese as they come with old wooden houses overlooking potato allotments down on the sandy beach.

Heading west from Tórshavn, Route 40 branches off left just beyond the Kollfjarðartunnilin tunnel bound for **Kvívík**, with its handful of Viking-age remains, and **Vestmanna**, a workaday fishing village, on Streymoy's west coast. Although not especially attractive in itself, Vestmanna is the departure point for one of the best excursions in the country: a trip to Vestmanna bird cliffs, which ranks as the highlight of any trip to Streymoy. These small boats wind their way under rock arches and around stacks to provide you with an unparalleled view of the sheer cliffs teeming with seabirds.

Although Vestmanna was once linked to Vágar by ferry, all traffic between Streymoy and Vágar now passes under rather than over Vestmannasund sound thanks to the new tunnel, which opened in 2002. On reaching this often overlooked island, Route 40 winds its way past the uneventful villages of Sandavágur and Miðvágur heading for yet another *vágur* (Faroese for 'bay'), **Sørvágur**, the best base on the island and also the home of the airport. It's from here that the main network of walking trails extends northwards towards Fjallavatn lake. West of here, the hamlets of **Bøur** and all-but-forgotten **Gásadalur** (until 2004 the last village without a road connection; a new tunnel has now been built), offer a plentiful taste of off-the-beaten-track Faroes.

However, it's **Mykines** that really steals the show. A must for any visitor to the islands, this remote outpost is quite simply the best of all the Faroes and you should allow it plenty of time, not least because the unpredictable weather out here often cancels ferry and helicopter departures. Brooding and sombre on occasions, alluring and seductive at others, this is the most verdant of all the islands and, without a doubt, the most enjoyable destination in the entire country. Spend a few days here exploring the delights of Mykines' rolling hills and precipitous cliffs; take a stroll out amid the puffin burrows of **Lambi**; cross the suspension bridge over to the islet and **Mykineshólmur** and gaze out at the open Atlantic from the lighthouse at the Faroes' most westerly point and you'll soon see what all the fuss is about.

GETTING AROUND

With the exception of Mykines and Gásadalur (until final completion of the tunnel), all destinations in this chapter are reachable by **bus**. Although bus services are generally frequent and operate all year round, there are only services during the summer months (late June to mid-August) to Saksun. When travelling between Tórshavn and Tjørnuvík you should make connections at **Oyrarbakki** which is served by #400 before continuing on to Eysturoy. In addition to the #400, Tórshavn city buses also operate to Kollafjørður. Gásadalur is accessible by helicopter from Vágar airport on the same circuit as Mykines.

In theory, Mykines can be reached by **boat** from Sørvágur between April and October. The frequency of services depends on the time of year, with daily sailings operating between mid-May and the end of August; at other times the boat sails only on Tuesday, Thursday and Saturday in both directions. However, it's important to remember that sailings are often cancelled. During my last visit to Mykines, for example, the boat hadn't sailed for a week due to bad weather and even the helicopter was cancelled leaving me stranded for several days. According to the timetable at least the **helicopter** is scheduled to fly out from Vágar to Mykines once daily on Sunday and Wednesday, twice on Friday; connections are available from several other places in the islands.

STREYMOY
Kollafjørður and around

Kollafjørður is a textbook example of a linear village, houses and the odd shop strung out in a long line along the main road which hugs the northern shore

THE COAST-TO-COAST HIKE: KOLLAFJØRÐUR TO LEYNAR

Stretching northeast from the head of Kollafjørður fjord, the narrow valley of **Kollafjarðardalur** marks the starting point of the 4.5km hike (allow 2.5 hours) over the hills to Leynar on Streymoy's western coast. The path begins at the Búnaðardepilin farming centre between the northern exit of the Kollfjarðartunnilin tunnel (which is served by buses #100, 300, 400 and city bus 4 from Tórshavn) and the roundabout where the road splits left for Vágar and right for Eysturoy. Follow the middle of three rivers, the Brekká, from the farming centre up the hillside heading for the cairn in front of you; the going is a little steep at this point. The path takes you over the old mountain road from Tórshavn, the Oyggjarvegurin (Route 10), towards the next cairn and on towards Skælingsvatn lake. According to legend a horse-like creature once lived in this remote mountain tarn which is also the meeting point for several walking trails. There are good views from here of some of Streymoy's tallest mountains: to the south Skælingur (763m), once mistakenly thought to be the island's highest; north to Sátan (621m; named after its resemblance to a haystack); and southeast to Stalur (614m). Now, following the cairns, it's downhill all the way to Leynar with some good vistas of Vágar and, a little later, of Koltur, out ahead of you. From Leynar bus #100 runs back to Tórshavn.

of the fjord of the same name. Although home today to around 900 people, the original settlement consisted of no more than a handful of dwellings tightly clustered around the timber church, which is still the focal point of the village. Built in 1837, a couple of years later than its near-identical neighbour in Kaldbak, the church shows the classic construction techniques of black-tarred walls, white windows, turf roof and white clocktower. There are generally subtle differences between all the wooden churches in the Faroes and the Kollafjørður example is no exception: the windows support an upper arch divided into three glass panes by radial bars. Admittedly, it's not a line that's going to make it onto your postcards home, but if you're passing, the church – and its windows – is worth a quick stop. Once you've seen the church, there's no real reason to tarry and it's probably wise to push on round the head of the fjord towards Hósvík.

Housed in the same building opposite the church, there's a food store, Matvørubúðin, which holds the key to the church, and a branch of the Føroya Sparikassi bank.

North to Hósvík and við Áir

Rounding Kjalnestangi point at the head of Kollafjørður fjord, Route 10 now meanders along the western shore of Sundini sound across which there are clear views of neighbouring Eysturoy. In fact, the next settlement along the road, **Hósvík**, was once the transit point for all traffic from Streymoy bound for Eysturoy and the northern islands. However, with the opening of the new bridge across the sound further north at Nesvík, the ferry which once shuttled over to Selatrað on the opposite shore has been taken out of service. During Viking times, Hósvík was known as Tórsvík, after the Norse god Thor, and was the site of a pagan worship place. However, with the introduction of Christianity the *hof*, as it's known in Faroese, was converted into a church which stood until the time of the Reformation. Today though, other than the waterfall which tumbles down the hillside behind Hósvík, there's little to see on this stretch of the road until you reach the former whaling station at **við Áir**, a couple of kilometres further on. Located beside two rivers which reach the sound here (*við Áir* means 'by the rivers'), the rusting reds and greens of the derelict corrugated iron buildings and winding gear may look like a Hollywood film set today, but until the late 1960s this place was buzzing with life. Harpooned whales were offloaded from ships onto the slipways to be unceremoniously sliced up alfresco ready for export; the last one came ashore here in 1984. Those days are now long gone, and við Áir is now a government research centre for fish farming specialising in salmon and smolt breeding; smolt are salmon hatchlings which can be placed immediately in salt water. Experiments are also conducted into the farming of halibut and into placing marked salmon into open water. In addition to its research activities, the centre also exports frozen fish.

Hvalvík

A further 6km north of Hósvík and home to around 200 people, Hvalvík (literally 'whale bay') nestles around the expansive mouth of the Stórá River, the Faroes' biggest river and renowned for its excellent salmon fishing; it's thought the village is named after the countless whales that have stranded on the estuary sands. Undoubtedly one of Streymoy's prettiest villages, Hvalvík benefits by being set back from the main Route 10, straddling instead the minor road which leads off to Saksun. It's the traditional houses, painted in subtle shades of red, yellow and green, that help to make the centre of the village so charming, dominated by the timber church which has been the focal point of Hvalvík since its construction in 1829. The oldest of all the wooden churches in the islands, this one was built of pine bought from a ship which stranded in nearby Saksun in 1829; earlier the same year the church that originally stood here was destroyed by a ferocious storm. Inside, the pulpit, which the church acquired in 1790, is quite something; built in 1609, it was originally used in the old church in Tórshavn until seized by French pirates during a raid in 1677. In fact it's said that slashes to the woodwork were caused by the pirates' swords. Certainly, the church with wild flowers growing in its turf roof is of striking elemental beauty, and its setting is wonderfully enhanced by the shady grove of trees decorating the churchyard behind.

Moving on from Hvalvík presents two opportunities: Route 592 to **Saksun** loyally follows every twist and turn of the wide but shallow Stórá, before finally crossing it at the point where the river finally reaches the valley bottom

NINETEENTH-CENTURY TIMBER CHURCHES

If you come to the Faroes looking for ancient architectural monuments such as those found in other European countries, you'll return home sadly disappointed. As in neighbouring Iceland, the main building material of the Middle Ages was untreated wood which simply didn't withstand the rigours of time and climate and rotted away. However, as the economic circumstances of the islands improved in the early19th century, building techniques were refined and a design of church was perfected which was more able to withstand the salty air and damp conditions that prevail in the midst of the North Atlantic. Between 1829 and 1847, around a dozen traditional **timber churches** were built across the country. Based on the same design, the churches are composed of double timber walls, which sit on top of a foundation of solid rock which is always painted white. In contrast, the walls are covered with black tar as protection against the weather and support a turf roof. Although the turf was originally laid on a layer of straw or birch bark imported from Scandinavia, a synthetic base is now used instead; all Faroese timber churches have turf roofs except those in Nes and Strendur whose roofs are made of slate and cement tiles respectively. A low wooden **belltower** which can be either parallel or perpendicular to the main entrance hall is found at the western end. A small staircase leads up into the tower and to a balcony which extends over the rear of the nave from behind the main door. Time has given the **nave**, plain in the extreme and usually made of unpainted scrubbed pine, a warm golden colour. Accessed through a second door, the nave consists of fixed wooden pews either side of the aisle which leads to a carved screen which stands in front of the altar and the font. The latticework adornments to the choral wall generally consist of various forms of crosses, flora and decorative patterns and were made by the same carpenters and boat builders who constructed the churches themselves. Normally the northern part of the choir is partitioned off by a wall forming a sacristy giving direct access to the pulpit, which in all Faroese churches is located on the northern side. Although all these churches are locked against theft, if you ask around in each village you'll eventually come across someone who keeps the key; you'll find the oldest-surviving examples in Hvalvík (1829), Norðragøta (1833), Strendur (1834), Kaldbak (1835), Kollafjørður (1837), Oyndarfjørður (1838), Sandur (1839), Nes (1843), Funningur (1847) and Porkeri (1847). Sunday service is usually held at either 11.00 or noon.

after tumbling down to sea level from the mountains above. The road then picks up the course of the Dalá River as it traverses the longest valley in the Faroes, **Saksunardalur**; a wonderful switchback ride through the austere beauty of the valley marked at its northern end by the popular fishing lake,

Saksunarvatn. Alternatively, Route 10 continues north to what the Faroese claim is the only bridge across the North Atlantic, the 220m-long Brúgvin um Streymin, which now carries all traffic heading over to Eysturoy. At this point, known as Nesvík, Route 10 swings east to Norðskáli, on the opposite side of the bridge, whereas Route 594 sticks to the shores of Sundini on its journey north to Streymoy's last two settlements, **Haldarsvík** and **Tjørnuvík**.

Hiking from Hvalvík to Vestmanna

From the centre of Hvalvík a 10km hike (allow 3½ hours) leads up through the remote mountain valley of Bjarnadalur over to Vestmanna on the western Streymoy coast. The trail begins where the Myllá River enters the village, roughly halfway along the village's one main road. Follow the north bank of the river through a gate and along a fenced track that's been used over the years for herding cattle. Look out for a cairn located after the Hvalvíkgjógv cleft. From here the path continues upwards towards Eggjarmúli hill where you meet the overhead electricity cables which serve Vestmanna and lead all the way there. From this point there are superb views of Saksunardalur valley running to the northwest. Next you'll come across a cairn built on top of a large rock known as Kellingarsteinur. At the next cairn you have a choice; the right path takes you on to Vestmanna whereas the trail cutting off to the left leads down to Kvívík. You now walk through Bjarnadalur valley between the twin peaks of Moskursfjall (624m) to the north and Loysingafjall (639m) to the south, about which there are several tales. One account is of a girl from Vestmanna who was found high on the mountain by a shepherd after she'd disappeared from home claiming she'd been led there by a mysterious ghostly figure dressed in white, whereas the other story concerns a young milkmaid who fell into the Gjógvará River hereabouts and was carried away down a waterfall. She was eventually found on the mountain wretched and naked and living in fear of the *huldufolk*, the Faroes' hidden elves and spirits.

Emerging from the valley at the Fossá dam, you have again two choices, though this time both paths lead to **Vestmanna**: either you can follow the road off to the left and walk down to an area known as á Fjørð, or you continue straight on, passing around the dam, still following the cairns and the Gjógvará River (of milkmaid fame) which then leads down into the village.

There's public transport to both ends of this hike: bus #400 runs to Hvalvík from Tórshavn and service #100 runs from Vestmanna back to Tórshavn.

Saksun

Barely 30 people today live in Saksun, a wonderfully remote hillside village, strung out along the banks of the Dalsá River close to Streymoy's northwestern tip, which has become a favourite summer day trip for many Faroese. The setting is austere in the extreme: high rocky knolls bear down on the tiny settlement on three sides creating the impression of a natural amphitheatre. The western end of the village overlooks the **Pollurin tidal lagoon**, a circular body of water virtually enclosed by sheer craggy cliff walls over which the Gellingará River tumbles into the lagoon.

Getting there and away

There are no facilities in Saksun at all. From late June to the middle of August, there's a twice-daily bus (#204) from Oyrarbakki at 07.40 and 13.05. If you want to spend more than half an hour in Saksun and intend to return by bus you will have no choice but to take the early-morning service to the village and return on the afternoon run. A much better idea is to take the afternoon bus to Saksun and then hike over the hills to either Tjørnuvík or Haldarsvík (see page 96) which are both connected by much more frequent service #202 back to Oyrarbakki and ultimately Tórshavn.

The village

At the entrance to the village, on the northern end of Saksunarvatn lake, there's a choice of roads: the left turn takes you over the river and down amongst the jumble of farm buildings and houses that make up the minute centre of Saksun, whereas the main road continues in a relatively straight line, on the eastern side of the river, to the village church and the Dúvugarðar museum (mid-Jun to mid-Aug daily except Thu 14.00–17.00; 30kr; tel: 42 23 03), an excellent snapshot of life on a Faroese farm from the Middle Ages to the early 20th century. Located by the main roadside opposite the church, the long stone walls and turf roof of the sturdy Dúvugarðar farmhouse are immediately apparent: around 300 years old in parts, this was the main building on the farm and was inhabited until World War II. After passing through a small outer porch you enter the main room, the *roykstova*, which traditionally served as an all-purpose kitchen, workroom and living room centred on the open fire which once burned in here on the dirt floor which has been preserved. Smoke escaped through a hole in the ceiling, which also provided the only source of daylight in the room. Alcoves in the walls served as beds for the farm workers. Although the present construction dates from around 1820, an older *roykstova* stood on the same spot. Next door, the *glasstova*, so called because it was often the only room in a house with a window, was used as both sleeping quarters for the farmer and his wife and a parlour where guests would be entertained on Sundays and holidays. This room was heated by an oven which was filled with embers through a hole in the wall behind the main fire in the *roykstova*. About 150 years ago, to coincide with the construction of the church in Saksun in 1858, an extension was made to the *glasstova* to provide living accommodation for the local priest who resided in Kvívík. Naturally known as the *prestastova*, or priest's room, the extension consisted of a kitchen, bedroom, dining and sitting room though it was only used when the priest visited once every two months or when the house was full of guests. Throughout the farmhouse you'll find examples of old tools and implements which once formed part of daily life: everything from weighing scales marked up in the former imperial Faroese measures to special combs for preparing wool for spinning. Although a handful of other smaller buildings are open to the public, such as a meat drying hut and a turf shed, it's worth remembering that they are all still in use by the current farmers, Jógvan and Richa, and you should show due consideration when wandering around their property.

Opposite the museum, the stone church enjoys one of the most dramatic positions in the whole of the islands standing proud high above the Pollurin lagoon from inside a turf-topped stone wall. Although a small chapel once existed in Saksun, it only survived until the Reformation after which people had to trek two hours over the mountains to neighbouring Tjørnuvík to attend church. In fact, the timber in today's church was shipped west around the headland from Tjørnuvík to help rebuild a church for the village. Unusually, one of the walls is composed almost entirely of vast rectangular windows allowing a generous view inside of the unadorned interior; unpainted pine walls, floor and roof create a picture of total simplicity.

Whilst you're in Saksun it's worth making the effort to walk down to the lagoon from where it's possible to continue on to the open sea. The best approach is from the western side of the Dalá River – remember, though, that you should not walk through fields of fresh grass (a precious resource for the two farms on this side of the river) when heading down to the lagoon; stick to the path and follow the river. At low tide it's possible to walk along the sandy shore of the lagoon around the headland which marks the neck of Pollurin round to the sea. At high tide, it's best to follow the path a little higher up the hillside; the surf crashing against the narrow sandy inlet to Pollurin is quite a remarkable sight.

Hiking from Saksun to Tjørnuvík and Haldarsvík

To reach the beginning of the walking trail (two hours) that leads from Saksun up over the Melin peak (764m) to Tjørnuvík and Haldarsvík on Streymoy's eastern shore, you need to press on from the Dúvugarðar museum to the farm at the main road. Once here, look for the stable block and you'll see a nearby fence; this is where you start. Cross the fence and follow the cairns and you'll begin to climb the steep hillside up behind Saksun heading slightly towards the northwest. At around 400m, the path splits to work around the base of Melin, giving you a choice. The left route heads north for Tjørnuvík along the eastern side of the Frammi í Dal valley, marked at its head by the Tjørnuvíksskarð pass; you pass through before heading gradually downhill southeast of the Heyggjurin Mikli peak (692m) for the steep grassy hillsides that form the backdrop to Tjørnuvík. The alternative path cuts off right for the Skipá River which descends back towards the Dúvugarðar farm; once over the river the path continues towards Haldarsvík by climbing through Skipádalur valley to the **Víkarskarð** pass squeezed in tight between the peaks of Víkartindur (703m) to the west and Gívrufelli (701m) to the east. The climb is now over and it's now a pleasant and gradual descent along a path known as Saksunarvegurin down to Haldarsvík. See *Getting there and away* above for details of buses back to Oyrarbakki.

Haldarsvík

Back in Hvalvík, Route 10 continues north to the bridge over to Eysturoy and the junction with Route 594 which heads out to Streymoy's northernmost settlements, Haldarsvík and Tjørnuvík. Although the road is well surfaced, it is extremely narrow in parts, predominantly after the small cluster of houses that is Langasandur, around which there are several large fish farms. Roughly halfway along its length, the Faroes' highest waterfall comes cascading down to sea level; connected to Víkarvatn lake high on the hills of the Vatnfelli peak above the road, the Fossá River falls majestically from a height of 140m over two rocky outcrops before passing under the bridge carrying Route 594 and finally reaching the waters of Sundini sound. There's a stopping place just after the bridge should you wish to pause and admire the spectacle. Beyond the falls, it's just another 3km further to Haldarsvík, an average-sized fishing village home to around 160 people, who, if the village's annotated road signs are anything to go by, evidently have different views about the name of their village than the cartographers who mapped it. Known locally as Haldórsvík, or even just plain Vík, the battle to convince the authorities in Tórshavn of their mistake goes on.

Most of the 50 or so brightly coloured houses here are tightly clustered around the small harbour, which provides superb shelter from the currents in Sundini, and the Kluftá River which flows down through the village from the hills above in a series of wide and lazy cascades. However, it's the highly unusual octagonal church, the only one in the country, that grabs your eye as you pass through the settlement. Built in 1856 on the instigation of the local Danish priest, Pruts, the curiously shaped white stone walls, heightened in 1932, are certainly an unusual sight. Inside the plain whitewashed interior, it's the striking painting by Tórshavn artist, Torbjørn Olssen, behind the altar that immediately catches the eye: sandal-wearing apostles at the Last Supper portrayed in sharp angular shapes and a mêlée of blues, greens, reds and yellows. The keyholder lives in the house opposite the church beside the main road as it climbs out of the village; she works at the kindergarten in the centre of the village.

Up on the hill behind the church, there's a contemporary monument erected in 1982 to all those who have lost their lives at sea; the work of Fridtjof Joensen, who intended it to symbolise eternity, the sculpture consists of stainless-steel arches twisting over a revolving metallic globe.

There are no facilities in Haldarsvík. For details of bus services, see the *Getting there and away* section for Tjørnuvík below.

Tjørnuvík

On leaving Haldarsvík and rounding the Víkarnes headland, excellent views open up across Sundini to Eiði on the northwest tip of Eysturoy. As you drive this exceedingly narrow stretch of road bound for end-of-the-road Tjørnuvík, it's easy to see why it was one of the last sections of the Faroese road network to be built; the soaring sides of Hægstafjall (470m) reach virtually all the way to the shore here leaving precious little room for any form of road or path; indeed the track which connected the two villages before the advent of the road was so steep and treacherous in parts that it demanded a steady nerve if you were to avoid a precipitous drop into the sound below.

Nestled at the head of a deep fjord which slices into the northern Streymoy shore, Tjørnuvík enjoys the most stunning setting of any settlement in the Faroe Islands. Surrounded on three sides by towering mountain walls and opening out to the sea on its eastern edge across the narrow fjord, the village lies in what the Faroese call a *botnur*, a glacial circular valley formed during the Ice Age, where the roar of the sea combined with the rushing waterfalls that descend behind the village is quite exhilarating.

Getting there and away

Both Haldarsvík and Tjørnuvík have a fairly decent bus service though there's a gap of around six hours in services between around 08.30 and 14.30; #202 runs seven times daily (Sat three daily, Sun two daily) linking the two villages with each other, and Oyrarbakki for connections to and from Tórshavn. If you're hiking over from Saksun, the last bus out of Tjørnuvík for Oyrarbakki leaves at 18.30 daily (Sun at 17.00). For details of the hike between Tjørnuvík (and Haldarsvík) and Saksun, see page 96. Other than the seasonal café and a public toilet, there are no facilities in Tjørnuvík.

The village

Tjørnuvík's steep hillsides have been responsible for a couple of natural disasters over the centuries; in 1633 and 1868 rockfalls virtually destroyed the tiny settlement, which even today barely counts 70 inhabitants. A network of dykes and stone walls behind the village now offers protection from falling rocks and enables the rich farmland at the foot of the mountains to be cultivated for hay and vegetables. Potatoes are also grown in the patchwork of allotments that lines the black-sand beach at the head of the fjord; incidentally, from here there are some superb views of the **Risin** and **Kellingin** sea stacks that lie just off the north coast of Eysturoy. Behind the beach a couple of narrow roads wind past a dozen or so turf-roofed old timber houses of the village and make a pleasant stroll; in summer there's a simple café, the accordingly named Lítla Café, with outdoor seating in the centre of the village near the modern church, serving coffee, tea, waffles and hotdogs for around 20kr. If you're looking though for the best views of Tjørnuvík's dramatic location, you'll find the descent into the village, after rounding the mouth of the fjord, provides the best place for photographs.

Although Tjørnuvík's greatest attraction is, arguably, its enchanting location, there's also one other thing of interest in the village: a **Viking burial site**. Excavation work of the poorly signed site, which lies beside a series of hay-drying racks and before the small car park and toilets on the right-hand side of the road, took place in the 1950s and astonishingly uncovered 12 graves which had been dug into an area of shifting sand. The bodies inside, all sadly in a poor state of preservation, were found lying on their backs; only in one case, that of a young woman, was it possible to verify the sex of the skeletons. Various everyday articles such as a fragment of a knife, a bronze buckle and a boat nail were also found, but it was a ring-headed bronze pin, common in the northwest Atlantic during the Viking period, that enabled archaeologists to date the finds to the 10th or early 11th centuries. This pin, which is of Celtic origin, is proof that links existed between the various Nordic settlements to the south in the British Isles and those in the Faroe Islands; today the finds are on display in the National Museum in Tórshavn and what remains in Tjørnuvík is a collection of moss-covered stones arranged in the shape of individual graves.

Tjørnuvík is also the departure point for one of the most unusual excursions in the Faroes: a trip to the nearby free-standing sea stack, **Stakkurin** (134m). Bookable through the Kunningarstovan in Tórshavn (dates of the tours are known in early spring), the outing involves a strenuous walk from the village up the heights of **Skoradalsheyggjurin** (448m) before reaching the stack, which forms the northernmost point of Streymoy and is used for sheep grazing. Animals and humans are carried from the mainland across to the stack in a basket which runs on pulleys across a suspended ropeway high above the crashing surf below; definitely not one for the faint-hearted. This excursion, which is primarily organised by the villagers to transport their sheep out to Stakkurin, runs only twice a year, always in July, though if you're around at the right time it certainly makes an exciting day out.

West to Kvívík and Vestmanna

With your own transport, it's worth considering taking the old mountain road, Route 10, north from Tórshavn for some fantastic views of several fjords and the mountains that form the backbone of this part of southern Streymoy. Although today the Oyggjarvegurin as it's known in Faroese (literally 'Island Road') is simply an alternative way of heading north from the capital and avoiding the Kollfjarðartunnilin, until 1992, when the tunnel opened, it was the only way in and out of Tórshavn. From its starting point just west of the Nordic House on the Norðari Ringvegur, the road climbs steeply up towards Hotel Føroyar and the couple of transmitters perched on the rocky hill behind, before swinging right and reaching a flat plateau at around 300m above sea level. From this exposed stretch of road there are superlative views east down over Kaldbaksfjørður. Here, high in the mountains at the head of the fjord, the Danes maintain a military base over which a giant red and white flag flies in the wind. Just beyond here, a left turn leads up to **Sornfelli** peak (749m), the site of the giant radar dishes that are NATO's early warning station in the Faroes. The mountain is also a favourite destination for the people of Tórshavn during the long light summer evenings who come up here to enjoy the fantastic views out over the surrounding islands. Incidentally, the fjord you can see stretching away to the east from here is Kollafjørður. Beyond here the road begins the gradual descent into the Kollafjarðardalur valley ahead; at its end it forms a T-junction with Route 40 which leads west to Kvívík, Vestmanna and the tunnel across to Vágar.

Kvívík

Twenty-eight kilometres northwest of Tórshavn, Kvívík sits prettily in a deep narrow valley formed by the Stórá River which flows through the middle of the village on its way down to the sea. The houses here, painted in eye-catching shades of blues, greens and reds, are tightly clustered either side of the river in two tiny streets. The white-walled village church and its neighbouring graveyard, encircled by a perfect dry-stone wall and a grove of gnarled and twisted trees, looks out over the tiny harbour beyond where a handful of small fishing boats bob on the Atlantic swell.

Getting there and away

Bus #101 runs from Tórshavn via the Kollfjarðartunnilin to Kvívík (continuing to Vestmanna) eight times daily (three daily Sat and Sun). All departures in and out of Kvívík must be booked ahead on tel: 34 30 30, otherwise the bus doesn't make the detour down into Kvívík from the main road, simply driving straight on to Vestmanna.

Other practicalities

Since there are no facilities in Kvívík other than a **village shop**, you should bring with you everything you think you will need. There is no accommodation in Kvívík.

The village

It was here in Kvívík church that a decisive step was taken towards making Faroese the official language of the Church: before a shocked congregation, **Venceslaus Ulricus Hammerschaimb** (1819–1909) gave his New Year's Eve sermon in 1855 in his native tongue (instead of Danish as had been the common practice until then) amid scenes of shock and uproar. In fact, the young minister was so taken aback by the indignant reaction of his flock, who considered the lowly Faroese tongue not worthy of the great words of God, that he didn't dare repeat his experiment. It took the best part of another century until the scriptures were finally translated into Faroese and an official Faroese Bible was published in 1961.

Attractive though today's village is, it's Kvívík's ancient past which people come here to explore: in 1942 remains of a **Viking longhouse** and **byre** were discovered close to the church at the foot of the village on the western side of the river. The knee-height remains, covered with turf, consist of a dwelling house and a cowshed alongside which both date from the late Viking period, around the 10th to 11th centuries. The main building, 21m long by 6m wide, has characteristically curved walls made of boulders, earth and gravel. The roof would have been made of birch bark and grass sods and supported by two parallel rows of posts, whose remains can be seen in the ground. In the middle of the floor area there was once a sizeable fireplace, around 7m in length. The byre is unique in the Faroe Islands since no other similar building from the Viking period has been discovered to date. Virtually identical to the longhouse in construction though it was split into two rooms; one was used as a storage barn, the other was divided into two rows of stalls for up to 12 cows opposite each other. During the excavations several tools were found which help to give a picture of what life was like at this time and serve as proof that the people who lived here not only spun wool but also wove the yarn: loom weights, spindles, ropes made of local juniper and a number of ornaments and decorations from the Kvívík site can be seen in the National Museum in Tórshavn.

Vestmanna

It's a further 13km from Kvívík on to Vestmanna, a busy modern fishing village that curves around a superbly sheltered natural harbour on Streymoy's western shore. A veritable giant in Faroese terms, Vestmanna is the second-largest town on the island (after Tórshavn) and home to around 1,200 people, many of whom work in the fish factory or down on the docks at the western side of the harbour. In fact the dockside area is relatively new, created by landfill to provide room for a couple of new quays and much-needed building land. The narrow strip of land between the harbour and the hills behind soon proved too limited for the rapid development that Vestmanna has seen in recent years; a filleting plant, fish farm, plastics company and building construction firm are just some of the businesses represented. Vestmanna is also the location for the Faroes' main **hydro-electric power** plants which use the waters of the Fossá River, which flows through the eastern part of town, to provide electricity for Streymoy including Tórshavn, Eysturoy, Vágar, Klaksvík and Suðuroy. Four dams high on the hills above the town (clearly visible from the walking path between Hvalvík and Vestmanna, see page 94) help to maintain the flow of water to the power stations.

Getting there and away

Bus #100 runs between Vestmanna and Tórshavn calling at Kvívík on request (tel: 34 30 30) eight times a day (Sat and Sun, three daily).

Where to stay and eat

Private bed and breakfast accommodation in Vestmanna can be arranged through the tourist office in Tórshavn; otherwise the closest option is the youth hostel, Á Giljanesi, at Sandavágur over on Vágar (see page 106).

Thanks to its relative size, Vestmanna is one of the few settlements on Streymoy outside Tórshavn to boast any form of eatery or drinking hole. Down on the harbourside, the pub-cum-café that is Café Bryggjan (evenings only: 17.00 to midnight) serves up a limited range of something-and-chips for around 60kr as well as beer. This place is at its liveliest on Friday and Saturday nights, when, seemingly, the entire population of Vestmanna is squeezed in here.

Other practicalities

The only other food available in town is the sandwiches and hotdogs sold at the Shell station. Vestmanna also has a post office and two banks, each with a cash machine; they're all located on the main road which runs through the centre of the village above the harbour. The swimming pool and sports centre is on Toftir, up behind the post office.

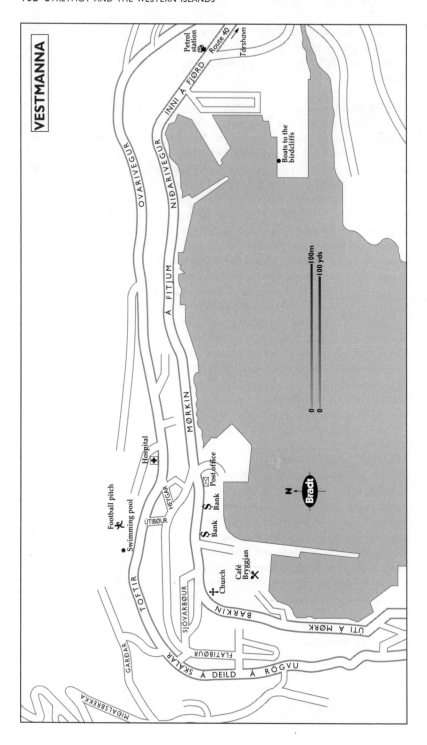

The town
Sadly Vestmanna's glory days are now gone; until 2002 all road traffic to and from the airport (as well as to other parts of Vágar, and, for that matter, Mykines) was forced to pass through the town since its regular ferry connections across the sound to the diminutive harbour at Oyrargjógv were the only means of reaching Vágar. The new sea tunnel, though, has put paid to all passing trade and Vestmanna now finds itself at the end of the road; to cross to Vágar you must backtrack to the mouth of the tunnel near Leynar, east of Kvívík.

Although Vestmanna can trace its origins back to pre-Viking times – its name is thought to come from the West Men or Irish monks who first settled here some time before AD1000 – there's little sign of this ancient heritage visible today, other than the paltry nondescript remains of a Viking-age house from around the same period close to the Gjógvará River in the western part of the village. In fact, Vestmanna, benefiting from its south-facing location for the growing of crops, remained a quiet agricultural backwater until the lifting of the Danish Trade Monopoly in 1856. Then, with the purchase of a number of wooden fishing vessels or sloops from England, the people of Vestmanna began to turn their attention to the sea and indeed haven't looked back since.

As you might expect from a working fishing village, there are no specific sights and the charms of Vestmanna lie more in wandering around the streets watching activities in and around the harbour rather than hurtling around taking in museums and galleries – there aren't any. However, what Vestmanna does have is some blockbuster scenery right on its doorstep.

Vestmanna bird cliffs
Indeed, it's the sea that provides the town with its greatest tourist attraction and one of the best excursions anywhere in the country: a boat trip to the Vestmanna bird cliffs and grottoes. Known as the **Vestmannabjørgini** in Faroese, these soaring cliffs, roughly halfway between Vestmanna and Saksun to the north, provide safe nesting places during the summer months (roughly May until late August) for thousands upon thousands of seabirds, attracted by the vast shoals of fish that gather here in the plankton-rich waters of the North Atlantic. Rising up to 600m above the turquoise hues of the churning sea below, the cliffs are characterised by their numerous clefts and green blankets of luxuriant grass and mosses. The boats that sail out here give you an unparalleled view of the cliffs and the birds – notably puffins, razorbills and guillemots – as they weave in between the numerous sea stacks and in and out of narrow straits bound by sheer rock walls (look up and you may well see sheep grazing quite undisturbed on the clifftops) and dark echoing grottoes where the sound of the squawking birds and dripping water is amplified to unnerving proportions.

Getting to the bird cliffs
Although two local companies run tours lasting a couple of hours to the bird cliffs, you'll find that those operated by the Skúvadal brothers, Gunnar (who also reads the news on Faroese National Radio) and Froði, together with their father,

Bjarki (tel: 42 43 05; email: skuvadal@puffin.fo; www.vestmannabjorgini.com; 175kr) are better equipped for non-Scandinavian speakers since they have a better command of English (thanks in great part to Gunnar's Australian wife, Jacqueline) than their rival, Palli Lamhauge (tel: 42 41 55; email: sight@sightseeing.fo; www.sightseeing.fo and www.seaservice.fo). Although there are four boats that sail out to the cliffs, it's worth trying to get one of the 12 places available on Skúvadal's atmospheric old wooden vessel, *Urðardrangur*, which was built in 1977 in keeping with traditional Viking design and was fitted with a new engine in 1998. Their other boat, the modern *Barbara* (28 passengers) from 1997 is the only boat in the Faroes to have been designed specifically for sightseeing: she has both an open deck and an inside lounge which allows you to escape the worst of the weather should the heavens open (likely) during the tour. Lamhauge's has similar if slightly older vessels: *Silja* (25 passengers) and *Friðgerð* (23 passengers). Both companies leave from the eastern end of the harbour, close to the Shell filling station at the entrance to the town; here the Skúvadals also have a kiosk which takes bookings and provides information about the tours (Jun–Aug daily 08.00–17.00).

Between June and August sailings for both companies operate daily at 09.40, 14.00, 17.00 and 20.00 and the boats await the arrival of the #100 bus from Tórshavn. If you intend to take either the 17.00 or 20.00 sailings, bear in mind that you will not arrive back into Vestmanna in time for the last bus to Tórshavn, which leaves at 18.15 (Mon–Fri) and at 18.55 (Sat and Sun). However, both companies can arrange transport back to the capital on demand.

THE WESTERN ISLANDS: VÁGAR AND MYKINES
Vágar
The third-largest of the Faroes with an area of 178km^2, Vágar is generally the first island you see when approaching the country by air. The terrain, although less dramatic than that of Streymoy and the northern islands, is certainly varied: broad green valleys, patches of cultivated land around the villages that are clustered on the south coast and dozens of small rivers flowing down from rounded hilltops. The highest point is **Árnafjall** mountain (722m) in the extreme northwest, whereas the centre of the island is dominated by a long valley running north–south where the island's two main lakes are found. Although Vágar isn't going to be the highlight of any trip to the Faroe Islands – it simply doesn't have enough attractions for that – it does have vast expanses of untouched wilderness, especially around the uninhabited north of the island, which offer first-class hiking and it's to that end that most people come here. However, Vágar is also of interest for two other reasons: it's the location of the Faroes' only airport, and it has a ferry connection to Mykines.

From the Vágatunnilin (180kr per car; fee payable only in the direction Vágar–Streymoy), as the new tunnel which links Streymoy with neighbouring Vágar is known, Route 40 climbs up the steep hillside en route to the island's first main settlements, the adjoining villages of **Miðvágur** and **Sandavágur**. From here the road, the only one on the island, hugs the southern shore, skirting Leitisvatn/Sørvágsvatn lake, as it heads west towards the airport and

THE STREYMOY–VÁGAR TUNNEL

The long-awaited tunnel beneath Vestmannasund sound linking Leynar on Streymoy with Fútaklettur on Vágar, and importantly the Faroes' one and only airport, finally opened in November 2002. Although initial construction work began in the late 80s, the ensuing financial crisis soon brought the ambitious venture to a standstill and during a period of 11 years the tunnel remained little more than a big hole in the ground. Then, in September 2000, the Faroese parliament announced that building work would recommence. Inspired by a similar undersea project north of Reykjavík in Iceland, Faroese contractors began work five months later on the 4.9km-long tunnel, 2.5km of which lie under the sound at a depth of around 100m. The tunnel has not only reduced journey times between Tórshavn and the airport by over an hour and cut the distance by 10km, but it will also make possible that great Faroese dream: to drive virtually the entire length of the central islands from Gásadalur in western Vágar to Viðareiði in northern Viðoy in one go. A new under-fjord tunnel between Leirvík in Eysturoy and Klaksvík in Borðoy, currently under construction, will complete the missing link when it opens. At a whopping cost of 240 billion kroner (1999 prices), the Vágatunnilin, as it's known in Faroese, is partly financed by hefty tolls (in the direction of Vágar to Streymoy only); expect to pay 180kr for the pleasure of a submarine experience. Tolls are payable at the booths immediately before the entrance on the Vágar side; credit cards are accepted.

the neighbouring village of **Sørvágar**, from where the boat sails to Mykines. Although there's not much beyond Sørvágar, the road continues west out to the farmstead of **Bøur** and ultimately through a new tunnel which at the time of writing was still undergoing completion, to Vágar's westernmost settlement, **Gásadalur**. On the deserted north coast, there are traces of two now-abandoned villages, **Víkar** and **Slættanes**, both of which can reached on foot (see below).

Sandavágur and Miðvágur

Sitting snugly around the head of the tooth-shaped **Vágafjørður** fjord, renowned as one of the best places in the Faroes for the *grindadrápur* whale hunt, the twin villages of Sandvágur and larger Míðvágur are essentially one and the same place and home to around 1,600 people.

Getting there and away

Bus #300 runs from Tórshavn to both Sandavágur and Mídvágur eight times daily (Sat and Sun six daily) before continuing on to the airport and Sørvágur; occasional services are extended beyond Sørvágur to Bøur, which can be useful for hiking tours.

WHAT'S IN A NAME? I SAY VÁGUR, YOU SAY VÁGAR

Vágar is named after the three deep bays or inlets, *vágar* in Faroese (compare with English 'way', as in Scalloway, and less obviously Walls, in the Shetland Islands), which characterise the island's south and west coast. However, on closer inspection, you'll notice that all Vágar's place names end in *–ur*, whereas the island's name itself has an *–ar* ending. This is because, in line with most other Germanic languages, Faroese doesn't add an *'s'* to form a plural; instead the ending of the word, in this case *–ur*, is modified: so, *vágur* becomes *vágar*. To further add to the confusion, Vágar is pronounced in true Faroese fashion – that's to say completely at odds with its spelling: approximately *vo-warr*.

Where to stay and eat

Míðvágur not only boasts one of the Faroes' few youth hostels but also an adjoining campsite. Situated to the east of the harbour entrance on the Giljanes promontory, the **youth hostel** (tel: 33 34 65; fax: 33 29 01; email: giljanes@post.olivant.fo; www.farhostel.fo; 120kr), is also, unusually, open all year. With 30 beds, the accommodation here may be plain and simple, but if you're looking for somewhere to stay on Vágar you'll find this place considerably cheaper than the sterile hotel at the airport. The hostel does have a kitchen but it's also possible to order meals in advance from the staff.

Other practicalities

Although, there are no other restaurants in either Sandavágur or Míðvágur, there are a number of small **food stores** where you can buy provisions. The **alcohol store**, Rúsdrekkasølin Landsins, is at Norðuri á Heiðum in Míðvágur (Mon–Fri 14.00–17.30, Thu until 19.00; tel: 33 31 77). Both villages each have a branch of the **Føroya Sparikassi** and **Føroya Banki** banks as well as a **post office**.

The villages

Of the two, it's **Sandavágur** which has the more interesting history; a runestone found by chance in 1917, now housed inside the tall wooden church, provides proof that the area was inhabited from at least the late Viking period. The inscription on the stone reads: 'Thorkæl Onundarson, East Man [ie: from Norway] from Rogaland was the first to build on this site'. Thankfully the farmer who discovered the stone in one of his fields and planned to smash it up, not realising what is was, was thwarted by a young farmhand who first came across its inscription and called in expert advice. Later excavations in the area uncovered the foundations of a dwelling house suggesting that there was indeed a settlement here in the early Middle Ages. Across the bridge from the church and in the village itself, there's a monument to **V U Hammerschaimb**, the minister who's credited as the creator of the modern Faroese literary language; he was born in 1819 on the local farm, á Steig, which from 1555 to 1816 was the seat of the *løgmaður*, the highest authority in the country. After collecting countless ballads and folk stories (in various dialects) from across the country, Hammerschaimb made it his life's work to write them down and give them a standard written form that would make them accessible to people right across the islands, no matter what their dialect.

From the village there's a pleasant walk out to the wonderfully named **Trøllkonufingur**, 'Witch's Finger' in English, a craggy cliff-top (313m) that stands guard over the entrance to the fjord to the east of Sandvágur. Although the path to the cliff is straightforward enough, climbing it is a completely different matter. According to local legend, the peak has only been scaled once; during the royal visit in 1844 of Crown Prince Fredrik, a young Faroese man did in fact manage to reach the summit in order to wave to the prince as he sailed past below. Tragically, when he returned to the peak to collect a glove he had inadvertently left behind in the excitement, the man lost his footing and was killed. To get to Trøllkonufingur, take the first left when heading from the monument to the church to reach the road above you. This road turns into a track, passing a couple of holiday homes, and soon heads out along the grassy slopes of the fjordside and over a river. From here there are good views not only of the imposing cliff-top, but also of southern Streymoy, Koltur and Hestur.

From Sandavágur, it's a short stroll of a kilometre or two west around the Giljanes headland to **Miðvágur**, the largest settlement on the island and location of most facilities and accommodation. Clustered around an extremely narrow bay at the head of the fjord, the village looks out over a sandy bay which is regarded as being the best place to trap pilot whales in the whole of the country; numerous sandbanks and a long sandy beach make it difficult for the whales to swim back out of the bay at low tide. However, local tradition has it that the women of the village don't start preparing their husbands' dinners the day of the *grind* until the whales are driven past the Presttangi headland at the southern entrance to the bay; once past this point there's no escape.

Once the site of the island *ting*, Miðvágur was also the residence of the priest of the western islands who lived in the building known as **Kálvalíð**, high above the town and now a museum (open on request; tel: 33 34 55 or 21 27 05). Built into the hillside, the walls of this curious turf-roofed house are made of local rock and blend effortlessly into the greens and greys of the surrounding countryside. Inside the building are just two plainly decorated rooms and a cow stall. To get here, take the first turn right after passing the sign announcing your arrival in Míðvágur. The path beyond the museum marks the beginning of an easy walk over the hill to Vatnsoyrar, a diminutive settlement at the northern end of the Leitisvatn/Sørvágsvatn lake where Route 40 veers sharply left for the airport and the only settlement in the country not located on the coast; the land here has been reclaimed from the boggy marshland where the lake petered out.

HIKING ALONG THE SHORE OF LEITISVATN/ SØRVÁGSVATN LAKE

A kilometre or so west of Míðvágur, Route 40 meets the shore of the Faroes' largest inland lake, bizzarely known by several names: Leitisvatn and Sørvágsvatn, though most local people simply call it **vatnið**, literally 'the water'. Over 6km long, this body of water, renowned for its extensive stocks of fish, makes a worthwhile walk of around an hour. At the point where the road meets the lake shore you'll see a couple of boat houses and small huts which were once used for storing peat. From here follow the bank southwards (the going can be pretty boggy in parts) and you'll have good views of the two peaks which hem the lake in on either side: Ritubergsnøva (376m) to your left and Borgarheyggjur (252m) across the water on your right. As you pass Ritubergsnøva, take care not to stray too close to the headland in front of you. Here, the promontory, Trælanípa, falls precipitously into the sea from a height of 142m marking the southernmost extent of the lake; during Viking times, slaves who were no longer capable of heavy labour, were simply flung off the cliff-top to their death on the rocks below. Close by you'll see the **Bøsdalafossur** waterfall, which carries the lake into the ocean after flowing over an area of basalt rock at the water's southern point. The ruins that you can see here are of buildings built by the British during World War II. Immediately offshore, the larger of the two free-standing rock stacks you'll spot is **Geituskorardrangur**, a pyramid-shaped point of basalt standing 115m above the sea. From here, it's possible to cross the Bøsdalaá River, which flows out of the lake by the using the stepping stones. From here you can walk up to the 115m peak which stands on the cliff edge. To return simply retrace your steps back along the eastern shore.

The airport and Sørvágur

It's another 8km west of Míðvágur until Route 40 reaches the airport, also known as Vága floghavn (for the linguistically minded, the form *Vága*, without a final –r, is not a spelling mistake but signifies a genitive plural, ie: Vágar's airport, literally 'the bays' airport'). Originally built by the British during World War II as a military landing strip together with the island's one main road, today's Route 40 (incidentally, the only road in the Faroes where driving on the left-hand side was permitted; British vehicles then switched to the right hand side when they reached Streymoy), this was once the most heavily guarded part of the country with up to 9,000 servicemen stationed here at any one time. Until 1944, civilians were forced to carry identity papers on Vágar and visitors from other islands had to seek permission from the military authorities before visiting. After the war the airport was modernised and extended and today consists of a terminal building with cafeteria, gift shop,

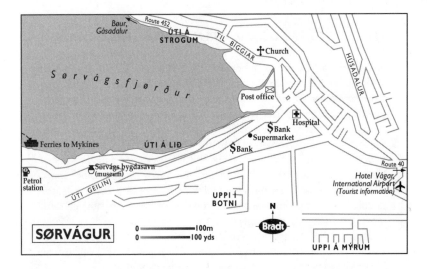

bank, travel agency and tourist information office, aircraft hangar (containing the Faroes' one and only private plane) and home of Atlantic Airways and a control tower. There are currently flights from the airport to Aberdeen, Billund, Copenhagen, London (summer only), Reykjavík and Oslo (summer only). The airport is also used as the departure point for the Atlantic Airways helicopter service, which serves the islands.

Getting there
Bus #300 runs here eight times daily (Sat and Sun six times daily) from Tórshavn, and continues (on request; tel: 21 56 10) to Bøur three times daily (Sat and Sun twice daily).

Where to stay and eat
If you need to stay at the airport, there's an expensive hotel, **Hotel Vágar** (tel: 33 29 55; email: hotel@ff.fo; www.ff.fo; 855kr), right outside next to the car park. However, it's a drab and dreary affair with block-like rooms and, frankly, you'd be better off staying in Tórshavn except in case of emergency. Private accomodation in the area is not to be recommended.

There's a restaurant at the hotel serving up run-of-the-mill uninspiring dinners and lunches. Other than this and a cafeteria in the terminal building up the hill, the only place to eat in Sørvágur is at the filling station down by the main quay, which sells a limited number of sandwiches and snacks.

There is, though, a well-stocked supermarket in the centre of Sørvágur on the main road winding down from the airport, 15 minutes' walk from the harbour.

Other practicalities
There's not much more to Sørvágur since all local services and activity are concentrated on the airport, leaving the town itself with little more than a couple of **banks** and a **post office**.

THE FAROESE NATIONAL AIRLINE: ATLANTIC AIRWAYS

As a symbol of national pride, it's hard to beat Atlantic Airways, a plucky little airline serving a home market of barely 45,000 people yet flying up to 30 times a week to five countries. Founded in 1988, the Faroese carrier aimed to break in to the lucrative Faroes–Denmark market and carry transfer passengers to Copenhagen, one of northern Europe's biggest airports and Scandinavia's main hub. Until then, the Faroe Islands were served only by the Danish airline, Maersk. By the mid-90s, business was booming and the airline opened a new route to Iceland, with services to Scotland and Norway following soon afterwards. Amid great patriotic jubilation in February 2000, Atlantic doubled its fleet (from one plane to two!) and two years later carried more than 100,000 passengers for the first time in its history. Many people put the success down to the fact that Atlantic was seen, in the Faroe Islands at least, as a more dependable airline. Why? Well, every Maersk departure from the Faroes used to be dependent on the plane first arriving in the islands from its home base in Denmark before making the return journey, whereas Atlantic planes are stationed in the Faroes and are able to leave immediately should there be an improvement in the weather, making them, in theory at least, less prone to delays. However in November 2004 things changed dramatically following the decision by Maersk to pull all routes from the Faroes and concentrate instead on southern Europe. They claimed the runway at Vágar was too short for their new planes. Atlantic now became the only airline to serve the Faroes and began eagerly plugging the gaps in the timetable left by the departure of Maersk, adding frequencies to the Denmark routes and doubling the season for London flights. The purchase of a third plane is a sure sign that one of Europe's smallest airlines is going from strength to strength.

However, the main purpose for coming to Sørvágur is to take the ferry to **Mykines**, which leaves from the main harbour just beyond the museum. Remember, though, that bad weather often delays and even cancels the sailings of the *Súlan* to Mykines, so it's wise to check the latest situation on tel: 34 30 00 or 34 30 30 before finding yourself stuck in Sórvágur – something you should avoid at all costs. Bus #300 runs here eight times daily (Sat and Sun six daily) from Tórshavn, and continues (on request; tel: 21 56 10) to Bøur three times daily (Sat and Sun twice daily).

Airport listings
Airport switchboard Tel: 35 33 00; email: airport@ff.fo; www.ff.fo
Atlantic Airways Ticket desk; tel: 34 10 10; flight information 34 10 20
Avis car rental Tel: 35 88 00
Bank Føroya Bank; tel: 35 88 30

Cafeteria Tel: 35 88 10
Flight information Tel: 34 00 70
Giftshop Gávubúðin Prýði; tel: 35 88 50
Hotel Vágar Tel: 33 29 55
Tourist information Kunningardiskurin; tel: 35 33 00
Travel agency Flogfelag Føroya; tel: 34 00 60

Sørvágur

So close is the airport to the town of Sørvágur that the western end of the runway is virtually in local people's back gardens. In fact it's just another 2km from the airport to Vágar's second-largest town, with around 900 inhabitants, which lies at the head of a 5km-long narrow fjord, Sørvágsfjørður. Unlike its eastern neighbours, though, the bay here is not suited to trapping whales since the sea bed is especially uneven. Sørvágur is a pleasant enough place to stroll around, its handful of streets supporting several small stores, and sooner or later you'll come across the local museum, **Sørvágs Bygdasavn** (open on request; tel: 33 32 84 or 33 28 93), on the southern side of the harbour at Úti á Bakka which has passable displays of the area's fishing and agricultural past. (Yes, the name of this museum is yet another mutant form of *vágur*: here, *-vágs* is the genitive singular.)

West to Bøur and Gásadalur

It's now worth making every effort to reach **Bøur**, just 4km west of Sørvágur along Route 452, one of the Faroes' prettiest villages. This tight huddle of tarred wooden houses with turf roofs snuggled up against the sheer mountainside behind that rises to a height of over 500m is not only picture-postcard perfect, but it also enjoys one of the best ocean views of any settlement in the islands. From its vantage point at the mouth of Sørvágsfjørður fjord, Bøur looks out over the steeply inclined grassy slopes on the opposite side of the fjord, several free-standing rock stacks, **Drangarnir**, as well as the uninhabited islands of **Gáshólmur** and **Tindhólmur**. Named after the peak (*tindur* in Faroese, hence 'mountain island') that rises precipitously to 262m, this tiny island was amazingly once inhabited, though today it is used only for grazing sheep. The larger island rising out of the sea beyond Gáshólmur is majestic **Mykines**; an island that looks so tantalisingly close but can be frustratingly far away when the unpredictable currents and eddies of Mykinesfjørður fjord, which separates the island from Vágar, are at their worst.

Getting there and away

Although bus #300 runs between Bøur and Tórshavn (calling at the airport) twice daily (Sat and Sun once daily on request; tel: 21 56 10), departure times are far from ideal: 06.30 and 18.00 (Sat and Sun 18.40 only).

Bøur

Bøur is best explored on foot since the narrow lanes that weave between the tiny houses are not suited to cars; it really is quite a small place, as barely 50 people live here. As you wander around you'll notice the profusion of flowers that are cultivated in the locals' gardens, which give the village such a charming appearance. The focal point of Bøur is undoubtedly its church, built in traditional Faroese style, and dating from 1865.

Gásadalur

Beyond Bøur things get pretty remote. Until recently, Gásadalur was the only Faroese settlement not accessible by road since it was considered too costly to blast through the rock and connect Vágar's most remote outpost, home to just 13 people, with the rest of the country. However, following a generous government rethink, engineers did just that in February 2003 and the tunnel to Gásadalur is expected to officially open by 2005, bringing the hamlet's blissful isolation to an end. Critics of the project claim as soon as the tunnel is complete it will encourage and enable the remaining people who still live in Gásadalur to up sticks and move to Tórshavn. The gaggle of colourful houses that comprise this remote community are grouped together on the only area of flat land for miles around on the gently sloping western side of the valley formed by the Dalsá River. Unusually for a Faroese village, there is no church here; services instead are held in the school. The sea, 150m below the houses, crashes and surges into the craggy inlet that is Gásadalur's window on the world. As a result of its off-the-beaten-track location, life here has changed little over the years and the settlement is still a fine example of rural island life. Indeed, until the tunnel finally broke through, the only (overland) way to reach Gásadalur was on foot using the old mountain mail route trodden by the local postman three times a week. Although it is possible to land a boat at the small point of land known as Reyðastíggjatangi just off the village, sea conditions and the offshore reefs often make this treacherous. In reality, Gásadalur's only link with the outside world has been the helicopter service to and from Vágar airport.

The old mail route: hiking from Bøur to Gásadalur

One of the most enjoyable, if difficult, hikes (allow two hours one way) anywhere in the Faroes stretches around 3.5km from the road out of Bøur down to Gásadalur, following the old mail route which rises to a height of around 430m. The path starts 3km west of Bøur at the point where the road, Route 452, splits in two. Ignore the turn that swings inland, and instead continue straight on sticking close to the edge of the mountain, taking extreme care not to get too close to the cliff edge. Here, you'll have superb views of the fjord, the islands **Gáshólmur** and **Tindhólmur**, and further in the distance, Mykines. The path now starts to climb the southern side of **Rógvukollur** mountain (464m) up towards a large stone known as *líksteinurin*, literally 'the body stone', which was used as a resting place by the men whose job it was to carry coffins along the path for burial in Bøur; Gásadalur only got its cemetery in 1873. The climb up to this point is rather steep and difficult going at times. The path now turns inland a little to pass along the northern side of the next peak, Krúkarnir (414m). Beyond here, you'll come to what's known as *risasporið*, 'the giant's footprint', an impression in the rock which, legend has it, was formed when a local giant decided to jump from this point across to Mykines. Just beyond here you see an intensely green valley open up before you with a handful of houses in the distance; 300m below you, this is Gásadalur. From here it's a zigzag downhill all the way to Gásadalur, though beware of loose stones on this stretch of the path which is rather steep.

Although the Atlantic Airways helicopter has flown to the hamlet three times a week (Sun, Wed and Fri), the tunnel looks set to make the need for air transport defunct. It's expected that the #300 bus will, instead, continue here providing transport back to Bøur if you don't fancy the climb back up the hill. Check with the Faroese tourist board in Tórshavn or at the airport for the latest information.

Hiking in northern Vágar: the Slættanesgøtan trail

One of the best hiking circuits (allow two days in total) in Vágar leads from **Gásadalur** east along the north coast past the now-uninhabited village of **Víkar** to the island's northern tip, **Slættanes**, opposite Vestmanna on Streymoy. Amazingly enough, this remote outpost was also occupied until 1964, when its isolated location became too much for the elderly people who remained here, and it, too, was abandoned. Experts considered it too expensive to run power cables out here and connect the handful of houses to the national grid. This trail, known as Slættanesgøtan (literally 'the Slættanes road'), passes through an area of outstanding natural beauty (the pasture on the floodplain around Víkar, for example, is exceptionally rich) and offers solitude in plenty; indeed, this isolated route was once the only way to reach these two remote settlements. From Slættanes, the path then leads south across the centre of the island, past Fjallavatn lake, for **Sørvágur**. This hike is certainly demanding and you should bring all provisions with you and be prepared to camp at Slættanes before moving on the next day down to Sørvágur along a much more straightforward path.

Gásadalur to Slættanes

From Gásadalur, take the path which winds its way along the valley up behind the village, following the river and climbing all the while, and in about an hour and a half you'll come to the pass (553m) which looks down on abandoned **Víkar**; this tiny place was only inhabited for around 60 years until 1914 when many of the men from the village were drowned in a fishing accident. Although it is possible to continue down to Víkar from the pass, it's a steep and rocky descent, and naturally, an even harder climb back up again. At this point there are sweeping views of the wild and barren north coast of Vágar. Now, turn right and follow the ridge east past a couple of rock clefts, after which point the path begins to descend into a valley bound by two peaks, Klubbin (352m) on the right and an unnamed hill on the left (322m). Beyond the peaks, the track descends towards sea level and **Viðvík Bay**. Continuing east from here can be boggy, but persevere and cross the Reipsá River emptying from Fjallavatn lake, sticking close to the sides of the mountain, Klubbin (455m) (though not the same as the Klubbin in Viðvík Bay). You now head up through a valley and cross one branch of the Botnáin River that flows down through it. At 426m you'll reach the mountain pass, Skoradalshálsur, from where it's a gradual descent down towards Slættanes, keeping to the northern side of the Grøv River.

Slættanes to Sørvágur

After spending the night in Slættanes, it's possible to continue south along the path known as Slættanesgøtan towards Sórvágur. From Slættanes, walk south around the foot of the hill, Eggin, passing Skáadalur valley coming down from the Skoradalshálsur pass and continue climbing up towards the point where the path divides on the slopes of the Tungufelli peak (563m). Take the right turn (the left one leads to Oyrargjógv and beyond towards Míðvágur) and the path begins to descend towards the southern end of Fjallavatn lake. From here it's a straightforward hike south, over relatively flat ground, crossing the Sjatlá River, towards Húsadalur valley and the Kirkjuá River which mark the approach to Sørvágur.

Mykines

Mykines really is something special. Geographically the Faroes' most westerly outpost, this rugged isle, barely 10km square, is certainly the most enigmatic of the 18 Faroe Islands and the one that ranks, time and again, as the absolute favourite among Faroese and visitors alike. Looking down the fjord from Sørvágur its craggy cliffs and hills rise precipitously out of the sea in a wall of lush green, turquoise and steely grey, the winds hurrying the clouds across the sky, changing the island's aspect as frequently as the light. Depending on the prevailing weather conditions, Mykines can seem bright and inviting or, at other times, sombre and threatening. Approaching across the turbulent waters of the **Mykinesfjørður** fjord, which separates the island from Vágar, Mykines can appear totally inaccessible, the south coast a remarkable series of unapproachable sheer cliffs and rocky clefts. High above this wall of rock, the peak, Knúkur (560m), bears down over the eastern end of the island, from where two rocky valleys, Borgardalur and Kálvadalur, tumble down to the sea drained by several serpentine rivers. As the land falls away to the west of the mountain, the rocky outcrops of the interior give way to a luxuriant valley of the deepest green that leads down gently to the island's only settlement. Some 150m below the village, hemmed into an alarmingly narrow cleft full of jagged reefs, the landing stage is regularly battered by the crashing Atlantic surf and surging waves; arrival in Mykines is not only an adventure but also something of an unpredictability, since, with southwesterly winds, the ferry may not be able to steer into the tiny harbour despite having sailed from Sørvágur with that very intention. It's not unknown for the island to be cut off for days, even a week or so, during particularly stormy weather. Charming though Mykines village is, it's the tremendous profusion of summer birdlife that is the real draw here. Seemingly everywhere you look there are birds: in the air, on the cliffs and hiding in nesting burrows on the hillsides. Indeed, the

FLEDGING TIMES OF BIRDS ON MYKINES
With thanks to Cornelius Nelo

The fledging time of puffins is roughly August 10–30, with the adults departing very quickly around the middle of this period. Black guillemots fledge around the same time (with a peak around August 20), but can still be seen in adjacent waters after the puffins have left for the open sea. Common guillemots generally leave the breeding cliff by the end of July, and most razorbills fledge around the same time, if not a bit earlier. Manx shearwaters fledge early in September, whereas gannets linger till the second half of September. At this time, both storm petrels and leach's storm petrel may still be seen and heard around the lighthouse. Fulmars check their territories all year long.

western point of the island beyond the harbour, known as **Lambi**, is a favourite location for puffin who gather here in uncountable numbers to hatch and rear their young. Beyond here, a narrow footbridge leads across to the neighbouring rectangular islet, **Mykineshólmur**, where the rock stacks, Píkarsdrangur and Flatidrangur, are home to the Faroes' only colony of gannets.

Incidentally, the correct pronunciation of the island's name is 'mitchines' and not 'mikines'; armed with this fact you're bound to impress the locals.

Where to stay and eat

The main accommodation option on Mykines is **Kristianshús** (tel: 32 19 85; fax: 31 09 85; email: mykines@post.olivant.fo; www.heima.olivant.fo/~mykines; 220kr), close to the public telephone box (tel: 32 07 30) and overlooking the village stream. Run by Katrina Johanessen (born and bred on Mykines) and her husband, Esbern, this glorified hostel has just four snug and cosy rooms upstairs reached by a set of steep wooden steps. Although space here is limited (be prepared to hit your head in the bathroom which is tucked up right under the eaves) it is a friendly place to stay and is also the only place to provide food: breakfast (included in the room rate) and evening meals (around 140kr). Although, it's strictly only open from May to the end of August, the chances are that Katrina will open up for you out of season as well. In the adjacent house, towards the harbour, there's a small kitchen which guests can use. The rooms in this rather spartan structure are also let out during the summer months. Other than the **campsite** (50kr) up behind the village (use of Kristianshús showers, 25kr, and kitchen, 60kr), the only other choice of accommodation is the yellow-painted **Gúla Húsið** (tel: 33 26 14; fax: 33 36 14; email: julianna@post.olivant.fo) which charges the same as its better-known neighbour.

Other practicalities

There is no general store on the island so it's imperative to bring all provisions with you – and bear in mind that you may get stuck here longer than you

THE BIRD HUNT ON MYKINES

Thirty species of bird nest on Mykines, but none is more common than the puffin. Indeed, from the beginning of July to the middle of August, roughly 25,000 puffins are caught on the island each year where they are plucked and prepared for sale ready for transport to Streymoy by boat. Although it's claimed that no birds are taken that are still feeding their young, in practice it can be quite difficult to work out which birds to catch. It's not uncommon to see dead chicks on the hillsides, their parents evidently no longer available for feeding duties, but the reasons for this are unclear.

From late August to early September, the islanders catch fulmars, though in much smaller numbers than puffins; only several hundred birds are taken. The gannet hunt takes place at night when the birds are asleep; the islanders sail out to the gannetry on the rock stack, **Flatidrangur**, and climb up its steep sides in order to net the birds, which are so startled by torchlight that they are easily caught. During daylight hunts, the men lower themselves down the cliff face of the **hólmur** and throw down the chicks to men waiting in boats below. Approximately 600 gannets are caught on Mykines each year, both on the rock stack and on the western reaches of Mykineshólmur.

Several decades ago the bird hunt on Mykines was an important source of food for the islanders, who would live off their booty during the long winter months. However, with the dwindling puffin population (as against an increase in gannet numbers), fewer birds are now caught and most are sold to bring in much-needed cash to the island.

anticipated if the weather closes in. For details of boat and helicopter transport to Mykines, see *Getting around* on page 90.

Mykines village

Undoubtedly one of the prettiest villages in the Faroes, the tiny settlement of Mykines is wonderfully photogenic: brightly painted wooden houses, interspersed with traditional tarred and turf-roofed structures, huddle together either side of a mountain stream which trickles down between them from the hillsides behind. There are no roads here, just a couple of footpaths, which wind among the houses and up to the 19th-century church at the top of the village. Built of sturdy white walls and topped with an unruly grass roof, the church is still used for services by the islanders, though the priest from Vágar does manage to make it over to the island twice a year to add a bit of authenticity. In his work *Barbara*, novelist Jørgen-Frantz Jacobsen puts the legendary appalling weather on Mykines and ensuing delays in boat traffic to good use; when the local minister finally manages to return to Vágar, after being stranded on Mykines for 11 days, he discovers his wife has run off with another man. It may only be a plot in a novel but during my last visit to Mykines reality bore an uncanny resemblance to fiction: both the priest from Vágar and I were stranded by truly atrocious conditions: one of the few occasions I have seen a horizontal windsock. Indeed, during stormy weather, foam from the crashing waves below the village is blown high up over the houses and into the outfield beyond giving the impression that you're witnessing a snowstorm.

When the church was built in the late 19th century, around 200 people lived on the island making a living from farming the land and fishing. Amazingly, by the 1960s, although there still was no electricity, the village boasted a school, meeting hall, a handful of shops and even a small hotel. However, Mykines's remote location, far from the bright lights and sophistication of Tórshavn, has always made life here difficult and the island has often been threatened with depopulation. Today barely nine people live here year-round, and as you wander around the village, you'll see that many of the houses are closed up, used only as holiday homes during the short summer months. Indeed, it's during the summer that Mykines is at its most lively, not only with tourists but also with returning islanders keen to keep their former family homes in good repair.

Although there are no sights as such in the village, sooner or later you'll come across a small dam in the stream at the back of the village, roughly on a level with the church. In jest, locals claim it's their swimming pool, and, indeed, it is possible to have a quick dip here, though preferably when the sun is shining to avoid hypothermia on getting out of the icy water! A stroll in the opposite direction will take you past the electricity generating station out towards the harbour, where a set of steep concrete steps leads from the couple of boat houses on the cliff-top down to the landing stage.

Hiking to Mykineshólmur

From the electricity generator, a path runs alongside the field behind, up the hillside you can see in front of you. Follow it to the top (it's quite steep) where it reaches the north coast of the island. Continue past a memorial on your left and a grass covered, cone-shaped hill on your right until about a hundred metres further on your right you come to some rocky steps. The monument was erected in 1939 in memory of nine fishermen from Mykines who drowned when the trawler *Neptun* went down, and their names are commemorated in the local church. Once through a wooden gate, the path continues on the cliff-side itself – a section of the cliff has been cut away to make this possible. It can be quite slippery here if it's wet, although there is a rope to steady yourself. From this section of the path there are breathtaking views of the sea below and of the cliffs further to the east (behind you). The path now weaves back towards the southern side of the island and begins to descend steeply towards the footbridge over the cleft to your right. This area is known as Lambi and it's full of puffin burrows; in the summer months the birds are everywhere here and you should tread carefully so as not to cave in their burrows and twist your ankle in the process. The stench of guano can be quite overpowering. You should now walk over the narrow footbridge, which spans the Hólmgjógv cleft between Mykines and its smaller neighbour,

Mykineshólmur. From its sheer northern coastline, around 130m above sea level, the tussocky terrain of this rectangular-shaped islet slopes gently to the south. Once over the bridge you have a choice of paths: either you follow the fence up the hillside and then west along the length of the island, or you stay close to the southern shoreline and walk west. Both tracks lead past more puffin burrows. The grass on Mykineshólmur is reputed to be the richest in the country; indeed, when the island was more extensively farmed than today, the cattle that grazed here were said to produce the tastiest meat. Amazingly, three families once lived on the island's westernmost extremity, where today's lighthouse stands. Built in 1909, this is one of the most important lighthouses in the country since it warns approaching shipping, that has sailed for days across the Atlantic without obstruction, that the Faroes lie ahead. Southwest of the lighthouse, the free-standing rock stacks, **Flatidrangur** (27m) and the slightly taller **Píkarsdrangur** (36m), together with the surrounding cliffs of Mykineshólmur, are home to the Faroes's only gannetry. The westernmost point in the Faroe Islands is now in front of you: the tiny blob of an islet, furthest in the distance and a little northwest of the stacks, is **Knikarsboði**; the last or first part of the Faroes depending on your point of view. It is here, on the boulders, little stacks and inside cracks of Knikarsboði, that you can spot some of the few razorbills to be found at Mykines. Binoculars are essential.

If you don't dawdle you can hike out there and back in around two hours, but it's much better to give yourself time to watch the puffins and other birdlife and enjoy the views, so allow perhaps double this. Remember, too, that the lighthouse is often buffeted by strong winds and the surf here can crash high up on the cliffs.

Other hikes: Knúkur peak and around

Rising to a height of 560m, and frequently obscured in low cloud, the **Knúkur** peak dominates any view of Mykines. By following the farm tracks at the top of the village out through the outfield and then up the hill beyond, it's possible to reach the peak in around an hour or so. From here there are superb views over the eastern end of the village, which can't be seen from the village itself. From Knúkur there are two further hiking options. With care it's possible to descend into Borgardalur valley, the easternmost part of the island by first heading southeast along a ridge for Heðinsskorarfjall mountain (433m). Following the cliffs it's a difficult descent down into the valley, best undertaken without a heavy rucksack. Heading in the opposite direction from Knúkur, heading north following a line of rock ledges to the east, it's a straightforward walk down into Korkadalur valley, location of what the islanders call the *steinskógir*, where basalt columns rise to around 60m in height, a veritable stone forest indeed as the Faroese name suggests.

Eysturoy

The second-largest island in the Faroese chain at 266km², Eysturoy is also one of the most densely populated serving as home to around 10,000 people. Connected to its bigger neighbour, Streymoy, to the west by the bridge over Sundini sound, it's thought Eysturoy was the second island in the Faroes to be settled; its name 'eastern island' suggesting that settlers came here from the west, ie: Streymoy. Today most settlements are concentrated in the south of the island, where **Runavík**, with nearly 2,500 inhabitants, weighs in as the Faroes' third-largest town after Tórshavn and Klaksvík. The surrounding countryside is dominated by the country's longest fjord, **Skálafjørður**, which virtually cuts the southern half of Eysturoy in two, reaching deep into the heart of the island. Although the scenery hereabouts is undoubtedly attractive, rich pastureland and low rounded hills gently sloping down to the fjordside, it's the mountainous north of the island which is the main geographical and geological attraction. Here, three majestic peaks, **Vaðhorn** (726m), **Slættaratindur** (882m) and **Gráfelli** (857m), bearing down over the scattering of local villages, and the imposing giant rock stacks **Risin** (71m) and **Kellingin** (69m) off the island's north coast, certainly provide a dramatic backdrop to this peaceful and remote northern corner of the island. East of here, Eysturoy's other great fjord, **Funningsfjørður**, slices deep into the island reaching within 7km of the head of Skálafjørður, leaving a flat narrow isthmus of land between the two fjords, the location of some fantastic hiking. Although Eysturoy has several attractions in its own right (see below), it's also a transit route for all traffic heading for the northern islands through the harbour at **Leirvík** on the east coast. However, work has already started on an undersea tunnel linking Eysturoy with neighbouring Borðoy due to open by 2006, similar to that between Streymoy and Vágar, which will then sadly do away with the need for the ferry between Leirvík and Klaksvík – one of the most dramatic ferry journeys anywhere in Europe featuring close-up views of the towering cliff-faces of no fewer than three different islands. Get here before the diggers do.

WHERE TO GO
The highlight of any trip to Eysturoy is the imposing rock stacks, Risin and Kellingin, situated just north of the magnificently located village of **Eiði**

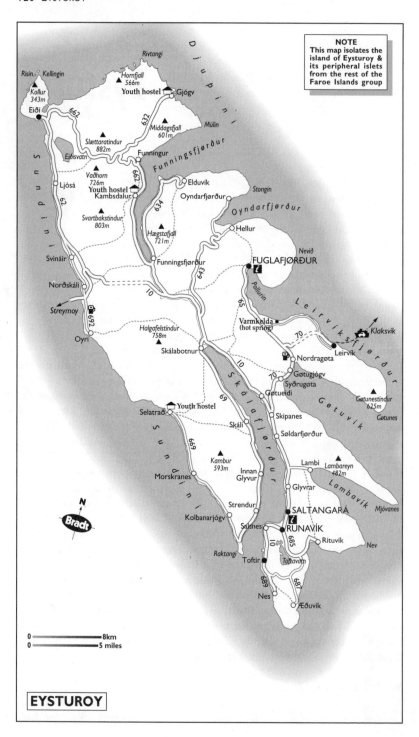

NOTE
This map isolates the island of Eysturoy & its peripheral islets from the rest of the Faroe Islands group

Rivtangi

Risin Kellingin

Kollur
343m

Eiði

Hornfjall
566m

Youth hostel

Gjógv

Djúpini

Slættaratindur
882m

Middagsfjall
601m

Múlin

Eiðisvatn

Funningur

Funningsfjørður

662

632

Vaðhorn
726m

Youth hostel

Kambsdalur

Ljósá

Elduvík

Oyndarfjørður

Stongin

634

Hægstafjall
721m

Hellur

Oyndarfjørður

Neviô

Svartbakstindur
803m

Sundini

62

Svináir

Funningsfjørður

FUGLAFJØRÐUR

Norðskáli

643

Pollurin

10

65

Leirviksfjørður

Streymoy

2692

Halgafelstindur
758m

Varmkelda
(hot spring)

Klaksvík

Oyri

Skálabotnur

79

Leirvík

Nordragøta

Gøtugjógv

70

Syðrugøta

Gøtueiði

Gøtunestindur
625m

Youth hostel

Selatrað

Skáli

Skipanes

Søldarfjørður

Gøtunes

Gøtuvik

69

Kambur
593m

Innan
Glyvur

Lambi

Lambareyn
482m

Morskranes

Glyvrar

Lambavik

Mjóvanes

669

Strendur

SALTANGARÁ

N

Kolbanarjógv

Sælnes

RUNAVÍK

Rituvík

Nev

Bradt

Raktangi

Toftir

Toftavatn

685

10

Skálafjørður

Sundini

Nes

Æðuvík

689

687

0 ――――― 8km
0 ――――― 5 miles

EYSTUROY

nestling between two hills on a narrow isthmus at the island's northwestern tip. Eiði is not only a good base from which to reach the two stacks but it also boasts an excellent hotel and restaurant; what's more, it's served by a frequent bus service from **Oyrarbakki**, the tiny settlement just over the bridge from Streymoy which functions as a transport hub with connections available in all directions. However, the island's most picturesque villages are **Gjógv**, best known for the dramatic rocky cleft which forms the harbour, and nearby **Elduvík**, whose huddle of brightly painted homes looks out dreamily over the swelling waters of **Funningsfjørður** fjord, are within easy reach on the opposite, eastern shore. **Elduvík** is also the starting point for the hike over the mountaintop to **Oyndarfjørður**. On the opposite shore of the eponymous fjord, another hike leads through a mountain pass and down into **Fuglafjørður**, an attractive fishing village with a busy harbour. For more cultural and historical attractions, **Norðragøta** with its timber-framed old farmhouse, now a museum, and **Leirvík**, which boasts Viking-age remains of four farm buildings dating from the 10th century, are both worth seeking out. The main reason to travel south along Skálafjørður to the cluster of settlements around Runavík is to potter around the shops and enjoy a meal in one of the handful of restaurants located here. Incidentally, if you're looking for knitwear, Eysturoy is a good place to start; two of the Faroes' main woollen mills are located here: Töting in Syðrugøta and Snældan in Strendur (see below).

GETTING AROUND

Eysturoy is blessed with a good and efficient bus network thanks to its relatively dense population. Operating directly from Tórshavn, #400 is the backbone of the service linking the capital with Oyrarbakki, Syðrugøta, Norðragøta, Leirvík and Fuglafjørður (connections are available in Leirvík with the ferry across to Klaksík). From Oyrarbakki, skeletal #205 runs a couple of times daily to Elduvík, Funningur and Gjógv, though check the timetable carefully before setting out. Bus #481 provides a regular service between Skálabotnur (at the head of Skálafjørður) and Oyndarfjørður and Hellur, whilst #480 runs from Skálabotnur to Strendur. Bus #481 runs from Søldarfjørður (on Skálafjørður) to Runavík and connects with all #400 services to and from Tórshavn. Until the tunnel opens across to Borðoy, Leirvík is also linked to Klaksvík by regular ferry (12 daily; 30min).

NORTHERN EYSTUROY
Oyrarbakki to Eiði

Barely more than a filling station and a straggly road junction, **Oyrarbakki** is inordinately important to the Faroese public transport network. This dot on the map just over the bridge from Streymoy is the connecting point for a good few bus services. Routes to Saksun and Tjørnuvík on Streymoy, as well as Eiði, Gjógv and Elduvík on Eysturoy, all originate here and the Tórshavn–Leirvík–Fuglafjørður service passes through providing connections to and from the capital. Despite the flurry of buses that stop off here, there's little reason to break your journey here and the settlement is best used as a starting point for the trip to Eiði along Route 62, a distance of around 11km. Clinging to the eastern shore of Sundini, the road provides excellent views of the Fossá River on the opposite shore, before passing the hydro-electric power station fed by the waters of Eiðisvatn lake above the hamlet of Ljósá, the only settlement along the entire road.

Sandwiched between two hills on a narrow isthmus of land, with a battered shoreline to the east and the precipitous end of Eysturoy to the west, **Eiði** (pronounced 'Eye-yuh') enjoys a magnificent location, gently climbing the hillside above the open waters of Sundini sound below. This diminutive fishing village is home to around 650 people – and one of the most windswept football pitches in the world.

Where to stay and eat
Enjoying a tremendous hilltop location right at the summit of the village, **Hotel Lonin á Eiði** (tel: 42 34 56; fax: 42 32 00; 700kr including breakfast) is a modern and friendly hotel whose rooms, although characterless, are perfectly comfortable and clean. Ask for one at the front and you'll have views out over the entire village, the harbour and the sound or at the side for views of the village, lake and open ocean beyond. A small **campsite** is located next to the hotel. The **restaurant** attached to the hotel is the best place to eat in town; the only other option is the **Pitstop** snack bar down in the harbour.

Other practicalities
Down in the village on the main road, a few doors down from the museum, the **Samkeyp supermarket** (Mon–Thu 09.00–17.30, Fri until 19.00, Sat until 13.00) sells food and a few other bare essentials. All buses stop next to the church.

Eiði
During the 19th century, this little place was second in size only to Tórshavn, making a tidy income from fishing, an industry which still remains Eiði's mainstay today; the fish factory down by the harbour provides most of the villagers with employment. Walk down to the northern shoreline, past the football field and Tjørnin lake, and you'll get a glimpse of the two sea stacks, **Risin** (71m) and **Kellingin** (69m) that have become one of the most photographed of all the Faroes' natural attractions and are the main reason to come here. According to legend, these are the remains of a giant and giantess who had come to the Faroes to tow them north to Iceland. However, things didn't go quite as smoothly as they had hoped and when the female giant climbed up nearby Eiðiskollur mountain to attach a rope, the mountain cracked (the crack is visible today), delaying matters, which finally came to an end when daylight turned the two giants into stone. With your own transport there's also a good viewing point, with a free telescope, up on the hills to the east of Eiði; simply follow Route 662 up towards **Gjógv** and high up on the plateau you'll come to a small lay-by on your left after about five minutes or so.

The centre of the village is a muddle of narrow lanes and streets and best not explored by car. Instead there is parking next to the sizeable church, a stone structure dating from 1881 whose marvellous painted interior of creams, yellows, browns and blues dangles model sailing boats from its ceiling – a common Faroese tradition, probably pre-Christian in origin and said to bring luck to local sailors. Close by, in a little walled garden, there's a poignant monument dedicated to all those who never came back from the sea. Whilst you're here, also have a look inside the homestead museum (Jun and Jul Sun and Wed 14.00–16.00; at other times by appointment on tel: 42 31 02 or 42 35 97; 20kr) known jointly as Eiðis bygdasavn and Látralonin. Originally used as a farmhouse until the 1950s, this stone building with a turf roof, right in the centre of the village, contains a wonderful jumble of gifts donated to the museum ranging from women's cotton knickers to a loom and various woodworking tools. If the museum is open, it's worth a look, but it's definitely not one to go out of your way to view.

Hikes around Eiði

From the village it's an easy half-day hike around the waters of Eiðisvatn lake, a couple of kilometres east of the village and reached by retracing your steps along Route 62 until just before the Breiðá River, where a lane leads to the lake itself. Sitting at a height of 130m above sea level, there are some good views to be had and the lake can be a pleasant place on a sunny dry day for a picnic.

In the opposite direction, an enjoyable walk of around two hours begins at the hotel heading for the steep grassy heights of Eiðiskollur mountain (343m) whose flat summit is marked by a broadcasting mast and the ruins of a watchtower from World War II. From here you have great views down on to the Risin and Kellingin sea stacks below.

Gjógv

Although it's tricky to get to and from Gjogv (pronounced 'dyeggv') by bus in one day, the surrounding scenery is worth the effort. With your own transport, the drive on to Gjógv is superlative and one of the most dramatic routes in the islands. From Eiði, Route 662 slowly climbs up on to the high moors to the east of the village heading for the Faroes' highest mountain, **Slættaratindur** (882m). As the road squeezes through the narrow pass, Eiðisskarð (392m), between the mountain and its southerly neighbour, Vaðhorn (726m), you might glimpse the path that leads up to the summit. It begins at the highest point along the road and climbs up the mountain's steep grassy slopes in a straight line to the peak. Although the climb is strenuous, it's relatively straightforward; the summit is so flat that the locals reckon it's even suitable for Faroese dancing (the Faroese name does indeed mean 'flat peak') and in summer the top is covered in Alpine buttercups.

After a couple of hairpin bends, the road meets the junction with Route 632, which swings off left to descend gently through the rich pastureland lining the long, straight valley created by the Dalsá River.

Getting there and away

Since getting to Gjógv requires perseverance, it's probably best to spend a night here to make your journey easier. If, however, you don't want to overnight in the village, the only way to do a day trip here is to take the morning bus from Oyrarbakki (late Jun to mid-Aug at 08.35; rest of the year at 07.00) so that you can then return from Gjógv at 11.50 (note this service only operates on request outside the summer times given above; tel: 42 22 69). Connections are available from Tórshavn; change at Oyrarbakki. Much better is to stay the night in Gjógv and arrive on the afternoon bus which leaves Oyrarbakki at 14.35.

Where to stay and eat

Gjógv is one of the few places in the Faroes to have a **youth hostel,** Gjáargarður (tel: 42 31 71 or Denmark +45 57 52 81 10; fax: 42 35 05; email: trygvisivertsen@email.dk; www.gjaarhostel.dk; open Jun–Aug; 400kr per double room; 120kr for dorm accommodation). Easily spotted by its large turf roof and Swiss-chalet-style appearance, this hostel is one of the first buildings you'll come to when descending the valley towards the village. The upper floor is arranged like a *roykstova* in an old Faroese house – combined kitchen and living room with box-beds; dorms here contain four beds. It's wise to make a reservation for any stay here as it's a popular place to spend a night or two. There's also a **campsite** behind the hostel. Although there's a kitchen at the hostel there's no food store in the village; the nearest shops are in Eiði.

The village

This quiet pastoral village, dauntingly closed in by mountains and with a harbour set in a deep natural cleft in the rock, is one of the Faroes' most charming – and most visited. In Faroese, *gjógv* means 'cleft' and when viewed from the walking paths which lead out on cliff-tops above the harbour, it does indeed appear as if the entire village is clinging to the edge of this 200m-long natural gorge. A set of 69 steep concrete steps leads down to the head of the inlet where often a couple of rowing boats are tied up on the concrete slope. In rough seas boats are winched out of the water to prevent them from smashing into the rocky walls of the cleft. Nestled either side of the Dalsá which flows right through the village, the majority of Gjógv's houses are modern in appearance, although a couple of older wooden turf-roofed structures can still be seen close to the steps down to the harbour. A village store operated in one of these buildings for over 100 years.

From the harbour, stroll past the couple of circular outdoor water tanks used for salmon breeding towards the village church dating from 1929, standing guard over the rocky coastline beyond. The lack of adornment of the church, simply painted white and green, belies its importance in the islands' history. It was here that the first consecration service was held in Faroese, marking a major milestone in the acceptance of Faroese, not Danish, as the national language. Behind the church you'll see a small fenced garden containing a small number of shrubs and plants. Inside is a stirring sculpture of a mother and her two children staring longingly out to sea, their expressions wretched with anguish; the names of all the local fishermen who lost their lives at sea are etched on plaques here. In 1870 half the adult male population of Gjógv was drowned when two eight-man boats went down.

A good day's hike from the village leads over to the hauntingly beautiful highland valley, Ambadalur. To get there, take the pass between the two mountains, Fjallið (469m) and Nøvin (490m) which form the western wall of the Dalsá valley above the village and then descend into the valley following the course of the Róvá River. The lonely shoreline here is dominated by the towering hulk of the Faroes' highest free-standing sea stack, **Búgvin** (188m). With care it's possible to walk back to Gjógv by following the coast eastwards around Fjallið mountain and back towards the harbour providing stunning views of the severe form of **Kalsoy** across the choppy stretch of water known as Djúpini. Just to the east of Fjallið you're likely to see a profusion of seabirds who gather on the cliff ledges here, predominantly puffins and fulmars.

Funningur and Elduvík

From Gjógv, it's 5km back up through the Dalsá valley to the junction with Route 662, which overlooks the funnel-shaped **Funningsfjorður** fjord, and its main settlement, picturesque Funningur, just 4km, four hairpin bends and 300m below, at the foot of the steep hillside which now opens up before you.

Getting there and away

Although Funningur and Elduvík can be reached twice daily by bus #205 (Oyrarbakki–Gjógv), the same restriction applies on making a day trip to either village – mornings only (see *Gjógv, Getting there and away*, opposite). With careful planning it is possible to combine a visit to Funningur, Elduvík and Gjógv (in that order), though, to be frank, there's more reason to visit Elduvík than Funningur, which then opens up the option of hiking onwards to your next destination. There is neither accommodation nor any facilities in any of the villages.

Funningur

The main reason to come here is to see the timber church, which enjoys pride of place in the centre of the village beside the Stórá River which empties into the fjord after its precipitous journey down from the heights of Vaðhorn peak high on the mountain plateau above. Built in 1847, the church closely follows the traditional late-19th-century design with its wooden interior. Inside make sure to see the now rather battered wooden carving of Christ. The figure, which has sadly already had its head glued back in place, once was placed on the altar, though now it's kept on the benches nearby. There's also a silver font in the church dating from 1735. Although Funningur is probably the oldest settlement in the Faroes – in fact **Grímur Kamban**, the islands' first settler, is thought to have once lived here – there's little to show today for this historical claim to fame. Indeed, once you've seen the church there's little reason to tarry and it's best to press on southwards along the new stretch of road leading to the head of the fjord. This route provides the only access to

Funningur during the long winter months when the steep descent from the junction above the village is too treacherous to attempt.

Funningsfjørður, named after the fjord on which it sits, is a modern settlement gathered around a tiny harbour established primarily to serve the fish farms which are found in the superbly sheltered waters at the head of the fjord. From here there's a choice of roads: Route 634 swings north to follow the fjord out to pretty Elduvík whilst Route 662 continues for another 2km to meet up with the main road across Eysturoy, Route 10.

Elduvík

Having reached the head of Funningsfjørður, it's worth retracing your steps back to the mouth of the fjord along Route 634 to reach one of the Faroes' most idyllically located villages, Elduvík. Tucked away around a couple of small headlands, the village is quite invisible from Funningur on the opposite side of the fjord giving the place a wonderfully isolated air. Barely 15 people live in the dozen or so houses here painted in cheery shades of red, blue and green which nestle at the foot of two peaks, Skoratindur (549m) and Múlin (244m). Although Elduvík is a dying village, there are still a few people who farm the land here and in summer you'll see that the lower slopes of the mountain are still used for hay production. Although most of the buildings here are relatively modern, there are still a couple of low-ceilinged wooden houses with turf roofs located close to the Stórá River that flows through the village.

Hikes from Elduvík

From Elduvík it's possible to hike to Funningsfjørður (and on to the main Route 10) or, alternatively, around Skoratinduer peak to Oyndarfjørður.

It's a well-trodden path of around 7km to **Funningsfjørður** following the course of the Stórá up through its valley to its source (parts of this can be quite boggy) before making a steep descent into the settlement. From here it's just a further 2km to pick up buses along Route 10 (#400 Tórshavn to Leirvík/ Fuglafjørður).

From Elduvík a second path, known as Sniðgøta, begins close to the foot of Skoratindur, on the eastern edge of the village, and leads along the fjord shore hugging the sides of the mountain until it reaches the inland end of the cleft in the coastline, Kolbanargjógv. Although the path is not difficult, care should be exercised at all times since it is very narrow and barely 50m above the sea below; in fact this was the route taken by the people of Elduvík to church on Sunday mornings before the construction of their own church in 1951. From the cleft it swings southeast and skirts the western edge of Oyndfjarðarfjall mountain (503m) before descending into **Oyndarfjørður**. This path should not be attempted in bad weather or during the winter months.

Oyndarfjørður and Hellur

At the mouth of the fjord bearing its name, Oyndarfjørður has a certain unkempt charm about it. Centred around a productive harbour, this little place of around 150 people is reached along Route 643 which cuts northwards for 10km from the main Route 10 near to the head of **Skálafjørður** fjord; the only other way in is the hiking route from Elduvík (see above) or the path from Fuglafjørður into Hellur (see below), which lies opposite Oyndarfjørður in the same fjord. Arriving in your own car, it's best to park on the edge of the village because it can be difficult to find somewhere to park in the narrow lanes that make up the central part of the settlement.

Practicalities

There is no accommodation available in either Oyndarfjørður or Hellur. However, if you have come to Hellur to walk over to Fuglafjørður, you will find a youth hostel just outside the town in nearby Kambsdalur (see page 128). Bus #482 operates five times daily (Mon–Fri only) from Skálabotnur to Oyndarfjørður and then Hellur.

Oyndarfjørður

Although it's possible to spend an hour or so wandering around the village admiring the brightly painted wooden houses and their luxuriant gardens or watching the comings and goings in the harbour, the main attraction here is the peculiar *rinkusteinar* (rocking stones) which can be found at the entrance to the village at the point where the two roads into the settlement divide. Follow the signed grass path down to the water's edge and you'll come across two large rocks about 100m off the shore. Quite bizarrely these massive boulders move with the slightest wave; a rope, with a stone at its end, is attached to the larger of the two rocks – watch carefully and you'll see the whole thing rock. Back in the village, take a stroll to the timber church, dating from 1838, down by the shore. Although it is constructed to the same design as the other wooden churches in the islands, it is curious for this one not to have black-tarred walls. Instead its white-painted walls and green windows make a refreshing change, as does its blue choir screen.

Hellur

Hellur, across the fjord from Oyndarfjørður and little more than a tight cluster of houses huddled together at the foot of the Rustarkambur peak (483m), is best visited as the starting point for the enjoyable 9km **hike to Fuglafjørður** (allow two hours one way) up through the Fuglfjarðarskarð pass (353m) between the mountain and the much higher Slætnatindur (625m) to the south. The path, known as Sjúrðargøta, is named after a giant and a local farmer's son who both shared the same name. Legend has it that Sjúrður the giant came to Oyndarfjørður from Suðuroy to test his strength. However, the giant was no match for the superior strength of the farmer's son, who beat the giant at his own game and was richly paid by his father for his efforts. Although the initial ascent out of Hellur is quite steep, the going becomes easier as you approach the pass, marked by two large cairns. According to an old custom, it is usual to throw three small stones at the cairns as you pass whilst saying out loud 'In the name of the Father, and of the Son and of the Holy Ghost' to protect you from getting lost and to bless the trip. Beyond here the path passes *malunar hav* (Malan's rock), named after a pregnant local milkmaid who, astonishingly, managed to lift the rock to prove her strength when teased by her friends for failing to keep up with them on the walk, before finally descending into Fuglafjørður.

Hellur (and Oyndarfjørður) are served by bus #482 from Skálabotnur; Fuglafjørður is connected to Tórshavn by #400.

Fuglafjørður

Tucked away at the head of a superbly sheltered fjord off Pollurin bay, a wide, open expanse of water on Eysturoy's east coast, Fuglafjørður is one of the Faroes' busiest fishing ports and an excellent place to base yourself to explore the rest of the island. Dominated by the three surrounding mountains, Slætnatindur (625m), Húsafelli (626m) and Borgin (571m), which bear down on the tiny village below, Fuglafjørður benefits from one of the best natural harbours in the country and boasts a fish-filleting factory, shipyard, oil depot and even a plant which produces state-of-the-art trawl nets for boats across the islands. A total of 20% of all Faroese exports pass through the harbour here. Although the population is barely around 1,500, the town appears bigger than it really is, with several shops, a couple of eateries, library and even a tourist information office; altogether an agreeable place to spend a day or two.

Tourist information

The friendly tourist information office (Mon–Fri 09.00–noon and 13.00–17.00, Sat 09.00–noon; tel: 44 48 60; fax: 44 51 80; email: infoey-f@post.olivant.fo; www.visiteysturoy.fo) is located in the town's library on the main road. Here you'll find a wealth of information about the surrounding district and also a map to help find the hot spring. The library, open the same hours as the tourist office, has free internet access.

Getting there and away

Buses (service #400) arrive and leave from beside the tourist office running directly to Tórshavn via the ferry dock at Leirvík for connections to the northern islands.

Where to stay and eat

For accommodation, there's the choice of a couple of self-catering **rooms** (same details as tourist office; www.framtak.com/eysturoy) in the town itself owned by the head of the tourist office, or the **youth hostel** (tel: 21 29 40; fax: 31 07 75; open mid-May to mid-September; 130kr) out in Kambsdalur, a couple of kilometres south of Fuglafjørður on the main road out of town (bus #400 goes by); cooking facilities are also available here.

For eating in town the best bet is **Muntra** (Mon noon–14.00, rest of the week noon–23.00), a cheap and cheerful café-cum-restaurant adjacent to the tourist office and run by the amenable Poul, who's been feeding the masses here since 1971; indeed this is the place to meet local fishermen, who come here for a big feed. Accessed by a door at the rear of the building and up the

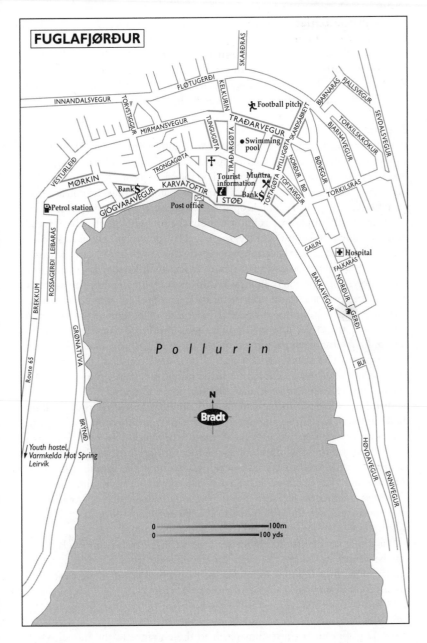

stairs, this eatery not only has great views over the harbour but also some good-value dishes: fish/chicken and chips (55kr), pork cutlet (85kr), set lunch (usually some kind of fish) 45kr; beer here is 40kr, a glass of wine 30kr. Alternatively, there's a **pizzeria** in Kambsdalur serving a good range of pizzas for 70–80kr, though it's only open evenings (17.00–21.00, Sat until 23.00).

Other practicalities

For self-caterers there are two supermarkets in Fuglafjørður: Samkeyp is adjacent to the tourist office on the main road whilst FK is up the hill behind the tourist office (look for the large sign on the building reading Keypsamtøkan). The bank, Føroya Banki (Mon–Fri 09.00–16.00, Thu until 18.00), with a cash machine, is also located on the main road.

The town

Fuglafjørður can trace its history back to Viking times. Excavations in the 1950s turned up remains of a farm on the beach at the mouth of the Gjógvará River in the western part of the town. The foundations of a hall dating back to the 10th century together with a collection of manmade objects such as pieces of pottery, glass beads and soapstone disks were uncovered during the excavations. Although little is known about the town before the Black Death in the middle of the 14th century, there is a tale of a man known as **Rádni í Lon** who owned a *knorr* (a simple wooden boat) and would regularly brave the stormy seas to sail across to Norway laden with goods for sale. Quite remarkably, the spot where he beached his boat for the winter, **Karvatoftir**, can still be seen; ask at the tourist office (see above) for precise directions. Although Fuglafjørður doesn't have any sights as such, there is one attraction you should try to get to whilst you're here: the Faroes' one and only hot spring, *Varmkelda*, which is located on the shore of Pollurin about 4km south of the town. The source, which has a year-round constant temperature of 18°C, is not really warm enough to bathe in but is certainly pleasant enough to dangle your feet in on a cold day. Although the tradition of meeting here on Midsummer's Eve to dance the night away on the flat rocks nearby has all but died out today, there is an attempt to revive it. To get here from Fuglafjørður, first retrace your steps back along Route 65, passing the new settlement of Kambsdalur on the way, until you come to a turn on the left. Take this road (actually the old road to Leirvík) which leads out to the southern shores of Pollurin and after a kilometre or so you'll come to a rock with the name *Varmkelda* marked on it. Here take the walking path leading off towards the shore and you'll see the spring just to the left of where the track ends at the shore; the tourist information office has a map showing the route.

For details of the hike to Hellur see page 127. The path from Fuglafjørður can be found by taking the road up the hillside from beside the tourist information office and then following the road which passes to the west of the town's football pitch.

Leirvík

From Fuglafjørður it's just 6km south to the entrance to the tunnel which carries Route 70 underneath Ritafjall mountain (639m) and a further 3km into Leirvík, the port for the northern islands with regular ferry traffic to Klaksvík. The tunnel is often busy with lorries and other traffic since all produce bound for and coming from the northern Faroes (including every bottle of beer made at the Föroya Bjór brewery) must travel through Leirvík and its 2km-long tunnel which opened in 1985; it was considered too dangerous to continue using the old road around Ritafjall due to frequent rock falls. A second tunnel is planned for Leirvík to link Eysturoy with neighbouring Borðoy; it's estimated to open by 2006 when ferry operations will cease.

Getting there and away
Bus #400 runs from here to both Fuglafjørður and Tórshavn. The ferry, *Dúgvan*, operates every 90 minutes across Leirvíksfjørður to Klaksvík; sailing time is 30 minutes and tickets can be bought on board.

Other practicalities
Although there is no accommodation available in Leirvík, **snacks and light meals** are available at the filling station, which also serves coffee, by the ferry dock. A **supermarket** and a **cash machine** can be found by continuing down the main street past the fish-processing plant.

The village
Leirvík's main attraction lies immediately opposite the loading bay for the ferry at the entrance to the village close to the filling station here: the knee-high remains of four buildings belonging to a Viking-age farm. Excavations on the site, known as **Toftanes**, from 1982–87 revealed that the stone foundations of the structures date from the 10th century. The main building, a longhouse with walls 20m in length, is characteristic of the period because it has double-built curved walls and was divided into two: the western half was used as a sitting area whilst the other half was a cow byre. Remains of a 5m-long fireplace in the middle of the sitting area and the intricate paved stairway by the main door can still clearly be seen, though the five pairs of roof supports close by are modern interpretations. Traces of ash and charcoal found behind the main house suggest that the small structure here was used as a fire-house. Today, the house walls stand five or six boulders high, covered in a layer of grass sods, giving a good impression of the layout of the site. Archaeologists also unearthed a good number of household implements used by the people who once lived here: bronze needles, stone weights for fishing and pieces of pottery all now on display in the Historical Museum in Tórshavn. A second dig in the 1990s uncovered one of the Faroes' best preserved ancient monuments: the remains of a chapel with an ancient burial place. Closed down at the time of the Reformation, this site known as *Bønhústoft*, located in a field in the village, is known to contain other such remains.

Norðragøta and Syðrugøta
Spreading a kilometre or so along Route 65 from the entrance of the Leirvík tunnel to the head of Gøtuvík bay, **Norðragøta** is another example of a Faroese linear village, but one that can trace its history back to the days of the *Færeyinga Saga*. According to the saga, which recounts the rivalry and ritualised violence amongst the islands' early settlers, it was here that one of the key men in Faroese history, the powerful chieftain Tróndur í Gøtu, once lived.

Converted to Christianity with a sword held at his neck, Tróndur is credited with building the Faroes' second church which once stood at nearby Syðragøtu before being moved to the site of the current timber church, dating from 1833 and one of the oldest in the country. The church stands at the centre of half a dozen superbly preserved timber houses resplendent with their black-tarred walls and turf roofs; inside one of them, the Blásastova (a former farmhouse dating from 1835), you'll find the Gøtu Fornminnissavn (homestead museum, open mid-May to mid-Sep Fri–Tue 14.00–16.00; 30kr) which provides a detailed and exemplary insight into Faroese life during the 19th century. The interior of the Blásastova has been lovingly restored to its original condition, including a traditional *roykstova*, and now contains a plethora of antique furniture and household and farm implements that would once have been used here.

Whilst you're in this neck of the woods, it's worth giving yourself over to a spot of retail therapy since one of the Faroes' biggest woollen mills, Töting (tel: 44 10 20; email: toeting@post.olivant.fo; www.toeting.com; open Mon–Fri 09.30–17.30, Sat 10.00–14.00) is located in nearby **Syðrugøta**, a kilometre or so further south along Route 70. Reckon on paying between 800 and 1,300kr for something warm and woolly with the higher prices reserved for more contemporary fashions. Attached to the mill, there's a decent café, the only place hereabouts serving food.

SOUTHERN EYSTUROY
Skálafjørður and around
At 13km in length, Skálafjørður is the longest fjord in the Faroe Islands, cutting deep into the heart of Eysturoy and all but joining up with Funningsfjørður to the north. The valley that separates the two fjord systems, barely 6km long and given over to the course of the Fjarðará River, is appropriately known as *millum fjarða*, 'between the fjords'. The superb protection the fjord offers to shipping was put to good use during World War II when the occupying British Forces chose to set up a naval base here. The underwater ridge that runs between **Strendur** and **Saltnes** at the narrow mouth of the fjord, a mere 25m below the surface, meant the inlet was effectively off limits to German submarines as a result. Today, around 5,000 people live here, concentrated in a series of small towns and villages at the fjord's southern tip. Although undeniably scenically dramatic, the Skálafjørður area is unlikely to be the highlight of a trip to the Faroes and the settlements which line its shores are predominantly modern affairs with little to offer the visitor other than a fair array of shops and restaurants which are singularly lacking in other parts of the island. The main places of interest are the woollen mill at Strendur, on the western shore, and the adjoining villages of **Toftir** and **Nes** on the eastern bank, known particularly as the location of the Faroes' international football ground. Since it is no longer possible to take a ferry across the mouth of the fjord between Strendur and Toftir, any visit to both banks will inevitably involve backtracking to the head of the fjord, Skálabotnur, and then continuing along the opposite shore.

Skáli and Strendur

Taking the head of the fjord at Skálabotnur (little more than a road junction, a couple of houses and a salmon farm) as your starting point, follow Route 69 down the fjord's western shore to reach the first settlement on this side of the water, **Skáli**. As you drive along this 6km stretch of road you'll notice that both sides of the fjord are totally uninhabited and it's only as you draw closer to Skáli that signs of habitation start to appear. This unkempt little hamlet consisting of a couple of streets of nondescript suburban dwellings owes its existence to the extensive harbour facilities, indeed the biggest in the country, which were developed along the fjordside during the late 1980s and early '90s. Tragically, the shipbuilding and repair businesses here went bankrupt during the ensuing financial crisis, and today the shipyard is all but empty; occasionally the odd Russian trawler puts in for repairs (paying in part in fish for the work carried out) though Skáli's heyday looks to be gone for good. A further 7km on, passing the pretty little timber church dating from 1834 in the hamlet of Við Sjógv and you'll reach the elongated settlement of **Strendur**, which guards the western entrance to Skálafjørður. Although visited predominantly for its spinning and knitting mill, Snældan, Strendur also enjoys wide open views of Tangafjørður fjord, which separates southern Eysturoy from Streymoy, and, indeed across to its sister settlement, Toftir, on the eastern side of Skálafjørður.

Getting there and away

Bus #480 operates fairly frequently (roughly a dozen services a day) from Skálabotnur through Skáli to Strendur, with just two services continuing on to Selatrað for the youth hostel: it's worth remembering, though, that one of these buses (15.45 from Skálabotnur) runs only on schooldays and the other one (19.20) only goes on demand (tel: 22 82 06 or 21 97 00).

Where to stay and eat

Although there is no accommodation in Strendur, a bed for the night is barely 10km further along Route 69 which now swings northwest and hugs the eastern shore of Sundini sound as it heads for **Selatrað**, the site of an ancient *ting*. The **youth hostel** (tel: 31 10 75; fax: 31 07 75; email: kfumskfo@post.olivant.fo; www.farhostel.fo; open mid-Jun to mid-Aug; 130kr) and adjoining **campsite** enjoy a wonderful location at the foot of a terrace of steep hills looking out over the sound to Hósvík on Streymoy; the hostel has a kitchen for self-caterers. Around 65 people live in Selatrað today and the youth hostel certainly brings life to a peacefully uneventful settlement which has seen busier days; during the 1960s one of the two ferries linking Eysturoy and Streymoy put in here from Hósvík putting tiny Selatrað on the main road to and from Tórshavn.

Strendur

Due to a lack of signposts Snældan (tel: 44 71 54; Mon–Fri 08.00–17.00, closed noon–13.00) can be hard to find: the mill itself is located in a grey concrete building with an aluminium roof above the old harbour on the main road through the village, though the adjacent shop, in a battered old building covered in corrugated iron painted yellow, is the place to find the shop. Inside there's a good selection of knitwear, everything from sweaters, scarves and gloves to coats and jackets of various designs which make one of the best souvenirs you can buy in the Faroe Islands. Over the years, the mill has at times been closed down due to various financial problems and today, although it provides many local people with work, the town's biggest employer is a fish-filleting factory. After you're done with woollens, it's worth heading to the southernmost tip of the western side of the fjord, Raktangi, a narrow grassy promontory jutting out into the mouth of Skálafjørður which affords superlative views across to the outskirts of Tórshavn. There's also a monument here in memory of all those who have lost their lives at sea.

Hiking from Skálabotnur to Selatrað

It's also possible to hike between Skálabotnur and Selatrað (7km) via the mountain pass, Millum Fjalla (344m) in around 3½ hours. From Skálabotnur the path begins a couple of kilometres south of the junction of Routes 69 and 10, at a stone quarry along Route 69 for Strendur. Here, you should climb the steep slope in front of you, passing through some quite rocky terrain known as Ennisstíggur. Beyond here the path then runs straight for several kilometres (though at times the ground can be quite marshy) offering good views, in clear weather, of the surrounding mountains as far afield as Slættaratindur (882m) near Eiði. After passing through the Millum Fjalla pass between the **Reyðafelstindur** (764m) and **Borgarfelli** (543m) peaks, the track then bears to the west following a series of cairns. Descend now towards the meadow fences ahead of you, cross the Breiðá River, pass through a gate and follow the cattle track which leads finally down to Selatrað.

Skipanes, Sóldarfjørður and Lambi

From Skálabotnur, it's an uneventful 6km down Route 10 along the eastern shore of Skálafjørður fjord, before the junction with Route 70 comes into view. This is the turn for all traffic heading for Norðragøta, Fuglafjorður, Leirvík and ultimately the northern islands. The small gaggle of houses at the intersection, **Skipanes**, is said to be of Viking origin; it's thought that the islands' first settlers, including Tróndur í Gøtu, once kept their ships here. The altogether larger settlement, which Skipanes runs into, **Soldarfjørður** is also one of the oldest villages on Eysturoy though it has a tragic history. The village was originally called Sólmundarfjørður after one of two brothers, sons of the chieftain, **Tróndur Tóralvsson**, who first settled here. However, Sólmundur fell out with his older brother, Skeggi (heir to the family's wealth) and unceremoniously pushed him to his death off the cliff known as Skeggjanøv; Sólmundur was later outlawed and driven out of the Faroe Islands for his crime. A couple of kilometres further on and you'll hit the junction for Route 683 which leads to the idyllically located hamlet of Lambi wedged between two cliff walls overlooking the steely waters of Lambavík bay on the island's eastern

Above Tjørnuvík beach, northern Streymoy (LP)

Below left Kirkjubøur harbour, Streymoy, looking towards Hestur (LP)

Below right The lighthouse at Skansin fort, Tórshavn (LP)

Above The view from southern Streymoy towards Koltur (GR)

Below Flat farmland in the mountainous Faroes is a precious resource (GR)

shore. Down at the harbour you'll see a large rock standing all by itself in the middle of the quay; when the harbour was being constructed, nobody dared move the stone because it was believed that the Faroese elves and spirits, the *huldufólk*, lived in it. In 1707, the bay witnessed the tragic shipwreck of the *Norske Løve* which foundered on New Year's Eve, and which belonged to the Danish East Indies Company. The ship's bell, together with a model of the vessel, can be seen in the cathedral in Tórshavn. Although over the years there has been much talk of raising the ship – rumours have circulated for centuries that there was a large cache of gold on board – to date the vessel lies buried on the sea bed under rock and earth after a series of landslips.

Glyvrar, Saltangará and Runavík

Back on Route 10 and a couple of kilometres after the turn for Lambi, one of the islands' biggest conurbations begins. Although this is not Los Angeles or London, in Faroese terms a veritable mass of people live here in the half-dozen small villages that have grown together to form a 10km-long centre of population that is home to around 3,500 islanders. First off, uninspiring **Glyvrar** is notable for its modern church, dating from 1927, of white walls and felt roof (though its more recent 1980s extension makes it look more like a giant folding concertina than a place of worship) and for its Bygdasavnið Forni (Homestead Museum, open Jun–Sep Mon, Wed and Sun 16.00–19.00; 20kr) situated beside the main road. Inside you'll find yet another collection of how-we-used-to-live paraphernalia such as black-and-white photographs of farming families, old wooden implements for tilling the ground and the ubiquitous child's doll sporting gaudy Faroese national dress.

Better, push on to the larger and more animated **Saltangará** and **Runavík**, virtually indistinguishable from each other, and home of a good number of services such as bakers, banks, restaurants, shops and the only alcohol store on Eysturoy (see *Other practicalities* below).

Tourist information

The tourist information office (tel: 44 94 49; fax: 44 91 80; email: infoey-r@post.olivant.fo; www.visiteysturoy.fo; open Mon–Fri 09.00–16.00), one of only two on Eysturoy, is located on the main road in Saltangará, close to the other shops and services. Inside you'll find plenty of information about local attractions and also the latest bus times if you're planning to hike around Nes or make connections back to Tórshavn.

Getting there and away

Bus #440 runs every one or two hours between Runavík (stopping outside the hotel), Saltangará and Sóldarfjørður where connections are available to Tórshavn; in the opposite direction it continues on to Toftir.

Where to stay and eat

For hotel accommodation, look no further than the pleasant, comfortable and recently renovated **Hotel Runavík Sjómansheimið** (tel: 44 74 20; fax: 44 88

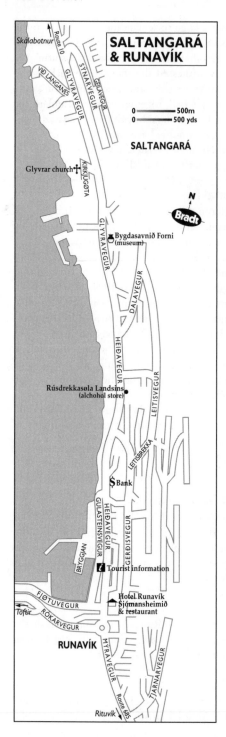

SALTANGARÁ & RUNAVÍK

SALTANGARÁ

Skálabotnur

Glyvrar church

Bygdasavnið Forni (museum)

Rúsdrekkasøla Landsins (alchohol store)

Bank

Tourist information

Hotel Runavík Sjómansheimið & restaurant

RUNAVÍK

Toftir

Rituvík

30; email: hotell@post.olivant.fo; 795kr including breakfast) on the main road in Runavík opposite the harbour, a 5–10-minute walk from the tourist office. This former seaman's home has undergone a tasteful makeover and now features neutrally decorated rooms with private facilities (grey carpet and cream walls) plus well-appointed bathrooms; try to get a room at the front, though, with a view of the harbour. For places to eat, the **hotel restaurant** serves a lunch buffet (60kr) between midday and 14.00, whereas in the evenings it mutates into a pizzeria (accessed through a separate side door on the right-hand side of the hotel, not through reception) serving pizzas (70–85kr), chicken/fish and chips (55kr) and burgers (40–55kr); this restaurant, which also does takeaways, is open 18.00–23.00.

Other practicalities

The Eysturoy branch of the Rúsdrekkasøla Landsins **alcohol store** (tel: 44 92 77; open Mon–Wed 14.00–17.30, Thu 14.00–19.00, Fri 10.00–17.30) is on the main road, Heiðavegur. There are two banks in the area: **Føroya Banki** in Saltangará and **Føroya Sparikassi** in Runavík, and a **post office** on the main road in Saltangará (Mon–Fri 09.00–16.00, Thu until 17.00).

Runavík

Although there are no sights as such to take in here, sooner or later you're bound to end up at the harbour in Runavík – one of the biggest and busiest in the Faroe Islands. It's here that the old cutter, *Høganes*, now spends her final days. Rescued by a group of enthusiasts from her former owners, who were planning to sink her, the *Høganes* has now been restored to her former glory and is available for viewing on the harbourside. However, should you wish to go on board and have a nosy round, you'll have to arrange an appointment (tel: 44 19 16 or 44 75 60 or 44 77 44). Remarkably, cutters like this were the backbone of the Faroese fishing fleet until the early 1970s.

Toftir and Nes

A mere 3km south around the headland from Runavík and you'll find yourself in **Toftir**, the last main town on Eysturoy which stretches in an ungainly fashion from the narrow strip of land up the hillside beyond. Indeed, it's this exposed rocky hillock that holds a special place in the heart of every Faroese football fan; it was here, following the quite sensational 1–0 victory of the Faroe Islands over Austria in the European Championship qualifier in 1991, that the islands' first proper football pitch was created. Blasting into the surrounding hillside created enough flat land to lay a pitch – with real turf – big enough to hold international matches and meeting all FIFA requirements. The stadium (tel: 44 80 68) here can hold the entire population of Tórshavn, around 16,000 spectators, who flock here in their thousands, despite the ferocious winds and rain that often whip in off the surrounding fjords, to watch both qualifying matches for the national team, local inter-island games as well as athletics events. From the main road in Toftir, follow the signs marked '*Ítróttarøki*' and later '*Tofta Ítróttarfelag*' up the hillside to the car park in front of a white building used as changing rooms. The international stadium is the second pitch you can see up here, located to the right of the main building. Locals proudly point out that the Toftir stadium is streets ahead of its rival, the new stadium in Tórshavn, thanks to the superior quality of the turf here, whereas in Tórshavn the grass still needs to bed down and is not yet suitable for international matches.

As you leave Toftir, it's worth stopping briefly at the modern church with its steep V-shaped roof, Fridrikskirkjan, built 1993–94, where, on the opposite side of the road, there's a moving memorial to all the local people who lost their lives at sea. The sculpture, in the form of curving metal strips, creates the form of a mother and child staring out to sea: a plaque here bears the names of those who never returned, most recently in 1994.

The handful of houses down the hill from Fridrikskirkjan make up **Nes**, a tiny hamlet which amazingly boasts its own much more beautiful timber church, dating from 1843 and one of the last to be built in the islands. With black-tarred walls and a slate roof, the interior of the church follows the same pattern as the other 19th-century churches in the Faroes with unscrubbed pine walls and a carved choral screen. Indeed, the church here has played an important role in Eysturoy's religious life; the minister for the whole of the island once lived here, a role fulfilled, most prominently, by **V U Hammerschaimb** (1867–78) who was instrumental in achieving official status for the Faroese language. Close by, just up the hill from the timber church overlooking the fjord, it's also worth having a look at the cannon that was erected here in 1990 to mark the 50th anniversary of the end of World War II. The gun, together with the surrounding bunkers and embattlements, was used by the occupying British forces during the war to defend the entrance to Skálafjørður. From this vantage point, there are unsurpassed views not only of the outskirts of Tórshavn, on the other side of the fjord, but also of the northern tip of Nólsoy.

Walks around Nes

From Nes, a pleasant hike of around three hours takes you out to Toftavatn lake, noted for its rich birdlife, and back to Nes via Runavík. The path begins close to the junction of the main road, Route 682 (which swings around Toftavatn), and heads to the lake's southeastern corner. As you walk you may notice a wind generator high on the moors off to your right; this is used to test wind speed for possible power generation. However, it seems that the wind on the Faroes is simply too strong for these turbines to operate. Once at the lake, the track turns into a small lane, which then heads north to join Route 685 back into Runavík, roughly 1.5km to the west.

Alternatively, a second path leads from the village of Nes southeast across Fossdalur valley, site of the wind generator, passing the hill, Vørðan (169m) on its western side, heading for the tiny settlement of **Æðuvík**, a distance of around 2–3km. This, the most southerly place on Eysturoy, is a hamlet of no more than a dozen or so houses perched right on the shore and alarmingly exposed to the ferocious Atlantic storms. Close to the tip to the north of the settlement, near the rubbish dump, the old Viking parliament site, *Tinghella*, can still be made out.

If you time your hike right, it's possible to hike one way from Nes to Æðuvík and then take bus #442 back to Runavík, a journey of around 20 minutes. Currently the bus leaves (Mon–Fri only) at 09.05, 12.15, 15.10 and 16.55.

Chamomile

The Northern Islands

The six northern islands (Norðoyar) that form the northeastern extremity of the Faroes are arguably the country's best-kept secret. These remote enigmatic islands, known as *norðoyar* in Faroese, receive little attention, even within the Faroe Islands themselves, and see even fewer visitors. Yet they are astonishingly beautiful islands, their geography of sheer sea cliffs and layer-cake mountains of scree and deep green valleys making them not only the most photogenic of all 18 islands but also the most alluring; although it takes time to get out here, it's well worth making the effort. Indeed, it also takes time to get to know the inhabitants of these remote outposts in the North Atlantic since any Faroe Islander will readily tell you they are known for their taciturn and even ill-tempered nature which is often, mistakenly, interpreted by outsiders as rudeness. Take the trouble, though, to chat to the people who scratch a living in the northern islands from sheep farming or crofting and you'll discover a genuine warmth of character and a shy curiosity about just what brings you out to these forgotten isles.

Of the six northern islands, an inner core of three are connected to each other. **Borðoy**, easily the most significant of the Norðoyar thanks primarily to the settlement of **Klaksvík**, the Faroes' second town, at its southern tip, is linked to neighbouring **Kunoy** and **Viðoy** by road-carrying causeways built atop the dams which stretch across the narrow Haraldssund and Hvannasund sounds respectively. Sandwiched between Eysturoy and Kunoy, the endearing skinny length of **Kalsoy** is the most westerly of the northern islands and one of the group's most appealing destinations due to its deep valleys and towering hillsides. However, it's the last two islands that really steal the show: **Svínoy** and its tiny neighbour **Fugloy** are undoubtedly the Faroes at their most remote, elemental and enchanting. Life here is totally dominated by the whims of the mighty Atlantic, the diminutive settlements clinging to the sheer rock faces of these barren islands in the face of adversity – and some truly appalling weather.

WHERE TO GO

The best place to base yourself in the northern islands is **Klaksvík** since it's here that you'll find the greatest (albeit still limited when compared with

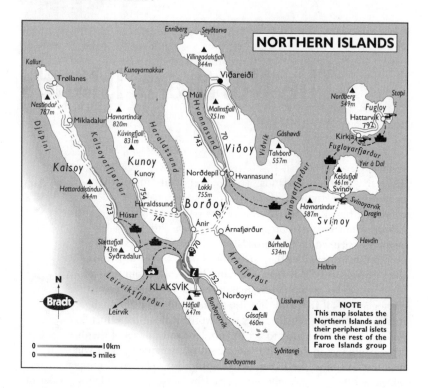

Tórshavn) choice of restaurants, shops and accommodation. Here, you'll also find one of the most spectacular churches in the Faroes as well as a museum – and a swimming pool for those rainy afternoons. In addition, all buses and ferries emanate from here so you'll generally be able to find a connection that suits. Klaksvík is also the entry point into the northern islands when arriving from the south; the regular ferry from Leirvík on Eysturoy arrives virtually in the town centre after nudging its way around the southern point of neighbouring Kalsoy, Gríslatindur (700m) and Kunoy (703m), a truly remarkable journey allowing close-up inspection from the upper deck of otherwise totally uninhabited and inaccessible layered coastlines of basalt. Striking out north from Klaksvík, Route 70 soon divides, heading west the short distance across the sound to **Kunoy**, an uneventful little place, whose best feature is the picturesque cluster of houses that make up the eponymous village overlooking the steely waters of **Kalsoyarfjørður**, perfect for photographs and barely 12km from the centre of Klaksvík. Alternatively, heading east, the road enters a series of tunnels before emerging high above the poetically named **Hvannasund** (angelica sound) off Borðoy's eastern shore. Before driving over the dam and road-causeway to **Viðoy**, consider a quick detour north to the now-abandoned village of **Múli**, just 6km from the junction with the causeway; a forlorn and neglected hamlet which stands as proof of the adversities of Faroese life. Across the causeway, the small harbour and jetty immediately to the east is the hamlet of Hvannasund; this is the departure point for one of the Faroes' most unforgettable boat trips aboard the alarmingly small *Másin* built in 1959 which chugs and splutters its way out to **Svínoy** and, weather permitting, to **Fugloy**, bobbing on the massive swells like a cork. From Hvannasund, Route 70 heads 8km north to **Viðareiði**, the most northerly village in the Faroes, and site of a truly remarkable collection of silverware presented to the villagers by the British government in thanks for their rescue of British sailors in 1847 as well as being the location of one of the highest perpendicular sea cliffs anywhere in the world, **Enniberg**. If you're after a boat trip that doesn't first involve taking a bus out to Viðoy, look no further than **Kalsoy** which is linked directly to Klaksvík by twice-daily boat; it's also the place to fully appreciate the Faroese obsession with blasting tunnels through their steep hillsides – this remote island is home to no fewer than five of them, making it an easy journey to Kalsoy's most northerly point and location for one of the best hikes in the entire northern islands and the best views anywhere in the country.

GETTING AROUND

Although the northern islands are not all linked to one another by road, getting around from one to another rarely poses a problem. The only thing to bear in mind when travelling in this remote part of the country is that bus and ferry services are not as frequent as further south and that the weather can, and often does, lead to helicopter cancellations. The ferries, though, generally run with little disruption in all but the most appalling of conditions.

The key **bus** services are #500 which operates from Klaksvík via Hvannasund to Viðareiði (Mon–Fri six daily, Sat and Sun two daily), #504 from Klaksvík to Kunoy (Mon–Fri four daily, Sat two daily) and #506 which operates on Kalsoy between Syðradalur and Trøllanes in connection with ferry arrivals from Klaksvík (generally twice daily). The bus to Hvannasund connects with ferry sailings to Svínoy and Fugloy.

Two **ferry** services operate in the northern islands: the ancient *Barsskor* runs out to Kalsoy from Klaksvík (roughly two or three daily with additional sailing most days of the week; a new ferry is set to relieve the *Barsskor* in the next couple of years) and the *Másin* sails out to Svínoy and Fugloy from Hvannasund following a timetable which changes frequently though generally follows the following pattern: always one daily (Mon–Sat) around 09.15 (bus connection from Tórshavn is possible by leaving at 06.20 for Leirvík, taking the 08.00 ferry to Klaksvík and then the 08.30 bus to Hvannasund) with additional afternoon sailings at certain times of year on certain days (see the timetable for precise details, and note that, due to sea conditions, arrival times at Svínoy and Fugloy are only approximate and not guaranteed).

Weather permitting, the Atlantic Airways **helicopter** links Klaksvík with Svínoy and Fugloy on Sunday, Wednesday and Friday, and can provide a handy way of getting between the two islands if you're trying to see both in one day; boat from Hvannasund to Svínoy, helicopter from Svínoy across to Fugloy, allowing you to return to Hvannasund by boat from Fugloy. Remember though that bad weather elsewhere in the islands can prevent the helicopter from taking off – during my last visit to Svínoy the helicopter was grounded at the airport on Vágar, unable to fly to Svínoy and pick me up, although the conditions in the northern islands were quite reasonable. If you can work it into your schedule, it's really worth trying to take a helicopter trip out here since the views of the northern islands from the air as you skim over their craggy forms are truly spectacular and a highlight of any trip to the Faroes.

BORÐOY
Klaksvík
Sitting snugly around a tight U-shaped inlet crammed with state-of-the-art ocean-going fishing trawlers, Klaksvík, with a population of around 5,000, is the second largest settlement in the Faroes and the economic and administrative centre for the northern islands. It's here that the entire population of the six surrounding islands comes to shop and go about their everyday chores, be it going to the bank, popping into the library or sorting things out at the district council. Klaksvík owes its pre-eminence to its superbly sheltered harbour, which, ever since the town was granted municipal status in 1908, has continued to grow steadily and today is the site of one of the Faroes' largest and most successful fish-processing plants served by the town's sizeable fishing fleet. Remarkably there's also a brewery in Klaksvík: Föroya Bjór (literally 'Beer of the Faroe Islands') was originally established by a local farmer and has since grown into the country's biggest and best beer producer brewing classic European-style lager from imported hops from southern Denmark; incidentally, the use of the *ö* in the spelling of the word *föroya* is an older version of today's Danicised *føroyar*.

Although Klaksvík can trace its history back to Viking times when a *ting* was held here to pronounce upon all things administrative, today's town effectively grew out of the four farms which were well established by the time a trading station was established here in 1838 during the Danish Trade Monopoly. It wasn't until the end of the 19th century that Klaksvík made the transition from farming to fishing and acquired the modern harbour which today provides the town with its window on the world; one-fifth of the the Faroes' fish exports originate here.

Tourist information
Handily located right outside the main ferry dock and arrival point for the *Dúgvan* from Leirvík, the Norðoya Kunningarstova tourist information office can be found at Nólsoyar Pálsgøta 32 (mid-Jun to mid-Aug, Mon–Fri 08.00–17.00, Sat 10.00–noon; rest of the year Mon–Fri 10.00–noon and 13.00–16.00; tel: 45 69 39; fax: 45 65 86; email: info@klaksvik.fo; www.kunning.fo). Inside, the friendly staff have maps and information about the town as well as the latest weather forecasts for the northern islands (a west-southwest wind generally brings clear sunny conditions to the northern Faroes). This is also the place to enquire and make bookings for cottages on some of the remoter islands as well as in Múli (see page 149). They can also help with bus and ferry timetables, essential if you're planning a trip to Svínoy and Fugloy.

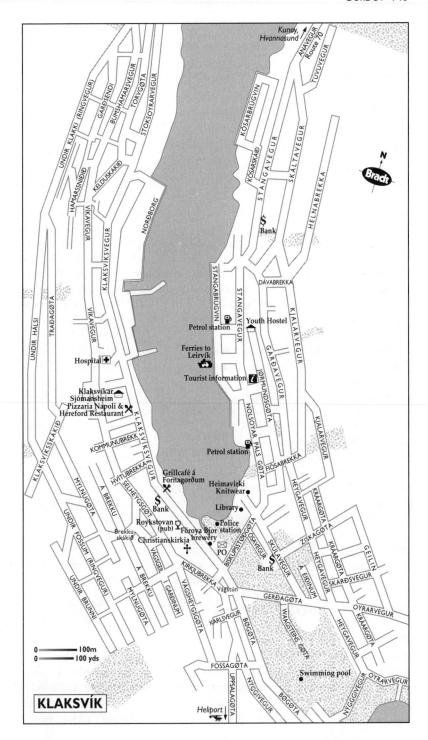

KLAKSVÍK

Getting there and away

Until the new tunnel opens, the only way into Klaksvík from the islands to the south is by ferry from Leirvík on Eysturoy. The *Dúgvan* sails 12 times daily across to Klaksvík; a journey of around 30min.

Where to stay and eat

Accommodation in Klaksvík throws up two options, one on each side of the harbour. The newly refurbished (though still scarily Stalinist in feel) **Klaksvíkar Sjómansheim** (tel: 45 53 33; fax: 45 72 33; email: hotelsjo@ post.olivant.fo; www.hotelsjo.fo; 795kr with private bathroom, 495kr with shared facilities) at Víkavegur 38 enjoys superb views out over the harbour but suffers from a bizarre obsession with alcohol; posted on each floor by the staircase is a no-nonsense sign in several languages pointing out that alcohol is banned on the premises. In a booth next to the reception desk is a cardphone for making and receiving calls; its number is tel: 45 69 83. Across the harbour, a couple of blocks up from the main road at Garðavegur 31, the friendly **youth hostel** (mid-May to early September; tel and fax 45 59 07; 120kr per dorm bed; 350kr double room with shared facilities), long in need of renovation, has now been taken in hand by its new owners, and work is under way to redecorate and modernise the building, which also has a kitchen.

Although eating is not exactly a pleasure to savour in Klaksvík there is at least a choice of more than one restaurant (all located on the western side of the harbour), which is more than can be said for all other towns in the northern islands. For a whopping plateful of school-dinner-style grub, it's hard to beat the restaurant inside the **Sjómansheim** at Víkavegur 38, which serves up no-nonsense buffets and meat-and-two-veg meals nightly for around 100kr; remember, though, there's no alcohol here. Alternatively, pizzas are available at the curiously misspelt **Pizzaria Napoli**, Klaksvíksvegur 45, for 70–80kr, calzone is 70kr; this place is also not licensed. For more upmarket dining, head for **Hereford** upstairs (same address as Napoli) open daily (except Mon) 18.00–23.00 – small and intimate, with soft lighting. The food here is not cheap (steak and fish dishes from 200kr, lamb from 175kr) though it is very good and is renowned as the best in town. The final option is the combined **Grillcafé á Fornagørðum** (downstairs) and **Fortuna** (upstairs) at Klaksvíksvegur 22. The greasy-spoon café on the ground floor serves up burgers and the like whereas the smarter restaurant above (with erratic opening hours; generally Fri–Sun only) has meat and fish dishes at slightly cheaper prices than the Hereford.

Nightlife and entertainment

Undoubtedly the best nights to be in Klaksvík are Friday and Saturday, when seemingly the entire town can be found crammed into the enjoyable drinking den that is **Roykstovan** at Klaksvíksvegur 41 opposite the Grillcafé á Fornagørðum. This smoky pub (11.00–23.00) which also serves up light snacks attracts everyone from seasoned seadogs to the town's trendy young things; come in here as a tourist at the weekend and it won't be long before someone strikes up a conversation with you wanting to know what you think about Klaksvík. Although it's not so busy on other nights of the week, if you're looking to have a beer this is definitely the best place to make for.

Quite unbelievably for such a small town, Klaksvík also boasts two **nightclubs**: Barok at Klaksvíksvegur 22 (tel: 45 88 80) and Klaksvíkar Klubbi at Uppsalagøta 23 (tel: 45 56 81) though they are only in operation at the weekends – and remember that Klaksvík is not exactly known for its big-city sophistication.

Klaksvík's **cinema**, Atlantis, can be found close to the head of the bay at Bøgøta 5 (tel: 45 69 00; www.atlantis.fo) though bear in mind that it is not open every night of the week. The excellent **swimming pool** and **sauna**, Svimjihøllin, are located off Gerðagøta on Jógvan Waagsteins gøta; despite what other bathers may do, you should follow the hygiene rules which apply to all swimming pools in the Faroes (as indeed a notice in Faroese posted up in the changing room dictates), namely, to shower naked, without a swimming costume, before entering the pool.

Listings

Alcohol store Rúsdrekkasølin Landsins, Bøgøta 38; tel: 45 64 77; www.rusan.fo. Open Mon–Wed & Fri 14.00–17.30, Thu until 19.00

Banks Føroya Banki, Klaksvíksvegur 7; tel: 45 63 77; Norðoya Sparikassi, Klaksvíksvegur 77; tel: 47 50 00 and Ósavegur 1; tel: 47 60 00

Bike rental J W Thomsen, Nólsoyar Pálsgøta 26; tel: 45 58 58; will also deliver bikes to Vágar airport for collection on arrival.

Bookshop Alfa Bókhandil, Nólsoyar Pálsgøta 2; tel: 45 55 33; Leikalund, Klaksvíksvegur; tel: 45 71 51

Car rental Autoshine, Stangavegur 1; tel: 45 74 74 or 28 74 74; Bilútleigan; tel: 45 68 68 or 45 80 80 or 22 52 00; email: arnafjord@post.olivant.fo

Doctor Klaksvíkar sjúkrahús hospital, Sníðgøta; tel: 45 54 63

Emergencies Tel: 112

Helicopter Ticket reservations; tel: 34 10 60

Internet At the library, Tingstøðin; tel: 45 57 57. Open Mon 13.00–19.00, Tue & Wed 15.00–19.00; Thu 13.00–18.00; Fri 15.00–18.00

Knitwear Norðoya Heimavirki, Tingstøðin; tel: 45 68 99. Open Mon–Fri 13.00–17.30

Library See *Internet*

Pharmacy Norðoya Apotek, Fornagarður; tel: 45 50 55. Open Mon–Fri 09.00–17.30, Sat 09.00–noon

Photography Photocare, Klaksvíksvegur 70; tel: 45 72 72

Police Corner of Biskupsstøðgøta and Klaksvíksvegur; tel: 45 53 48. Open Mon–Thu 09.00–16.00, Fri 09.00–15.00

Post office Klaksvíksvegur 2; tel: 45 50 08. Open Mon–Wed & Fri 09.00–16.00, Thu until 17.00

Swimming pool Svimjihøllin, Jógvan Waagsteins gøta. Open Tue, Thu & Fri 15.00–20.00, adults only from 17.30; Wed 15.00–17.30; Sat 10.00–17.00, adults only

from 14.30; tel: 45 60 37; 20kr
Taxi Bil; tel: 45 55 55 or 21 29 00
Travel agent Fonn Flog, Nólsoyar Pálsgøta 28; tel: 45 63 63; email: fonnflog@post.olivant.fo; www.fonnflog.fo. Open Mon–Fri 09.00–17.00

The town

Although, in Faroese terms, Klaksvík is a steaming urban metropolis, it's still pretty hard to get lost here since the town consists essentially of just one main road (Nólsoyar Pálsgøta later becoming Klaksvíksvegur) which winds its way from the harbour entrance around the head of the inlet and back towards the open sea on the other side of the bay. Indeed, it's a pleasant place to stroll, taking in the shops and the busy goings-on in the harbour, perhaps worth a day or so's exploration before heading on to the remoter islands which lie beyond.

From the ferry berth, Nólsoyar Pálsgøta leads past the tourist office towards the town centre passing a couple of clothes stores, a bakery and a bookshop along the way. Just beyond here, on the right-hand side, you'll come across one of the best places in the islands to buy home-made Faroese sweaters: Norðoya Heimavirki (tel: 45 68 99) located in a small square known as Tingstøðin beside the town library where you'll also find internet access. Inside, there's not only a good selection of knitwear from Töting and Snældan but there's also an array of jumpers hand-knitted by the women of Klaksvík; if they appeal and you make a purchase, it's certainly satisfying to know that you are helping the local economy as the women receive direct payment from the sale of their sweaters. Incidentally, there is no tax on home-made woollens.

From here, Nólsoyar Pálsgøta mutates into Biskupsstøðgøta as it curves around the head of the harbour, passing the Norðoya Sparikassi bank at the corner of Ósavegur and Faroese telecom, Føroya Tele, who sell phonecards. Up behind the bank, occupying part of the narrow neck of land dividing the main harbour from Borðoyarvík bay to the east, is the swimming pool and sports ground. At the corner of Biskupsstøðsgøta and Klaksvíksvegur, which now runs the entire length of the western side of the harbour, you'll find the post office, the police station and the brewery whose small store opens daily (Mon–Fri) at 14.00 for the sale of bottles of beer and, occasionally, promotional goodies such as T-shirts and towels.

Klaksvík church

Opposite Föroya Bjór stands one of the Faroes' most imposing churches and Klaksvík's main sight, the **Christianskirkjan** church (Jun–Aug daily 10.00–11.00 and 14.00–15.00; at other times contact the tourist office), named after King Christian X of Denmark and consecrated in 1963. Although designed by Danish architect Peter Kock, from the outside it's easy to make out the Faroese shapes that have given this modern re-creation of a traditional church its unusual form: the tall gable walls, made of natural stone, at either end of the church are based on those at Kirkjubøur, whereas the vast floor-to-ceiling windows which punctuate the lengths of the building are representations of the gable ends of Faroese boat sheds. The extravagant interior holds a whopping altar fresco of *The Last Supper*, which, although originally painted by Joakim Skovgaard in 1901 for the church in Viborg in Denmark, somehow ended up being donated to the church in Klaksvík. The traditional wooden eight-oared boat hanging from the ceiling was once the largest such vessel in the islands. Built in 1890, the boat has quite a history, being used not only by the local minister who sailed out in it from his home in Viðareiði to the remoter islands to hold his sermons but also by the people of Fugloy as a fishing and whaling boat. At Christmas 1913, this boat and three others were caught in a ferocious storm whilst out fishing; as the others went down, this boat limped home carrying the only survivors: two boys aged nine and 11 and an old man in his 70s. Coming just a fortnight after another maritime disaster off nearby Svínoy, 13 widows with over 40 children under the age of 15 were left without husbands and fathers. The other item of note inside the church is the font which is thought to be up to 4,000 years old. Originally made during the Stone Age in Denmark, this granite bowl was donated to Christianskirkja by the Danish National Museum in Copenhagen.

Norðoya Fornminnasavn: Klaksvík Museum

Continuing past the church, the Seaman's Home and the hospital, you'll soon reach the other main sight in town: the Norðoya Fornminnasavn museum (open mid-Jun to mid-Sep Mon–Sat 13.00–16.00) which occupies the black-tarred building at Klaksvíksvegur 86 of the Danish Trade Monopoly which dates from 1838. To be honest, though, the pot-pourri of exhibits inside is rather pedestrian and is perhaps only worth a look on a rainy day. Divided into two rooms, the museum's contents are split between the pharmacy on the first floor, which operated until 1961 and is today still stuffed with its original lotions and potions and curious bottles and tools, and a couple of other exhibition rooms which contain, predictably, all the usual suspects: fishing nets, grindstones, hooks and other equally dull bits and bobs from a previous age.

Hikes from Klaksvík

To fully appreciate Klaksvík's highly unusual geographical location wedged between two inlets on a narrow strip of land no more than a kilometre wide, it's worth climbing up the hills on the western edge of the town for a better perspective. The easiest viewpoint is at **Hálsur**, a mountain pass at 245m immediately behind the Sjómansheim and the hospital. To get here follow Uppsalagøta south out of town heading for the heliport (look for the windsock to guide you), then turn into Niðan Horn and look out for an unmade road branching off to the right and leading back in the direction of the town along the slopes of Hálgafelli mountain (502m) past a couple of water tanks. Follow this track and you'll come to the pass between Hálgafelli and the mountain, Klakkur (413m), in front of you. From this vantage point there are superb views not only of Klaksvík and its two bays, Vágur and Borðoyarvík, but west through the pass across to Eysturoy. From the pass there's easy access to the two mountains, Hálgafelli and Klakkur, but sadly, in all but the best weather, their peaks are often shrouded in mist.

Out from Klaksvík: northern Borðoy

The main road out of Klaksvík leads past the tourist office and the ferry berth north (turn left when coming off the ferry from Leirvík) along Borðoy's western shoreline affording grand views out towards Kunoy. Barely 3km from the town centre, Route 70 splits: left drops down to sea level to cross to Kunoy, whereas Route 429, to the right, enters the single-lane 1.7km-long Árnafjarðartunnilin tunnel (the second to be built in the Faroes, in 1965) to access the island's east coast. However, after emerging blinking in the bright daylight (there's no lighting in Faroese tunnels), you're immediately plunged into Borðoy's second tunnel, Hvannasundstunnilin, dating from 1967 and just over 2km in length. Should you wish to break your journey and stretch your legs, there's a hiking path up to Áarskarð (429m; the mountain above the first tunnel) which begins beside the mountain stream on the short stretch of road between the two tunnels. Although the path is well marked with cairns, the climb is quite steep at times and, indeed, until the opening of the tunnel, provided the only access between Klaksvík and the small villages to the north. The views from the top of this mountain, however, are stupendous; on a clear day you can see most of the northern islands from up here, their peaks stretching far into the distance. Incidentally, it was also in this area that a German bomber crashed into a mountainside after bombing Klaksvík harbour during World War II.

After the second tunnel, Route 70 descends past the precipitous slopes of another of Borðoy's high mountains, Lokki (755m), towards a cluster of houses either side of Hvannasund sound, which separates the island from neighbouring Viðoy. These twin villages, **Norðdepil** on Borðoy and **Hvannasund** on Viðoy, have together formed a single town since the construction of the causeway between them in 1972. Although the main road races past Norðdepil towards the causeway, it's worth turning off and heading into the village, home to around 200 people, to see the pretty collection of old wood-panelled houses reflected in the still waters of the sound. Economic life here is totally dependent on the impressive fish factory, one of the biggest in the Faroes, which has helped to prevent depopulation. In sharp contrast to Hvannasund across the water, Norðdepil, which consists of no more than a couple of narrow streets, dates only from the reforms of 1866 when land was made available for settlement and cultivation. Life here on the northern side of the sound has always been tougher than on the sunnier southern side around Hvannasund, where land has been cultivated since the Reformation. The harbour has always been Norðdepil's lifeblood, whereas more climatically favoured Hvannasund has been able to exploit the flat land around the sound for agriculture; the results are clear to see, for bar a couple of wooden houses, modern concrete structures with small gardens dominate in Norðdepil.

North to Múli

Just 6km north of Norðdepil along Route 743, the now abandoned hamlet of **Múli**, three weather-beaten wooden houses built tightly together as protection against the wind and rain, bear silent witness to man's final surrender to the unforgiving forces of nature.

Practicalities

Without doubt, Múli is remote, but its location is also hauntingly beautiful, and should you wish to stay here, it's possible to rent one of the houses (the red one) through the tourist office in Klaksvík; available all year round and sleeping eight people, reckon on around 600kr per night, though remember that the furniture and fittings inside are rather old-fashioned. There is no public transport to Múli – bus #500 operates only as far as Norðdepil from where you would have to walk the 6km to the hamlet if you didn't hire a car.

Múli

Just one generation ago, this was a thriving community of 30 people, working the crofts that once lined the shoreline here, and fishing. However, with their menfolk often away at sea for days or weeks at a time, it soon became evident that life here was unsustainable and one by one the families of Múli drifted away for the bright lights and security of Klaksvík – at the time, Múli wasn't even reachable by road, only by boat from Klaksvík (the *Másin* which now operates from Hvannasund to Svínoy and Fugloy was originally built to work in the northern islands and operated a circuitous route linking Klaksvík with Haraldssund on Kunoy, Múli, Viðareiði, Norðdepil, Svínoy, Fugloy and Árnafjørður). Ironically, once the road was built out here the last people finally moved away and the hamlet was finally abandoned in 1998. The last inhabitants were two elderly couples in their 80s and 90s, who simply were unable to exist in such a remote location. Indeed, this finger of land is one of the best places in the Faroes to experience nature in the raw: turn off your car engine, stand outside and listen to the eerie silence, disturbed only by the cries of seabirds, the crashing of the waves on this exposed shoreline and the howl of the wind off the Atlantic.

VIÐOY

The most northerly of all the 18 Faroe Islands, Viðoy, although not large at just 41km^2, is certainly one of the most impressive. Although the western coastline (location for the island's one and only road) is relatively flat and even, barely a couple of metres inland from the sea the terrain starts to rise steeply, most spectacularly around the pyramid-shaped Malinsfjall mountain (751m) which faces Múli across the northern end of Borðoy. Craggy mountaintops and soaring vertical sea cliffs can be found across the island, yet they are at their most magnificent close to Viðoy's northern tip: the third-highest mountain in the Faroes, Villingadalsfjall (844m), rears up just north of the main settlement, **Viðareiði**, conjuring up true geological splendour. From here it's possible to walk along a ridge to the Faroes' most northerly point, the **Enniberg** sea cliff which plummets vertically to the sea over a dizzying height of 754m; naturally it's a favourite nesting spot for thousands upon thousands of seabirds which create, during the short breeding season, a truly cacophonous din from the ledges at the top of the cliff. The island's other main geographical feature is the long and desolate north-facing bay, **Viðvík**, which is a veritable trap for driftwood (the Faroese word for timber is *viður*). In a country where trees simply don't grow, driftwood was highly prized as both building material and a source of fuel. Such unforgiving terrain has naturally rendered large parts of Viðoy inaccessible; indeed, there is only around 8km of road on the entire island. Access to the island is across the causeway from Borðoy whence Route 70 passes through the modest settlement of **Hvannasund**, one of only two on the entire island, and notable as the departure point for the *Másin* which sails from here out to Svínoy and Fugloy; the jetty is located immediately to the right of the causeway when crossing from Borðoy and the ferry leaves from its right-hand side. If you're around when the boat is in the harbour, be sure to watch the deft loading operation which sees milk churns, bags of cattle feed and other essentials for island life being winched from the quay on to the boat, much to the amazement of visitors who find it hard to believe that there's room on this tiny boat for anything other than a couple of passengers. Whilst you're in Hvannasund, wander along the main road which runs parallel to the sound and admire the neat allotment-style gardens adjoining many of the houses in the town (the southern aspect particularly favours the growing of potatoes, vegetables and flowers) and the painstaking work that has evidently gone into restoring some of the older wooden dwellings to their former glory.

Viðareiði

From Hvannasund, Route 70 presses on north clinging to the eastern shore of Hvannasund sound bound for Viðareiði, a desolate stretch of road punctuated only by the former landing stage at Leiti, roughly two-thirds of the way between Viðoy's two villages. Depending on the sea conditions it was sometimes impossible to land at Viðareiði and so an alternative landing was needed. Indeed, the landing stage was not only used by the ferry which once ran from here around the northern islands back to Klaksvík, but also the villagers from Múli on Borðoy who would row across the sound on Sundays to attend church in Viðareiði. Beyond Leiti, the road swings inland around the northwestern slopes of Malinsfjall before entering the green and pleasant isthmus of land, barely 1.5km wide, which is home to the Faroes' most northerly settlement.

The views from Viðareiði are truly wonderful – across the isthmus to the east you can clearly see Fugloy, whereas, in the opposite direction, beyond the church, framed by the sea and the hills of Borðoy, there's now-abandoned Múli. Indeed, it's no surprise that Viðareiði is located here since this is the only place on the entire island flat enough to allow modern agriculture including the rearing of cattle. The main sight in the village, other than the natural surroundings, is the church and adjoining turf-roofed vicarage. Inside the church, which dates from 1892, is a breathtaking collection of altar silverware including a baptismal font donated to the congregation of the village by the British government in acknowledgement for the charity and hospitality they showed the crew of the British brig, *Marwood*, wrecked in the Faroes in January 1847. Look out too for the impressive silver crucifix hanging on the wall, donated by the Hamburg merchant Thomas Köppen in 1551. Although the silver is kept in a safe in the church, if you find the keeper of the church

Above Roykstovan farmhouse, Kirkjubøur, Streymoy (GR)

Right Door detail, Roykstovan farmhouse, Kirkjubøur, Streymoy (LP)

Below right Even the most remote island has its own postal service (GR)

Below left Bird sculpture, Tórshavn (LP)

Above Nólsoy sheep: the animals gave the Faroe Islands their name (LP)

Below The Risin and Kellingin rock stacks, northern Eysturoy (LP)

key (in the adjacent house) or ask at the vicarage; there's every chance you'll
be shown Viðareiði's pride and joy.

Getting there and away
Bus #500 runs between Klaksvík and Viðareiði (Mon–Fri six daily; Sat and
Sun two daily).

Where to stay and eat
Unusually for such a remote location, Viðareiði has accommodation: **Hotel
Norð** (tel: 45 12 44; fax: 45 12 45; 775kr) is a surprisingly plush place with
superb views from most rooms and a restaurant attached; both hotel and eatery
are open only June–August. The only other place to eat is **Matstova hjá
Elisabeth**, open noon–21.00, located at the main junction in the village
centre; there's also a small shop here selling coffee, tea and biscuits.

Other practicalities
Opposite the hotel, the **Samkeyp supermarket** sells more substantial
provisions (Mon–Fri 09.00–noon and 13.00–17.30, Sat 09.00–13.00). Viðareiði
also has a branch of the **Norðoya Sparikassi** (Mon, Wed and Fri
11.00–16.00), once again in the centre of the village.

Hiking to Villingsdalsfjall and Enniberg
Without a doubt, the hike up Villingsdalsfjall mountain (844m) and on
towards the vertical sea cliff, Enniberg (754m), ranks as one of the highlights
of any trip to the Faroe Islands. The steep hike up the mountain and the ridge
walk leading out to Enniberg certainly requires stamina, plenty of time (ideally
six or seven hours to make the return trip) and – most importantly – good
weather. The precipitous drops that dominate the northern end of Viðoy can
naturally be dangerous in poor visibility. However, once you've made it all the
way up to the top of Enniberg, the chances are you will never see anything
quite so breathtaking anywhere else in Europe – standing at the summit of
Enniberg, high above the agitated waves of the North Atlantic, with a sheer
drop of over 750m immediately below your feet, is a totally exhilarating
experience.

Begin your hike by following the small road that leads northwest from the
hotel and finally peters out after crossing two rivers, the second one being the
Bólsá. Now follow the clear line of cairns which leads up the southern ridge
of Villingadalsfjall – it's steep going all the way to the top but the summit does
flatten out eventually. Once up here you'll have a bird's-eye view on a clear
day of all the northern islands and will immediately appreciate the unforgiving
geology of these remote outposts. From the summit, the trail leads westwards
and then swings to the north and heads around a cleft in the rock. From here
head north again towards Enniberg and take extreme care when approaching
the cliff edge. In theory, it's possible to return to Viðareiði by descending from
Enniberg down through Ormadalur valley (the valley you saw to your left
when you walked around the cleft in the rock) and then along a path along the

coast close to sea level; however, it's probably wise to check the viability of this route in the village before setting out. If in doubt, return via the same way you came.

KUNOY

Much more than any of the other Faroe Islands, Kunoy consists entirely of a single ridge of mountains which runs down the spine of the island at a height of between 700 and 830m; from the top of Kunoyarnakkur, which forms the island's northernmost point, it's a sheer drop of 819m to the sea below, making this not only the Faroes' tallest sea cliff, but also one of the highest anywhere in the world. This unforgiving terrain has made human habitation here all but impossible since there are few spots with enough flat land to make both house building and farming viable; the entire island barely measures 35km². Although the east coast is characterised by a number of *botnar* or rounded valleys studded with rivers, it's not been possible to live here either, because the mountainsides are simply too steep and prone to avalanches. Indeed, there are only two settlements on Kunoy, one on either coast, both linked by a 3km tunnel which opened in 1988 and, together with the causeway across to Borðoy which opened the year before, effectively prevented total depopulation which was threatening the island until then. A third hamlet, Skarð, bravely located between two rounded valleys at the foot of Teigafjall (825m), was abandoned in 1919 and today makes a wonderful destination for an easy hike up the east coast (see below).

Kunoy is approached from neighbouring Borðoy along the causeway, which takes Route 754 across Haraldssund sound separating the two islands. Immediately over the sound, you arrive in the diminutive settlement of **Haraldssund**, notable as the probable location of an earlier Dutch settlement. A couple of kilometres south of today's hamlet there are indeed ruins of houses, known as *Hálendabúðir*, where it's thought earlier settlers may have once lived. There's no real reason to linger here and it's better to push on into the tunnel and emerge on Kunoy's west coast, opposite Kalsoy, where one of the country's most picturesque villages is more demanding of your attention.

Getting there and away

It's easy to visit the island as a day trip from Klaksvík thanks to a regular bus service; #504 runs here four times daily (Sat twice daily; Sun no service). Indeed, an area of new housing at the entrance to the village is proof of the popularity of Kunoy as a place to live with many people choosing the commute to Klaksvík to work, some by bus. There is no accommodation on Kunoy.

Kunoy village

Kunoy, the main settlement of the island, enjoys a fantastic location at the foot of a rounded valley framed by layer-cake crenellations of the sheer rock walls of Lítlafjall (374m) high above the village. Originally formed of three farms, today's village has faithfully kept to these earlier boundaries and can be neatly divided into thirds. The main centre of the village is undoubtedly the most attractive area of Kunoy: a couple of narrow winding streets, encircling the wooden church dating from 1867, tightly lined with wooden houses whose gardens are seemingly overflowing in summer with sweet-smelling flowers and gnarled trees forced into ever more curious shapes by the wind. Alongside, the crystal-clear stream, which tumbles down from the mountains above, adds to the perfect tranquillity.

In theory it is possible to hike from Kunoy up over the mountain ridge and down to the abandoned village of **Skarð** on the east coast. However, on looking up at the rock walls and almost perpendicular mountainsides that bear down on Kunoy, you'd be forgiven for thinking that such a feat was ever possible. Be that as it may, the villagers of Skarð would indeed make this daunting trip every Sunday to attend church in Kunoy, returning the same way they had come. Should you be tempted to follow in their footsteps, the path first climbs the long hillside behind Norður í húsi, the third and most northerly cluster of houses that make up Kunoy village, before reaching the summit of Middagsfjall (805m). The rest of the path down to Skarð is incredibly steep, almost vertical in parts, and is only recommended for the most determined and experienced; before setting out you should be sure to ask the advice of the villagers as to the best way to tackle the descent and bear in mind that the course of the path is now no longer shown on maps of the area; this was always one of the Faroes' most difficult paths to negotiate. An altogether easier approach to Skarð begins north of Haraldssund, from where a track follows the eastern shoreline passing no fewer than seven cascading rivers falling from the mountain ridges above; be prepared to negotiate the water with suitable footwear and allow around three hours for the return hike. An area of flat grassland dotted with a few ruined walls is now all that remains of Skarð after it was abandoned in tragic circumstances nearly 90 years ago. On Christmas Eve, 1913, all the men of the village were out fishing when they were caught in a ferocious storm with three other boats; they never returned, reducing the number of males in the hamlet to just two boys aged nine and 11 and a man in his 70s. The inhabitants of Skarð struggled on but finally gave up their battle six years later and moved away; as far as land use was concerned, Skarð had always been a marginal settlement and fishing was always required to maintain an existence here. Following the deaths of the men of the village it was sadly only a matter of time until the hamlet also died.

KALSOY

The most westerly of all the northern islands, Kalsoy, weighing in at just 31km², is not only one of the easiest in the group to reach but it is also one of the most beguiling. This long slender finger of an island has the benefit of regular ferry connections to Klaksvík and some great hiking, making it a popular day-trip destination. Like its easterly neighbour, Kunoy, this island is also composed of a single ridge of mountains, which run north to south down its centre. The peaks plummet, often perpendicularly, to the sea along the west coast, rendering it entirely inaccessible, whereas the gentler east coast, where

Kalsoy's four settlements are to be found, is characterised by a number of *botnar*, whose deep rounded nature has allowed some agricultural activity to take place.

Getting there and away

Bus #506 runs the length of the island from Syðradalur to Trøllanes generally two to three times daily in connection with ferry arrivals and departures. There is no accommodation and you should bring all provisions with you. Kalsoy is totally devoid of facilities, so it pays not to get stuck here. Time your hikes carefully and don't miss the bus back to the ferry or you'll be faced with a very long wait, and possibly nowhere to spend the night.

The island

Kalsoy was once regarded as the best place in the Faroes to grow corn; look at a map today and it's quite inconceivable to think that the now-abandoned hamlet of Blakskáli, clinging to the steep slopes off the island's southwestern tip, enjoyed this privilege. An avalanche in 1809 soon persuaded the four families living there that they were better off moving to the opposite coast and they founded the village of **Syðradalur** which today serves as the new ferry harbour for Klaksvík. Until the completion of the new jetty, the ferry arrived at Kalsoy's second settlement, **Húsar**, a couple of kilometres to the north. Indeed, arrival at either of these two villages by boat offers a spectacular view of the steep mountainsides of the rounded valleys, which bear down on three sides over the houses huddled together for protection at sea level.

From Húsar, Route 723 runs north for 11km heading for the island's main village, **Mikladalur**. During the early '80s, tunnel mania gripped Kalsoy and no fewer than five tunnels were bored through the length of Kalsoy to facilitate communication between the settlements; accordingly, the island is now known to the Faroese, endearingly, as the 'recorder', due to the large number of holes that have been drilled through its length, whereas neighbouring Kunoy, which has been bored through from east to west, is known as the 'flute'. Don't think of these tunnels as wide, well-illuminated, tarmacked underpasses that can be whizzed through at top speed; they are instead potholed, one-lane, unlit passageways, which should be negotiated with care. There is always priority in one direction only; vehicles coming in the opposite direction should pull over into the meeting places provided allowing those with priority to pass. Judging the distance in the pitch black between meeting places is a skill which even many Faroese drivers have yet to master.

Mikladalur enjoys an imposing location at the foot of a wide and fertile rounded valley looking out over the sea. Around 70 people live here in a couple of dozen brightly painted houses gathered around the village's stone church dating from 1856. Indeed, religion is alive and well in the village, as too is the abstinence movement and any consumption of alcohol is frowned upon; the Good Templars association has been active here since 1883. Although farming the flat lands of the valley floor has been the main occupation here for centuries, things became considerably easier in 1985 with the construction of yet another tunnel into Djúpadalur valley, directly north of Mikladalur, to allow local sheep farmers to graze their animals on the valley's rich pastures; shortly after this extravagance, the money for such ventures finally dried up and the Faroes lurched towards financial bankruptcy. Until the construction of the island's fifth tunnel connecting up Kalsoy's most northerly settlement, **Trøllanes**, with the rest of the island, the only way north out of Mikladalur was to scramble up the sheer mountain path to a height of 480m before carefully negotiating the vertical slope of the rear wall of Djupadalur's rounded valley and the eastern slopes of Hádegisfjall mountain (576m) before descending, exhausted and greatly relieved, into Trøllanes; naturally, during the long winter months, deep snow made this route impassable. Today, just three families live in this agricultural hamlet, and surprisingly for such an isolated location, it's not threatened with depopulation. It's a cheerful sort of a place with the farmers' children playing in the lanes and fields which wind between the dozen or so barns and tool sheds, giving the hamlet the appearance of one big farm. Exposed to the swells of the Atlantic, landing a boat has always been difficult here, hence the arrival of the road in 1986 was a cause for great celebration. Indeed, the descent into Trøllanes is particularly picturesque as the road winds round a couple of hairpin bends as it passes the boundary of the outfields giving superb vistas, not only of the village, but also of Kunoyarnakkur mountain (819m) across on Kunoy, and in good weather, even all the way to Enniberg (754m), three islands away on Viðoy.

Hiking to Kallur lighthouse

One of the most pleasurable things to do on Kalsoy, and certainly the best way to experience the wild nature of the island, is to hike. From Trøllanes, an easy walking path (unmarked) leads out to the northernmost promontory of Kalsoy where the lighthouse, **Kallur**, enjoys what is without a shadow of a doubt the most awe-inspiring view anywhere in the country. To get there, head north past the red-painted farmhouse and the former heliport towards the hill you can see in front of you. Go through the red gate and climb the steep hill, always keeping to the right of the Borgarin peak (537m). After around a quarter of an hour, the land begins to flatten out and you should veer slightly to the left, at which point the lighthouse will come into view. Although there is no path as such to follow and the ground in parts is rather soggy, it's an easy hike out across the tussocky grass of the promontory where you're likely to come across large numbers of snipe. Once at the lighthouse you'll be rewarded with a truly amazing view of no fewer than five islands: to the west you'll see the village of Gjógv, the Risin and Kellingin stacks off Eysturoy, as well as the Tjørnuvíksstakkur in the far distance off Streymoy, whereas in the opposite direction you have Kunoyarnakkur (819m) at the tip of Kunoy, followed by the Múli headland of Borðoy and finally, far in the distance, the village of Viðareiði and the Enniberg sea cliff of Viðoy. However, from this vantage point, it's not just the northern capes of the islands that impress; it is the backbone of mountains which runs down virtually every island in the northern chain that is equally demanding of your attention. Peak after peak, lined up in perfect silhouette, is clearly visible. Enjoy the spectacle; there are few places in the world that offer such stunning views.

NORTHERN OUTPOSTS: SVÍNOY AND FUGLOY

The journey that everyone who comes to the Faroe Islands wants to make is the combination of bus and ferry that leads to the country's two most remote islands: Svínoy and Fugloy. Indeed, much of the attraction of these two last places far out in the North Atlantic lies in the getting there. The weather in this exposed northeastern corner of the country often plays havoc with timetables and arriving here at all is a major achievement. A journey out here is not something to be undertaken on a whim; it requires careful planning, perseverance and not least a large amount of luck. It's certainly not a journey that is recommended to anyone who suffers from seasickness; not only are the rolls and swells in this part of the Atlantic particularly unsettling, there is also no proper harbour on either island, which means that passengers must take their life in their hands and leap ashore from the *Másin* at just the right moment as the boat rises and falls up to three metres on the swell and ricochets off the quay only to be catapulted back towards the jetty as she strains on her moorings. If all this sounds alarming, and indeed it is all the more so in a northeasterly gale, rest assured that there is always someone on land to give you a hand as you fly through the air on to dry land – an experience that is likely to stay with you for quite a while. In a strong tide, the roughest parts of the journey will be when the boat turns out of the sheltered Hvannasund sound to pass through the narrow stretch of water, Svínoyarsund, between Bergið on southern Viðoy and Tangarnir on Svínoy, as well as the final stretch across the open water of Fugloyarfjørður between Svínoy and Fugloy when the boat, quite literally, bobs like a cork. Quite remarkably, there has not been an accident on this route for many years.

Getting there and away

Sailing from Hvannasund, the *Másin* is the workhorse of the northern islands. Built of oak in Tórshavn in 1959, she had an engine refit in 2001, and has several more years left in her yet. This wonderful old mail boat consists of an open deck out front where cargo is loaded, a saloon to the rear with portholes (which more often than not are covered in spray and seawater) and further seating down below – only recommended for those who don't get seasick. The upper deck, open to the elements (and the waves) is accessed by an outdoor staircase from behind the rear saloon, where there's also a small toilet. If you do venture up here, be sure to hold on tight. All passengers board and alight from the front deck; be careful when doing so in choppy seas since the cargo has an unnerving ability to slide across the deck and slam into the sides as the boat rolls and pitches – even when moored. Always check the timetable when leaving for Svínoy and Fugloy as it changes frequently. In general though the boat sails first to Svínoy, putting in at **Svínoyareiði** (occasionally sea conditions force her to sail around the island to land in Svínoy village instead) and then continues on to **Kirkja**, and if required, to **Hattarvík** on Fugloy. On most sailings the boat then returns from Fugloy via Svínoy, though this is by no means certain. Depending on tide conditions journey times are as follows: Hvannasund to Svínoy 40 minutes–1 hour; Svínoy to Kirkja (Fugloy) 20min, with another 10min to reach Hattarvík. Bus connections to Hvannasund are available in Klaksvík, and, if coming directly from Tórshavn you can always make the 09.15 sailing from Hvannasund (daily except Sun) by taking the 06.20 bus to Leirvík followed by the ferry to Klaksvík.

Where to stay and eat
Through the tourist office in Klaksvík it's possible to rent one of the houses in **Svínoy** for around 700kr per night; it sleeps six to eight people. Remember to bring all provisions with you whether you plan to stay here or not, since there are no facilities. Other than the tiny hut adjacent to the helipad, which you might be able to shelter in should it start to rain (ask around to find the keyholder), there is nowhere else to shelter from inclement weather in Svínoy.

Although there is no accommodation in Kirkja on **Fugloy**, the tourist office in Klaksvík does rent out one of the handful of homes in Hattarvík for around 700kr per night; sleeping six to eight people it must be booked well in advance. Although there is a small shop with erratic opening hours selling simple provisions in Kirkja, it's best not to rely on it and bring everything you need with you from Klaksvík. It's also worth bearing in mind that should you choose to take the ferry to Fugloy and return by helicopter, there is nowhere in Hattarvík to shelter from the rain or wind; when the wind blows in from the sea here it can be surprisingly cold so it's worth bringing extra woollies with you should you be left out in the cold waiting for a delayed helicopter.

Svínoy
From the landing stage on the island's western coast at Svínoyareiði, Svínoy's main village is nowhere to be seen. Don't let this put you off, since it's a straightforward walk of around ten minutes or so across the isthmus which sits between the island's two main peaks, Keldufjall (461m) to the north and Knúkur (460m) to the south, to the main settlement, the appropriately named Svínoy. The constrained yet unusually fertile neck of land barely 33m above sea level you're traversing can often be inundated by Atlantic storms; there is no land between here and the west coast of Norway to brunt the full force of the waves. Arriving in the village, you'll be struck by the lush pasturelands all around; true, like most places in the Faroes, the mountains are not very far away, but what makes this village different is the wide open expanses of green so suited to agricultural use; indeed this is the largest area of flat land available for farming anywhere in the northern islands. In addition to the couple of dairy and sheep farms, the island also supports a salmon-breeding plant; you'll see the large green circular containers for this purpose to the south of the harbour. Curiously, for an island named after pigs (Svínoy means literally 'swine island') there are no pigs to be seen anywhere. Instead, the name refers to an ancient legend, according to which Svínoy was once a floating island that drifted around in the sea. An old woman tied a bunch of keys to her sow's tail

so that when it next swam over to Svínoy to mate with the boar that once lived here, the island could be locked and finally anchored down.

Although there are no sights as such in Svínoy, sooner or later you'll turn up at the **church** dating from 1878. It's worth looking inside for the gravestone of **Svínoyar-Bjarni**, renowned in Viking times as the uncle of the hero of *Færeyinga Saga*, Tróndur í Gøtu. When the previous church was torn down in 1828, a gravestone bearing a cross, though no other inscription, was discovered under the floor. Its existence was well known to the islanders who have always referred to it as *Bjarnasteinur* or Bjarni's stone. Once you've wandered around the village, the best thing to do on Svínoy is to take a hike out to the island's northeastern coast from where there are good views of Kirkja across on Fugloy. From the church take the path which gently climbs along the hillside on the northern side of the bay, **Svínoyarvík**. Along the way you'll pass a number of disused sheep huts before the land gradually falls towards the shoreline; the climb to the highest part of path is only 137m. The path now descends through a wide low valley, Yvir á dál, which was once used for peat cutting. In fact, the promontory to the left of the valley, opposite Kirkja on Fugloy, is known as **Kallanes** or 'calling point' since it was from here that the people of Fugloy, who used to come over to Svínoy to cut peat, would call back to their village for boats to come to collect them.

Fugloy

The last Faroe Island, lost far out in the gyrating mists and fogs of the North Atlantic, Fugloy is a favourite with many visitors. Barely 11km² in size, this squat lump of basalt easily repays the effort in reaching it and has a charm all of its own. Approaching from the sea, the 30 or so weather-beaten houses which constitute the main village, **Kirkja**, home to just ten people, make a perfect picture postcard as they climb steeply up the hillside behind. The faded yellows, blues and blacks of the wooden walls merge with the greens of turf roofs and the whites of the clouds to conjure up a resonant image. Named after the church which once stood here in medieval times, Kirkja is still dominated by its church, though today's structure only dates from 1933; inside there's an altar painting by the Faroese artist, **Sámal Joensen Mikines**, of Christ walking on water. Although a new road now links Fugloy's two villages, it's much more enjoyable to follow the old cliff-top footpath, marked by cairns, to reach the island's other settlement, **Hattarvík** (allow about an hour one way). Although this path is not difficult, there is a story of one old woman in Kirkja who was well into her 70s before she ventured along the path; it was her wish before she died to at least see the neighbouring village of Hattarvík. From the eastern end of Kirkja, close to the tiny power-generating plant, follow the overhead power cables steeply up through the homefield to reach the beginning of the track which then loyally follows the coastline eastwards in line with the power cables and even meets up with the road at one point. Although the path is quite indistinct at times, the cairns always serve as a guideline. From up here, high on the cliffs of Fugloy, there are superlative views out over the churning waves of **Fugloyarfjørður** across to Svínoy, and if you time things right, it's an amazing sight to watch the tiny *Másin* rolling and pitching and she battles her way through the swell. After roughly 30–40minutes, the hamlet of Hattarvík will come into view, superbly sheltered on three sides by the steep terraces of a rounded valley and frighteningly exposed to the Atlantic on the fourth. Less picturesque than Kirkja, the 15 or so houses here, all sitting on foundations of basalt as protection from the damp ground, are unimaginatively painted in drab browns and greys. Home to just six people, many of the houses here are now used solely as holiday homes and as a result the village appears forlorn and unkempt. Even the stone church, dating from 1899, with its white and blue painted interior, is overtly spartan in appearance. To be frank, there's not much to detain you in Hattarvík once you've had a quick look around and it's perhaps a better idea to press on and take in some more of Fugloy's wonderful scenery. This is not a big island and with determination you can see most parts of it on a day trip. Although there are no marked paths, it's an easy walk from Hattarvík north to the Eiðsvík bay: simply follow the road out of the village, past the heliport and up to the edge of the homefield; from here it's a straightforward walk down to the bay ahead of you. Alternatively you could head northeast from this point for Eystfelli peak (449m) and its lighthouse, from where there are arresting views of the Faroes' most easterly point, the rock stack, **Stapin** (47m), where there is another lighthouse. A third option, albeit from Kirkja, is to climb to the top of Klubbin mountain (621m), which lies directly north of the village; the ascent through Vatnsdalur valley is steep and rocky in parts though not difficult. From the plateau, steep cliffs known as Norðberg (549m), making up a large part of the island's west coast, plummet to the sea and are home to thousands of seabirds which come here to nest.

Mossy saxifrage

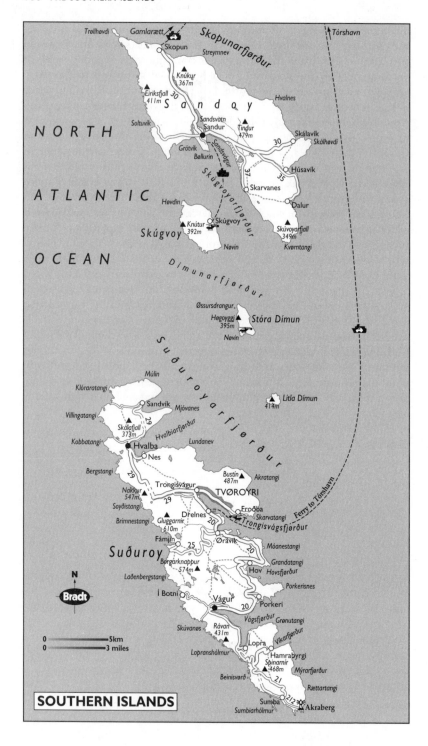

SOUTHERN ISLANDS

The Southern Islands

The five southern islands that make up the Faroe chain exist in a world of their own. Separated from the central group around Streymoy and, indeed, from each other, by some of the most turbulent seas you'll encounter anywhere in the North Atlantic, life here has changed little over the past decades and retains an enviably sedate quality. Immediately south of Streymoy's southern point, **Sandoy** is the first of the five, and at 112km² is the fifth-biggest of all the Faroe Islands. As its name suggests, Sandoy is known for its sweeping sandy beaches and, accordingly, this is one of the most gentle of all the islands. Here the countryside is characterised by rich undulating pasturelands and low rounded hilltops; a more striking contrast to the vertical cliffs and layer-cake mountains of the northern islands is hard to imagine. Indeed, Sandoy's highest peak, **Tindur** (479m), is barely half the size of mountains further to the north. Marooned in the sea off the island's southern coast, **Skúgvoy**, an egg-shaped lump of rock measuring a mere 10km², is about as remote as you can get in the southern islands. Although its western shoreline consists of 400m-high cliffs which rise like a wall out of the sea, the eastern side of the island, location for the one and only village, is altogether less severe and the relatively flat lands around the Áldarsá River, which drains the island's peaks, have been successfully cultivated. However, Skúgvoy is best known for its rich birdlife, in particular its colonies of auks and guillemots. To the southeast lie the two smallest of the Faroe Islands: **Stóra Dímun** and **Lítla Dímun**. Quite incredibly, the larger of the pair, Stóra Dímun, an imposing tooth-shaped island, whose scenic cliffs plummet precipitously to the ocean making sea landings all but impossible, is inhabited. A single family farms the flat land on the mountaintop – their link with the outside world is provided by the Atlantic Airways helicopter which calls in here three times a week bringing much-needed supplies. Of all 18 Faroes, only Lítla Dímun is uninhabited; consisting of angular cliffs which rise together to form a craggy peak, human occupation here is simply not possible. Consequently, there is no public transport to the island, though there are arresting views of this barren rocky outcrop from the ferry which sails from Tórshavn to **Suðuroy**, the most southerly of all the Faroe Islands. It's claimed that the weather here is a little warmer and more stable than elsewhere in the country, and although this may well be true, you're unlikely to notice any appreciable difference in the climate. Characterised by four deep fjords which have gnawed their way into the heart of the island, the rugged and dramatic coastal scenery here is truly spectacular: soaring peaks, bleak moorland studded by mountain tarns which glitter a brilliant blue, and majestic sea cliffs teeming with birdlife. Indeed, if the wind is blowing hard on Suðuroy, the seascape is memorably dramatic.

WHERE TO GO

Since Sandoy scarcely has any accommodation, it's best visited as a day trip from Streymoy. The first place to head for is the main village, **Sandur**, a short drive of around 8km from the ferry port, **Skopun**, on the north coast. The unusual wooden church here, dating from 1839, is the main draw; archaeologists have now established that no fewer than six churches have stood on this spot since the 1000s. Thanks to Sandoy's gentle terrain, the island is perfectly suited to hiking: an easy coastal path leads from Sandur south to the hamlet of **Skarvanes** before striking off across the island's southern reaches towards the picturesque village of **Dalur**. From here it's possible to continue on to **Húsavík**, where remains of a medieval manor house stand beside a beach of black-basalt sand. Another hike leads west to the untrammelled delights of **Søltuvík**, a remote windswept bay of jagged shores which offers some of the best coastal scenery anywhere in the Faroes. There's more superlative hiking to be had on neighbouring **Skúgvoy** – an ideal destination for a day trip, particularly popular with birdwatchers, from Sandur on board the regular ferry across Skúvoyarfjørður. Since Stóra Dímun can only be visited with permission from the farmer who works the land here, it's probably best to move on in favour of Suðuroy where both **Tvøroyri**, a busy harbour village, and **Vágur**, a pleasant little place close to some superb hiking routes, make agreeable places to base yourself. If hiking doesn't appeal there's a handful of other sights to take in here, notably the original Faroese flag which is proudly displayed in the church in **Fámjin**, on the west coast; a traditional wooden church in **Porkeri**; and, arguably best of all, the daunting expanse of the Atlantic which reaches out before you as you stand at the Faroes' southernmost point, **Akraberg**, perfectly marked by two towering radio transmitters and a red-domed lighthouse.

GETTING AROUND

All ferry routes to the southern islands begin from Streymoy. Skopun on **Sandoy** is connected to Gamlarætt on Streymoy by the new boat, *Teistin*, which sails between the two islands roughly six times a day; journey time is 30 minutes. Once daily (not Sun) the boat also links Hestur with Sandoy; currently the boat sails from Hestur at 17.35 for Skopun. It's therefore possible to spend the day on Hestur (take the 08.45 sailing, daily except Sun, from Gamlarætt) before continuing on to Sandoy in the late afternoon. Remember there is limited accommodation on Sandoy at present. From Sandur, the *Sildberin* makes the 35-minute journey over to Skúgvoy twice daily with additional sailings on certain days of the week (see the timetable for this route for precise details). If you're planning to visit the island as a day trip from Streymoy, you will need to be on the first boat out of Gamlarætt bound for Skopun (currently 07.30) in order to reach Sandur for the 08.30 sailing to Skúvoy. For details of the bus service on Sandoy see below.

Getting to Suðuroy is a much more drawn-out affair since sailing time from Tórshavn aboard the *Smyril* is 2 hours 15 minutes. Generally there are two sailings daily (morning and evening) to **Drelnes**, the harbour for Tvøroyri. The sea conditions down to Suðuroy are more often than not rather sporty – taking a seasickness pill before setting off is no bad idea. There is no ferry link between Sandoy and Suðuroy – the only way to sail between the two is to backtrack to Tórshavn. However, it is possible to fly between Skúgvoy and Suðuroy on Wednesday and Friday on board the Atlantic Airways helicopter. The helicopter also flies between Tórshavn and Skúgvoy on Sunday, Wednesday and Friday before continuing on to Stóra Dímun. Suðuroy is only connected to Tórshavn by helicopter on Wednesday and Friday.

Bus services in the southern islands in general are good. On Sandoy, bus #600 runs several times daily (connecting with ferry sailings) between Skopun–Sandur–Skálavík complementing the #601 which operates Skopun–Sandur–Húsavík–Dalur. On Suðuroy, the main services are as follows: #700 Sumba–Vágur–Tvøroyri, #702 Tvøroyri–Sandvík and #703 Froðba–Tvøroyri–Fámjin.

SANDOY
Skopun
Roughly 1,600 people live on the island of Sandoy, predominantly in two main villages: Skopun and Sandur. It's the modern settlement of Skopun, that handles all ferry traffic to and from Streymoy. Indeed, as the ferry swings into the harbour here, good views of the couple of streets that serve as the village centre slowly unfold, banking up the hillside beyond in tight neat rows. Barely 150 years old, Skopun's fortunes are closely linked with the hulking fish factory dominating the quayside, processing the fish landed by the village's modest fleet of trawlers. Other than stopping for a bite to eat in the nameless café on the main road through the centre, which serves up burgers and hot dogs for 20kr, pancakes for 7kr and coffee also 7kr, there's little reason to linger in Skopun and it's a better use of time to have a look at Trøllhøvdi, a tiny island off Sandoy's northernmost point. Once part of the farm of Kirkjubøur, incredibly there's grazing for around 50 or so sheep on the island's steeply sloping hillsides that peak at a height of 106m. However, it's certainly no easy task bundling the sheep into boats in the autumn when it's time for the annual round up – the only way down from the grazing areas is via a ladder, which is anchored into the rockface. You can hike out to Høvdasund, the sound which separates the island from Sandoy, in around an hour from Skopun; take the road which leads up past the church (and later turns into a walking path) leading up towards Gleðin mountain (269m) which you can see in front of you; you climb to the plateau at a height of 200m, and before the land falls away steeply to the sea, you'll have a wonderful view of Trøllhøvdi. According to

legend, the island is actually the head of a troll who was trying to fasten Sandoy and Nólsoy together by pulling on a rope. However, after putting the rope around his neck, he tugged a little too hard and his head fell off.

Sandur

From Skopun, Route 30 climbs up away from the sea to approach the pass which leads into Traðadalur, the lush broad V-shaped valley which runs the length of this western part of Sandoy, one of the most fertile areas in the whole country. Incidentally, the switchback route through the valley was the first road to be completed in the Faroes, in 1917. At its southern end, the valley is punctuated by two small lakes, Gróthúsvatn to the west of the road, and the larger Sandsvatn to the east, a favourite spot for autumn anglers when spawning sea trout struggle up the short stream that connects the lake to the sea. Beyond the lakes, Sandur strings out in an ungainly way across the narrow promontory, which separates the two bays, Grótvík and Sandsvágur. Named after the dunes of black-basalt sand – the only ones in the Faroes and the only place in the country where marram grass, *ammophila arenaria*, grows – at the head of Sandsvágur, Sandur is not an immediately appealing place, though it is the only village on the island to have any services to speak of.

Tourist information

The helpful tourist office (Jun–Aug, Mon–Fri 09.00–11.00 and 14.00–16.00; rest of the year 15.00–17.00; tel: 36 18 36; email: sandinfo@post.olivant.fo; www.visitsandoy.fo) is in the centre of the village, just off the main road close to the bank, and beyond the junction for the road to Skálavík. The staff here have the latest information on the island's limited accommodation options.

Where to stay

For years, the **Ísansgarður** guesthouse in Sandur has been in and out of business – quite simply, there aren't enough visitors to provide a steady income. At the time of writing, the guesthouse had closed down yet again, but there was talk of it reopening under new management. Sandoy is one of the few islands to offer accommodation out in the wilds; the wilderness stay at **Norðasti Hagi**, formerly accommodation for sheep farmers whilst out tending their flocks in the outfield, is a perfect opportunity to get back to basics. There's no electricity or flush toilet in this simple wooden hut with three rooms northeast of Sandur, but what it lacks in mod cons, it more than makes up for in terms of location. Perched on the Borgin hills on Sandoy's totally uninhabited northeastern shore, this is the place to come to commune with nature. Access is only on foot; reckon on two to three hours hiking from either Sandur or Skálavík; the tourist office can make bookings (200kr per night). Should you wish for something a little more comfortable, the tourist office also rents out entire houses across Sandoy for between 400 and 550kr per night. The tourist office can also help with planning a trip across to Skúgvoy, including accommodation, and has further information about some of the hiking routes listed below.

Other practicalities

There are no cafés or restaurants in Sandur, but there is a small **Samkeyp supermarket** selling all the everyday essentials. There are two banks in the village, **Føroya Banki** and **Føroya Sparikassi**, both situated on the main road. Inside the former (closest to the tourist office), which is also the location of the post office, there's a public telephone (tel: 37 16 25).

The village

Located by the side of the main road at the entrance to the village, the Bygdasavn homestead museum (Jun–Aug Sun 16.00–18.00; 20kr), housed in a traditional turf-roofed dwelling with coarsely hewn floorboards and low ceiling (ideal for keeping in the heat) dating from 1812, that was once the home of a local fisherman and farmer, is Sandur's main attraction. The house was occupied until 1938 and today provides a snapshot of what life was like in the Faroes in the early 20th century; both rooms in the house have been kept exactly as they were when the occupant died: everything from pots and pans, woodworking tools to an elegant old grandfather clock dating from 1860 are on display. Close by, overlooking the still waters of Sandsvágur bay, the village church is the other building of note. Though this fine example of wooden church architecture with black-tarred walls, turf roof and white-painted belfry dates only from 1838, the site has been occupied by no fewer than five earlier churches; the first church was built according to traditional Norwegian stave design during the Viking period of AD1000–1100. Whilst here, take a wander around the graveyard and look for the gravestone that is encircled by a low stone wall; during an archaeological dig in 1989, experts discovered an extremely well-preserved grave containing the remains of a skeleton, thought to be that of a woman, dating from the Viking period. Her headstone now stands inside the wall.

West to Søltuvík

Just 3km west of Sandur along an un-numbered single-track lane that begins just before the village museum, the remote and wild bay, Søltuvík, is one of the most beautiful spots in the whole of the Faroes and is a must for any visitor to Sandoy. The perfectly formed arched bay, backed by a sandy beach littered with boulders and curiously shaped rocks and tiers of low green hills, is truly idyllic. The wide and open nature of the landscapes around the bay are quite unusual for the Faroe Islands, noted more for their jagged and rocky mountains. From the end of the lane, a path leads down to a wooden gate giving access onto the beach. There can be few more tranquil places in the islands from where to watch the sun go down over the Atlantic on a warm summer's evening or to watch the waves crash with tremendous force onto the shore here. However charming the bay may look on a warm sunny day, this stretch of coastline is noted for a series of shipwrecks, which have claimed many lives over the centuries. Perhaps the most tragic occurred in November 1895 when the steamer, Principia, foundered on rocks during an atrocious storm. She had been on fire and drifting for three days before running aground in Søltuvík, where the single survivor managed to cling to a plank of wood and float across to Kirkjubøur on Streymoy where he was finally rescued. The table that stands in the roykstova in the farmhouse at Kirkjubøur is made from this piece of wood. From beyond the solitary house which enjoys views out over the bay, a hiking path leads north following the coast to Tröllhøvdi (see page 163) and ultimately back to Skopun.

South to Skarvanes

Eight kilometres south of Sandur along Routes 30 and 37, the picturesque hamlet of Skarvanes boasts one of the best views in the Faroes. From this exposed hillside location on the western shore of Sandoy, you can see four different islands stretched out in the distance: Skúgvoy, followed by both Stóra and Lítla Dímun, and finally, Suðuroy. The hamlet itself is equally appealing: a cluster of just seven brightly painted wooden houses, huddled beside a waterfall cascading down from Gjófelli mountain up above the settlement, makes a perfect picture-postcard scene. Sadly though, Skarvanes (whose name probably originates from the shags which once gathered on the promontory here) today belongs to one of the ever-increasing number of Faroese dying villages. During the early 1800s, the place was known as the home of the bird painter, Diðrikur á Skarvanesi, who no doubt painted the shags for which his village was known.

East to Skálavík, Húsavík and Dalur

Back on Route 30, just 2km after the junction with Route 37 to Skarvanes, there's a choice of directions: southeast leads to Húsavík and ultimately to Dalur, whereas northeast heads to **Skálavík**, a workaday fishing village that over recent years has lost a quarter of its inhabitants. The result is a dreary little place, devoid of life, which has little to offer the visitor in itself. However, Skálavík is one of the access points to the wilderness stay at Borgin on Sandoy's northeast coast. From the village, take the lane running to the northwest through the outfield, which eventually peters out and becomes a walking path. Stout waterproof shoes are required to tackle this route since it crosses a number of rivers as it climbs up the mountain of Tvøfelli from where you can see the cliffs at Borgin.

Húsavík

At the Skálavík road junction, Route 35 heads southeast to the endearing little village of Húsavík, an altogether more attractive place which occupies a commanding position at the head of a sandy beach. Although the village itself, home to around 90 people, is pretty enough, consisting of both modern and traditional turf-roofed houses, it's the remains of a medieval farm that have really put this little place on the map. Before the beach, at the entrance to the village, you'll come to a narrow footbridge which leads over a small stream to the remains of *Heimi á Garði*, reputed to have been the home of the legendary **Guðrun Sjúrðardóttir** of Bergen, once the richest woman in the Faroe Islands. Over the centuries various folk tales about her have been handed down from generation to generation and naturally it's impossible to know exactly where the truth lies. However, according to one version of events, she had two of her servants buried alive for committing a minor offence. Another story claims that she was nothing more than a poor peasant girl from Skúgvoy who had the good fortune to find a golden horn belonging to local chieftain, **Sigmundur Brestisson**. Guðrun then dutifully sent her newly found treasure to the king who rewarded her with so much money that she could afford to buy not only all the land in Húsavík but also a good slice of Shetland, too. You have to hunt around a little in Húsavík to find the remains, which consist of a stone floor and surrounding low walls: cross the footbridge to the church and head for the wooden houses on your right-hand side with the gabled roof. Close by, the tiny house built of basalt, known as *á Breyt*, is a typical example of an early 20th-century Faroese family dwelling; originally it was planned to open the house as a museum, but as yet, nothing has come of the idea. Whilst the doors remain closed, take the liberty to peek through the window to see the extremely simple interior: a kitchen with an earthern floor and a wood-panelled sitting room with a couple of stoves for heating. Walking past the church towards the beach, you'll find a collection of 200-year-old *gróthús* or wooden storage sheds once used to keep fish and meat. Painted ochre red and standing side by side on the grassy foreshore, these huts have been impressively restored, preserved for posterity and make a great photograph when viewed with the church as a background.

Dalur

From Húsavík it's a hair-raising 5km journey around the towering headland, Kinnartangi, on a single-track lane with blind corners that hugs the side of the mountain high above sheer cliffs before finally dropping down into Dalur, one of the most picturesque places in the southern islands, sheltered in a perfectly formed bowl-shaped valley. This delightful cluster of multi-coloured houses sits contentedly at the foot of a river, which empties into the sea by the harbour on the eastern edge of the village. The main reason to come here is to walk out to the cliffs at Sandoy's southern tip, **Skorin**, from where there are great views towards Skúgvoy and the two Dímuns. The trail out here begins where the river enters the village, close to the point where the main road swings east to enter the village proper. The minor road out to Skorin was built during World War II to help defend the islands from German attack, passing to the west of Skúgvoyarfjall mountain (349m) before leading all the way out to the cliffs (the highest point, known as Nakkur, is 251m) which are a good place to watch birds. Unusually for a place so off the beaten track, Dalur has summer (Jun–Aug only) accommodation: **Eiriksgarður** (tel: 36 14 02) offers one large youth-hostel-style room with mattresses laid on the floor (bring your own sleeping bag) and a kitchen; reckon on around 150kr per person.

Hiking in southern Sandoy: Dalur to Húsavík/Sandur

Thanks to its relatively flat terrain, Sandoy makes for some great hiking. The best trail on the island leads from Dalur back over Gjofelli mountain to

Skarvanes before following the coast north through Djúpidalur valley and leading back into Sandur. Alternatively, after leaving Skarvanes it's possible to head off to the northwest and hike over to Húsavík instead.

From **Dalur** the path begins at the western end of the village at the point where the lane down to Skorin branches off south; go straight on heading west. Here the path starts to climb as you ascend the hill in front of you; at the summit (300m) you'll see a lake to your left, Vatnsdalsvatn, surrounded by boggy marshland. The climb is now over and you make a steep descent down the southern slopes of Gjofelli into Skarvanes. If you opt to walk east back over to Húsavík, you'll find the path right in the village climbing immediately up the hillside behind the houses here. As you climb, hope for good weather because the ascent offers superlative views – in clear conditions you can see out past Grótvík bay on Sandoy all the way to Mykines far in the distance. Continue past the small tarn, Dúnjavatn; the path then skirts the western slopes of Dúnjaheyggjur hill before coming to Klovastein, two large rocks which appear to be a single large stone cut clean in two. According to local superstition, anyone who walks between them will die before the year is out. Pass the sheepfold that lies ahead of you and you'll reach Route 35 which runs between Sandur and Húsavík. Bus #601 runs from here to both destinations.

Alternatively, from Skarvanes it's possible to continue north heading straight for **Sandur**. Take the main road, Route 37, out of the village to the point where it begins to swing inland a little; if you reach Stóravatn lake in front of you, you have gone too far. At this point you'll come to a footpath which hugs the coast and weaves around the western edge of the lake through Djúpidalur valley. Pass the rocks you can see immediately offshore and you'll soon come to the main road, Route 30, into Sandur; when you reach the road it's around 2km further into the village.

SKÚGVOY

Settled during the early Viking period, the 10km² island of Skúgvoy (also spelt Skúvoy) may not be one of the larger of the Faroes, but it's certainly made its mark on the country's history. It was here that one of the main characters of *Færeyinga Saga*, **Sigmundur Brestisson**, lived and farmed. Indeed, he is accredited with the building of the first church in the islands in line with the Christianisation of the country around AD1000; sadly, nothing remains of this first church, and the unremarkable church on the island today dates from the last century only. According to the *Saga*, however, Sigmundur's farm was raided and set on fire by his arch rival, the heathen **Tróndur í Gøtu**, whose men then harried Sigmundur, leaving him no option but to throw himself into the sea from the northern end of the island, **Høvðin**, to escape imminent death. Bizarrely, with the coast of Sandoy within sight, he washed up instead down in Sandvík in northern Suðuroy, no doubt the unfortunate victim of the unpredictable Faroese tides. Exhausted and suffering from hypothermia, he set foot ashore only to be cut to the ground by local farmer, **Tórgrímur the Evil**, who then stole Sigmundur's gold ring. His body was brought back to Skúgvoy and his grave can still be seen in the graveyard, Ólansgarður, a little south of the present church (near the heliport) where Sigmundur built his original church. A stone cross, known to the islanders for centuries as *Sigmundarsteinur* (Sigmund's stone), is considered to mark his final resting place.

Getting there and away
The ferry, *Sildberin*, sails from Sandur to Skúgvoy roughly twice daily, with additional sailings on certain days which often have to be booked in advance (tel: 50 52 07). There is a helicopter service to and from Skúgvoy on Sunday, Wednesday and Friday.

Where to stay and eat
The tourist office in Sandur has two houses for rent on Skúgvoy; 500kr per night. There is also a small food shop in the village as well as a post office.

The island
Today, Skúgvoy is an altogether less bloodthirsty sort of a place and is better known for its rich birdlife; the island's Faroese name is 'island of the skuas'. Although many of these birds no longer frequent the island, there are still other large colonies of seabirds on the island's western cliffs waiting to be discovered. The people of Skúgvoy once made a living from bird hunting, and, although many species are now protected by law, there are calls for a complete ban on the island. However, the gathering of birds and eggs by hunters suspended on long ropes dangling down the vertical cliffs is still practised today. Although it's not fully known why, the vast numbers of guillemots which once bred on the island have been greatly reduced – it's thought they're victims of dwindling fish stocks rather than hunting. One of the best places to watch birds is around the northern end of the island; from the main village, take the farm track which leads up through the homefield to its end, then head off west up the hill, Klettarnir (256m), with **Hælsiða** bay to your right. Here, there are large numbers of puffin burrows. Descending from the hilltop towards an area of flatland on the northwest coast, you'll see the sea cliffs which form the headland, Høvdin (134m), to your right where there are still good numbers of guillemots to be seen. Look out also for cormorants, fulmars and razorbills, which can all be seen here. You're likely at this point to come under attack from frighteningly large numbers of Arctic tern, the pluckiest of all the island's birds, intent on delivering a sharp blow to the top of your head with their pointed beaks. Protect yourself by carrying a stick above your head, or by raising your arm in the air; the birds will then strike this, as the highest point, instead of screeching towards your tender scalp. From this point, it's possible to continue south along the bird cliffs of Skúgvoy's west coast, which fall away vertically into the sea from a height of around 400m, towards a hill at the southern end of the island, Heyggjurin mikli (300m). A farm track begins by the lake here and leads back towards the southern end of the village.

STÓRA DÍMUN

The Faroes don't get any more remote – or indeed breathtakingly dramatic – than Stóra Dímun. A diamond-shaped island fortress halfway between Sandoy and Suðuroy, this enigmatic island measuring barely 2.5km² has fascinated sailors for centuries. The entire length of the west coast is one vertical sea cliff, reaching a dizzying 395m at its highest point, the wonderfully understated, **Høgoyyggj** ('high island'). The rest of the island is no less forbidding; in fact at no point are the perpendicular cliffs lower than 100m, which makes landing a boat here a highly hazardous business. This is the most difficult landing in the entire country, and, until the helicopter began flying here in the 1980s, the islanders often didn't set eyes on the supply boat which bravely attempted to put in at Stóra Dímun for months at a time. The island's southern landing stage can only be used in calm conditions or in a northerly wind which shelters it from the ferocious swell (the only other suitable place is the exposed headland, Breiðanes, on the eastern coast, although this is not commonly used). From the landing stage, a set of steps, chiselled into the 100m-vertical rockface, leads steeply up to the farmhouse which is surrounded by 2m-thick stone walls, anchored down with steel ropes against the brute force of the wind. In winter, when the weather is at its worst, walking outside the protective enclosure requires stamina.

Getting there and away

Since the farmer doesn't permit camping or rent out rooms, it's not possible to spend the night on Stóra Dímun. However, if time allows, it's worth making every effort to get out here because this really is one of the world's last places. Either take the helicopter from Tórshavn en route to Suðuroy, which calls at Stóra Dímun on the way, and make do with a quick look out of the window whilst it lands to unload supplies; or better, get out and pick up the helicopter again on its return trip to Tórshavn. This option, only possible on Wednesday and Friday then gives you around an hour on the island – time enough to be totally overwhelmed by the unforgiving geography and absolute isolation of this remote outpost.

The island

In fact, the only human habitation is found on the island's southern slope, where, in addition to the farmhouse there's a lighthouse and a helipad – and that's it. Quite incredibly, the farm here has been occupied since the days of the Settlement, although the current farmer's family only managed to live here year-round once the regular helicopter service was established. From behind the farmhouse a steep slope streaks upwards towards the island's flat top where the lush high pastures are considered to be some of the best in the entire Faroe Islands. In its heyday, the farm here supported up to 50 cattle, over 600 sheep and 36 people, who survived on collecting eggs and birds from the cliffs as well as farming the land. Life was never easy here, and many people fell to their deaths from the cliff-tops or died at sea; it's even claimed that since Viking times barely a handful of inhabitants of Stóra Dímun have died of natural causes in their beds. Indeed, in 1874 the minister of Sandoy, who was duty-bound to visit the island twice a year to hold a service in the island's church, fell to his death whilst climbing the steps from the landing stage and was killed instantly. Ruins of the last church to stand on the island, dating from 1873, can still be seen close to the farmhouse; it was torn down in 1923 to make room for a new structure which never saw the light of day because the farmer himself was killed.

LÍTLA DÍMUN

The baby of the Faroese family, Lítla Dímun, with a total area of just 1km², is the only Faroe Island never to have been inhabited. With little wonder, as resembling a volcano rising out of the sea to a height of 414m, this round cone-shaped lump of rock is an island too far – even for the Faroese. Its precipitous cliffs and lack of farming land make it only suitable for sheep grazing – indeed, since Norse times sheep have been brought out here in boats to graze during the summer months. In fact, the island once supported an unusual breed of black sheep brought by the Irish hermits who first settled the Faroes and known for their short coarse wool, until they were all slaughtered in 1866 to make room for another variety. Although there has never been any permanent human habitation on Lítla Dímun, the Faroese have long been drawn here in search of birds and eggs and there are plenty of stories of those who came but became stranded by bad weather, forced to kill birds and sheep to survive until they could next put to sea to escape. Undoubtedly the most infamous of the island's visitors was Viking chieftain, **Sigmundur Brestisson**, who also grazed his sheep here. In the summer of 1004, whilst he was on the island to round up his animals, he came under attack from **Tróndur í Gøtu**. Cunningly, Sigmundur managed to give Tróndur the slip and escape in his boat, leaving his arch rival marooned and forced to light a fire to signal for help, and ultimately, rescue. The southwestern point of the island is still known as **Sigmundarberg** (Sigmund's mountain).

Since there is no public transport to Lítla Dímun, the best way to appreciate this uninhabited island is to see it from the sea; as she journeys between Tórshavn and Suðuroy, the *Smyril* sails along its eastern cliffs allowing unsurpassed views of the towering rock walls, which like those of its big brother, Stóra Dímun, rise sheer out of the water for around 100m, before tapering towards the island's peak. Incidentally, the name Dímun is of Celtic origin (*stóra* and *lítla* are Faroese for 'big' and 'little'), composed of two elements: *di* meaning 'two' and *muin* signifying a 'ridge' or a 'mountaintop'. The name occurs elsewhere in the Nordic region, and also in Shetland, to describe this readily identifiable geographic feature.

SUÐUROY

The biggest and best of the southern islands, Suðuroy, is the fourth-largest Faroe Island and the chain's most southerly. A good two-hour journey by boat south from Tórshavn, this island is a world apart – the islanders are claimed not only to be the most friendly of all the people in the Faroes, but also the most emotional, a quintessentially un-Faroese trait, taking readily to flailing their arms and hands around, in true Mediterranean fashion, when in discussion. As a visitor you'll be warmly welcomed across the island, not least because Suðuroy sees so few tourists, but also because the islanders are at pains to point out how different their lives are from those of the 'city-slickers' in Tórshavn. Bemoaning their fate as the Faroes' most southerly (read, forgotten) island, is also a well-rehearsed sport. The new ferry to sail between Suðuroy and Tórshavn, the fifth in the long line of *Smyrils* (the retiring *Smyril* once sailed the North Atlantic operating the route currently served by *Norröna* and was therefore deemed too old and uncomfortable to continue operating all the way to Suðuroy) is the latest sop from the government to keep the southerners smiling.

At 30km in length, but barely ever more than 5km in width, this is an up-and-down sort of a place; there's only one road which runs across the island from coast to coast. Virtually the entire west coast consists of steep bird cliffs which rise to a height of 472m in the northwest, where Prestfjall mountain sits precariously right on the cliff edge. In contrast, the tamer east coast is altogether more accessible and it's here that most of Suðuroy's villages and agricultural land are found. The highly indented eastern shoreline is likely to be where you'll spend most of your time, namely between the main settlements, **Tvøroyri** and its satellite villages in the north, and **Vágur** in the south from where some of the southern islands' best hiking trails radiate. Until recently, the *Smyril* put in at Vágur once weekly; now though all sailings are to the newly constructed ferry jetty at **Drelnes**, on the western shore of Trongisvágsfjørður, immediately opposite the main town, Tvøroyri, which is the best place to start your wanderings.

Tvøroyri and around

Another textbook example of a linear settlement, Tvøroyri, stretches over 2.5km or so from the head of the superbly sheltered, **Trongisvágsfjørður** fjord, to its mouth at Høvðatangi point. Its streets run in parallel lines banking steeply up the green hillsides behind which reach a height of around 300m. All activity takes place on the one long main road and down on the harbourside; the busy goings-on and the sheer number of small craft moored on the jetties here are good indicators of the town's prosperity.

Tourist information

The tourist office (Mon–Fri 09.00–noon and 13.00–16.00, also Jul Sat 10.00–noon; tel: 37 24 80; fax: 37 18 14; email: sout-inf@post.olivant.fo; www.kunning.fo), Kunningarstovan á Tvøroyri, can be found on the main road between the museum and the church. Though there's a limited amount of printed matter available here, the staff are very friendly and know the island like the back of their hand.

Getting there and away

Access to Tvøroyri and indeed the rest of Suðuroy is most easily done by the twice-daily ferry *Smyril* which sails direct from Tórshavn taking around two hours. However, it is also possible to fly by helicopter to Froðba, just east of Tvøroyri, three times a week.

Where to stay

For accommodation, you need to decide whether you want to be in the town or outside. The spick, span and convenient **Hotel Tvøroyri** (tel: 37 11 71; fax: 37 21 71; 650kr including breakfast) is right at the heart of things, just a stone's throw from the shops, overlooking the harbour, whereas **Hotel Øravík** and **Gistingarhúsið við Á** (tel: 37 13 02; fax: 37 20 57), together on the same spot in Øravík, offer youth-hostel-style accommodation (120kr per person in the **Gistingarhúsið**) and more upmarket rooms with private facilities in the hotel section (625kr with breakfast); bus #700 runs here from Tvøroyri. There's a public telephone in the hotel section, number 37 17 29. The guesthouse section is popular with walkers since many trails begin at Øravík.

Where to eat and drink

Eating in Tvøroyri, unfortunately, is limited to the hotels. By far the best option is the **restaurant in Øravík** where a two-course fish dinner goes for 195kr though, to be honest, it's a little too pricey for the quality of the food served; alternatively there are better-value pizzas (takeaway also) for 70–80kr; the restaurant is open Mon–Sat 17.00–22.00, Sun noon–22.00. With a little cajoling, you might be able to persuade **Hotel Tvøroyri** to conjure up something fishy, though essentially, the room below the hotel is used as a bar rather than a restaurant. The main drinking den in town is **Tvøroyri Klubbi** (open Wed 22.00–midnight, Fri 17.00–19.00, Sat 17.00–02.00, and Sun 17.00–midnight), close to the church, which also has occasional live music. Although this is really a members' only place, the chances are that as a new face in town you'll be greeted with open arms – and an empty glass.

Listings

Note: there are currently no street names in Tvøroyri. A government committee, however, has been appointed to give all streets in the town a name.

Alcohol store Rúsdrekkasøla Landsins, Drelnes; tel: 37 26 77; www.rusan.fo. Open Mon–Wed & Fri 14.00–17.30, Thu 14.00–19.00

Banks Føroya Banki; tel: 37 10 32; Føroya Sparikassi; tel: 37 10 40

Bookshop J Nolsøe; tel: 37 10 44

Hospital Tel: 37 11 33

Pharmacy Suðuroya Apotek; tel: 37 10 76. Open Mon–Fri 09.00–17.30, Sat 09.00–noon

Police Politistøðin; tel: 37 14 48

Post office Posthúsið; tel: 37 10 18. Open Mon–Wed & Fri 09.00–16.00, Thu until 17.00

Taxi Tel: 37 21 10 and 37 11 71

The town

It was Tvøroyri's protected location on a deep fjord that gave rise to the establishment in the mid-19th century of a branch of the Danish Trade Monopoly – an event which, in effect, created the town of today, the fourth-largest in the Faroes. Following the dismantling of the Monopoly in 1856, the town received a couple of fishing sloops, bought secondhand from England, which took a leading role in creating the Faroese industrial revolution. A fish factory, still in existence today, was soon required to process the tons of fish being landed in Tvøroyri, which, together with today's modern ocean-going trawlers stationed here, have helped create the basis for the town's economic advance. The best place to get to grips with the town's history is at the **Tvøroyrar Bygda- og Sjósavn** museum (May–Aug Sun 15.00–18.00; 20kr) in the town centre, close to the harbour. Located in the former doctor's residence and surgery which dates from 1852, the museum canters through the most significant periods of the town's development. Inside, the evocative black-and-white photographs depicting local women washing the fish their husbands had landed before it was salted and sent for export are certainly an instant reminder of the past. It's worth glancing too at a few of the museum's other curiosities: a pair of old leather football boots from 1932 (the first Faroese football club was founded in 1892); the whopping 35cm-long shoes, size 53, once worn by a former Suðuroy policeman, Martin Christiansen; and the first typewriter ever used on the island from 1910 which involved the user typing with one finger and moving a pointer to the desired key on the keyboard before striking the character – such was demand for the new-fangled machine that it had to be shared between the local post office and town hall who each received it for one or two days at a time.

Tvøroyri church

The other sight in Tvøroyri lies a further five minutes' walk east along the main road: the village church (get the key from the tourist office, see above). Unusually, the current structure, dating from 1908, was built in sections in Lillestrøm in Norway before being shipped in sections to the Faroes. Its Norwegian influence is clear to see and its form is quite unlike any other in the islands. This monumental structure, with room inside for 600 worshippers, was donated to the town by a local family of merchants, and became an arresting sign of their wealth – they owned a fishing fleet of 30 or so ships and ran stores in several villages up and down the island.

Continuing a further couple of kilometres past the church towards the mouth of the fjord will bring you to the original Viking settlement of **Froðba**, now essentially an overspill village. The hamlet is named after one of the area's earliest settlers, the Danish king, **Froði**, who actually never had any intention of coming to the Faroes. He was en route for Ireland when he ran into fog, and, drifting helplessly, arrived in the mouth of Trongisvágsfjørður where he settled, naming his new home, in true egotistical Viking fashion, after himself and his farmstead or *bø*. Marking the eastern end of Froðba, the promontory, **Skarvatangi**, is the place to look for one of Suðuroy's most unusual geological features: continue past the helipad and round a sharp left-hand bend and you'll come to an entire row of vertical basalt columns formed in the rock that look like stone tree-trunks growing out of the sea. From Froðba, a narrow road, built by the British for defence purposes during World War II, leads up the hill behind the settlement to a viewpoint known as Nakkur (325m) from where there are stirring views out over the Atlantic north towards Lítla and Stóra Dímun, Sandoy and also Skúgvoy; reckon on about an hour on foot to reach Nakkur. However, for those wishing to continue, a footpath leads off to the northwest scaling the heights of **Froðbiarkambur** mountain (487m), the tallest peak on the entire east coast.

Whereas the northern shore of Trongisvágsfjørður is relatively densely settled, the southern coast of the inlet is all but devoid of habitation. Other than the ferry quay at Drelnes (the blue hut here occasionally functions as a tourist office when the *Smyril* arrives during the summer months), the only place of note is **Øravík**. Sooner or later you'll end up here because this is one of the few places in and around Tvøroyri to eat and stay. Barely more than the guesthouse and an adjoining farm, it's a wonderfully wild location to visit with views out over the sea in one direction, back towards some of Suðuroy's craggy peaks in the other.

Hikes from Tvøroyri

The two most popular hikes from Tvøroyri both begin from **Trongisvágur**, the tiny cluster of houses that nestles around the head of the fjord. One leads northwest to **Hvalba**, the other southwest to **Fámjin**. Bus connections are available in both destinations to bring you back to Tvøroyri: #702 from Hvalba and #703 from Fámjin.

The path to Hvalba (6.5km climbing to a height of 350m; reckon on 2 hours one way) begins a couple of kilometres outside Trongisvágur along Route 29 to Hvalba. Look out for two solitary huts either side of the road just after you have passed a river flowing down from the hills on your right. From the right-hand hut, take the path up through the ravine here, Mannagjógv, between the two peaks Tempilsklettur (493m) to the left and Eggin (389m) on the right; the worst of the climb is now over. From here the track becomes less steep and is quite level as it goes over **Hvalbiarfjall**. Arriving at the highest cairn, there's a small rise in the terrain, which allows tremendous views east to the two Dímuns, Skúgvoy, Sandoy and the lake, Vatnsdalur, which attracts many birds during the summer months and is a good place for watching ducks and waders; to the west you can clearly see Hvalba. In the distance you should be able to make out the three large rocks known as *Sigmundarsteinar* after the Viking chieftain, **Sigmundur Brestisson**, of *Færeyinga Saga*. According to the *Saga*, he carried them up here and local folklore has it that anyone who walks between them will either become suddenly old, or, if that wasn't bad enough, die before the end of the year. Should the weather turn whilst you're up here, be sure to follow the cairns. In the winter of 1917 one man became stranded up here when the fog came down and it began to snow. To pass his time, whilst waiting to be rescued, he dismantled and then rebuilt one of the cairns time after time to give himself something to do. Beyond the rocks, the path descends down Káragjógv ravine and it is quite steep in parts. It finally meets up with Route 293 near the hamlet of **Nes** in Hvalbiarfjørður east of Hvalba, from where it's a walk west of around a kilometre or so into the village itself.

The trail to Fámjin begins on the southern side of Trongisvágur just north of the couple of houses that are Líðin. This hike is roughly two hours in duration one way and covers similar terrain as that to Hvalba. Begin by climbing the gentle slopes of Oyrnafjall mountain (443m). Don't go all the way to the top; instead you follow the path as it skirts the western side of the peak squeezing through the Valdaskarð pass which you can see in the distance. The fabulous rounded valley you have to your right up here, Hvammabotnur, has sides reaching a magnificent 569m, making them the highest point on the island. Once through the pass you're into another rounded valley dominated by the blue waters of Kirkjuvatn lake at its foot. The path now leads down the eastern side of the lake into the village of Fámjin.

North to Hvalba and Sandvík

From Trongisvágur, Route 29 heads northwest through a particularly lush valley, where there's even a plantation of trees to spot on your left as you leave the town behind. Soon the road enters Hvalbiartunnilin, the very first road tunnel (around 1.5km long) to be built in the Faroes, in 1963, which connects the harbour of Tvøroyri with the more rural agricultural lands to the north of Suðuroy. As the road emerges from the tunnel, the narrow lane to the right leads to the islands' only still-functioning coal mine where four pitmen still produce modest amounts of the black stuff. Begun as early as 1780, the seam covers an area of around 20km^2 between Trongisvágur and Hvalba where over the years a number of mines were sunk to extract the coal. During World War II the Faroese exported it to England to help with the war effort. The coal is, however, of poor quality and is today used only for the home market. As you drive the last couple of kilometres between the tunnel exit and Hvalba you will see remnants of three former mines that, tragically, all collapsed.

Hvalba spreads right across Suðuroy at a narrow isthmus, a fertile hospitable shelf of land whose rocky, sea-battered old landing place, among the cliffs on the western side, is well worth a look. It was here at Hvalba in 1629 that Algerian pirates made a surprise attack, looted the village and took many of the inhabitants to be sold as slaves. The Faroese were too poor to raise the ransom money and the unfortunates were never seen again. However, one of their three ships foundered on the rocks and the bodies of 300 of those on board were washed ashore in the village. They were buried in graves along the beach known as *Turkagravir* which can still be seen today.

From Hvalba, it's a further 5km to end-of-the-road **Sandvík**, the most northerly settlement on Suðuroy, enjoying superb views out to Lítla Dímun, which is today still owned by local farmers who graze some of their sheep there. According to *Færeyinga Saga*, Sigmundur Brestisson, who had brought Christianity to the islands, was surprised by his pagan enemies on his farm in Skúgvoy. To save his life, Sigmundur had to jump into the sea and swim for it (albeit with two of his men on his back). He managed the shore at Sandvík some 15km away and collapsed on the sandy beach here. But, just to prove there's no justice in the world, the first person to find him, a local farmer aptly named Tórgrímur the Evil, immediately cut off his head. Indeed, the land around Sandvík, so named after its sandy beach, was once the pasturelands of the Hvalba farmers until 1810, when the first settlement was founded here. The picturesque wooden church, dating from 1840, which today stands at the centre of this tiny hamlet beside a traditional farmer's cottage (closed to the public but perhaps worth a peek through the window into the large kitchen which takes up the lion's share of the building) is really the only reason to tarry.

Sandvík is one of the best places in Suðuroy to see puffins: take the narrow road up out of the village to the west where it peters out at the foot of Glyvraberg mountain (366m). From here a footpath leads out to the coast, where, off to the right, you'll see the rock stack, **Ásmundarstakkur** (109m). Its flat grassy top is a favourite nesting place for hundreds of these comical birds.

West to Fámjin

One of the nicest spots on Suðuroy, **Fámjin** is a beautiful small village, ringed on its eastern side by a series of low-stepped hills that gradually merge up into the mountains at the centre of the island. It's not solely the picturesque quality of the harbour and the houses here that makes Fámjin so special to the Faroese. Instead, it's the presence of that potent symbol of nationhood, the flag, that brings car loads of misty-eyed home-grown tourists here. Ask around in the village for someone to open the church (dating from 1875) for you, and you'll see what all the fuss is about. In a glass cabinet hung on the rear wall is the original Merkið or **Faroese flag**. A red cross fringed with blue on a white background, this flag was the brainchild of local student **Jens Oliver Lisberg** and two of his friends, who were studying at Copenhagen University when they hit upon the radical idea of creating a flag for their country to further their own dreams of independence for the Faroes. Although it was first flown following a church service in Fámjin in June 1919, it took several more decades until the flag was officially recognised. During World War II, the occupying British forces forbade all Faroese shipping to fly the red-and-white flag of occupied Denmark, instead encouraging the islanders to fly their own flag instead. The Faroese skipper, **Hans Mikkelsen**, sailing to Aberdeen from the Faroes during the war under a British escort, became the first man to raise the flag at sea. Ignoring protests from the Danish authorities, a British government announcement made on the BBC on April 25 1940 effectively made the move official, to much jubilation in the Faroe Islands. Ever since, this day has been celebrated as 'flag day'; with the advent of Home Rule in 1948, the Merkið had finally come of age and was adopted as the national flag of the Faroe Islands. Just outside the church entrance, Jens's grave can be seen; his gravestone was erected by the Faroese Students' Association to mark his death in 1920 at the age of just 34.

If the 9km drive to Fámjin from Øravík along the very windy Route 25, which climbs up through the Øraskarð pass between the two peaks, Snæválsheyggjur (469m) and Nónfjall (427m), doesn't appeal there's an excellent hike that will also take you to Fámjin, beginning at the hotel in

Øravík. It leads steeply up the hillside behind the hotel towards the Øraskarð pass where it meets up with Route 25. Unlike the road, the path doesn't weave around hairpin bends to make the ascent, it just goes up and up until its reaches the summit of the pass. From here, the going is considerably easier and the trail leads around the southern slopes of Snæválsheyggjur before dropping gracefully into Fámjin, arriving a little south of the church. Remember that there are no facilities in Fámjin, and it's therefore a good idea to bring with you everything you think you'll need. Bus #703 runs back to Tvøroyri.

Vágur and around

From Øravík, Suðuroy's main road, Route 20, winds its circuitous way around the Høvðaberg and Grandatangi headlands, which separate **Trongisvágsfjorður** from **Hovsfjørður** fjord to the south, before reaching **Hov**, today an innocuous small village but which, during Viking times, served as a heathen place of sacrifice. According to the *Færeyinga Saga*, the powerful chieftain, **Havgrímur**, once lived here. Today, amazingly, it's still possible to make out his burial mound, which lies in a field above the village. During the late 19th century, an excavation of the mound was made and remains of bone and iron fragments were discovered. The other notable feature in Hov is the wooden village church, which was moved here in 1942 from Vágur where it first stood from its inauguration in 1862. From Hov it's a straightforward drive of 5km to unusually named **Porkeri,** inhabited since Viking times. Although the main road passes the village by from above, it's worth the small detour into this busy fishing settlement to see the tar-walled, turf-roofed church, dating from 1847, and its small collection of trinkets inside donated by sailors who were rescued by local people when their ships foundered. The overgrown churchyard, which surrounds the church, is particularly pleasing to the eye and makes a charming photograph when viewed with the sea as a backdrop. Route 20 now hugs the shoreline of Suðuroy's second great fjord, **Vágsfjørður**, bound for the island's second town, **Vágur**, a thriving shipbuilding centre, fishing port and wool-spinning town that is home to around 1,400 people.

Where to stay and eat

To be honest, there's not much to delay you in Vágur, but should you wish to stay here as an alternative base to Tvøroyri, you'll find comfortable and well-appointed accommodation at **Hotel Bakkin** (tel: 37 39 61; fax: 37 39 62; 550kr including breakfast) whose 11 brightly painted rooms (two have private facilities; six have views of the fjord) contain tasteful modern Scandinavian furniture. Although this place serves more as a hotel for shipyard and fish-factory workers than tourists, you'll be assured of a warm welcome. There's also food available here: lunch is served from noon–13.00 and generally consists of soup and a fish or meat dish with coffee (100kr); in the evening the hotel serves up traditional open sandwiches. The only other eating option is **Pizza Kokkurin** (open evenings only from 17.00) located at the entrance to Vágur when approaching from the north.

Other practicalities
There are two **public telephones** in the Hotel Bakkin: the upstairs one (tel: 37 42 65) takes coins, whereas the one downstairs (tel: 37 37 25) only accepts phonecards. Vágur also has a **post office** (Mon–Wed and Fri 09.00–16.00, Thu until 17.00) and two banks, **Føroya Banki** and the local **Suðuroyar Sparikassi**. The **library** and the **swimming pool** (Mon and Wed 19.00–21.00, Sat 15.00–18.00) can be found in the village school near the church.

The town
What activity there is here is concentrated on the one main road; you'll find a small stone memorial near the shipyard celebrating the launching in 1804 of *Royndin Fríða* ('The Good Endeavour'), the first sea-going ship to be built and owned by the Faroese since the early Middle Ages – a tribute to the efforts of national hero, **Nólsoy Páll**, who led resistance to the Danish Trade Monopoly in the 19th century. The main sight in Vágur is the rather fanciful new Gothic stone church built in 1927, which replaced the town's former church now moved to Hov. Whilst you're in town, it's worth having a quick look in Suðuroy's two main knitwear stores: the Heimavirki (Mon–Fri 09.00–17.30, Sat 09.00–noon) and the Ullvirki, which specialises in hand-knitted traditional sweaters; you'll find them both in the town centre.

South to Sumba and Akraberg
To be frank, the real reason for coming to southern Suðuroy is not to linger in Vágur but rather to press towards the country's most southerly village, **Sumba**, and the Faroese equivalent of Land's End, **Akraberg**. On the way, Route 21, which leads south of Vágur, passes close to the **Beinisvørð** cliffs which, at 476m above sea level, are Suðuroy's highest vertical sea cliffs and worth the short detour from the main road. To get here, take Route 21 from the tiny hamlet of **Lopra** up the hillside in front of you instead of driving through the tunnel leading to Sumba. As the road climbs you'll reach a radio transmitter at a bend in the road from where it's possible to walk to the cliffs. The road then continues down into Sumba, long one of the Faroes' most isolated villages where traditions are still strong; the place is known across the islands for its talented group of **chain dancers** who, over the years, have brought international recognition to this peculiarly Faroese art. From Sumba, it's barely another 2km along the un-signposted road, which climbs up out of the village to Akraberg and the most southerly point of the Faroe Islands. This wonderfully remote rocky promontory, which juts out proudly into the crashing waves of the North Atlantic, is a suitably enigmatic spot. Dominated by two towering radio transmitters, which pump out the medium-wave signal for Faroese radio across the country, and a red-domed lighthouse, it's a great place to sit and contemplate not only the breathtaking beauty of these 18 barren and windswept islands lost in the North Atlantic, but also their remoteness: from Akraberg, the nearest landfall is the Shetland Islands, 300km (162 nautical miles) to the southeast.

Appendix 1

LANGUAGE

Faroese, a member of the family of Germanic languages, is most closely related to Danish, Icelandic, Norwegian and Swedish. Speakers of the above languages will notice many words and grammatical structures in common with Faroese. The closest language to Faroese is Icelandic; indeed, when Faroese and Icelanders speak to each other in their native tongues there is a good degree of mutual comprehension, much as there is between Spanish and Portuguese. The distance between Faroese and the continental Scandinavian languages, Danish, Norwegian and Swedish, is so great that there is no common ground for comprehension.

Although English is also related to Faroese, it's unlikely that you will be able to understand much written or spoken Faroese because, over the centuries, both languages have evolved along different lines. Whereas English lost its original case endings, inverted word order and genders, Faroese has maintained these and other grammatical features which, initially, make it difficult for English native speakers to learn even the simplest phrases. However, with perseverance, it is possible to learn some rudimentary phrases even if the complexities of the grammar remain beyond your grasp. Having said that, it's not necessary to speak Faroese to enjoy a holiday in the Faroes since most islanders speak at least some English (knowledge of English is at its most extensive in and around Tórshavn and the other main towns), and where no English is spoken, there's always the possibility of falling back on one or other Scandinavian language (notably Danish and Norwegian) if you can. However, mastering a couple of phrases in Faroese (at the very least, the bare essentials: hello, thank you, goodbye etc) is sure to impress – manage more and you'll have Faroese jaws dropping at your every turn.

Pronunciation

Since Faroese was first written down in only 1846, the spelling of many words is based on their etymology rather than their current pronunciation. This naturally confuses matters for anyone trying to learn the language. Below is a guide to the pronunciation of vowels and consonants, though, naturally, the best way to perfect your pronunciation is to listen carefully to native speakers. Stress in Faroese usually falls on the first syllable of a word. Vowels followed by a double consonant are pronounced short, whereas those followed by a single consonant or none at all are long. We have excluded vowels and consonants where pronunciation is similar to that of English.

á	as in French *oi* in *moi*
av + consonant	as *ow* in exclamation ow!
ð	is never pronounced except when before *r* becoming *g*. Otherwise incorporated into surrounding vowels
ðr	as *gr* in *grey*
ei	as *eye*
dj, ge, gi, gy, gey, gj and **ggj**	as *j* in *jam*
g	silent when between vowels
hj	as *y* in *yellow*
hv	as *kv* when at the beginning of a word
í and **ý**	as in French *oui*
ke, ki, ky, key, kj	as *ch* in *chat*
ll	as *dl* in *saddle* and similar to Welsh *ll* in Llandudno
rn	as *dn* in *hadn't*
rs	similar to *sh* in *ship* though softer
sj, sk, ske, ski, sky, skey, skj	as *sh* in *ship*
tj	as *ch* in *chat*
ó	as in *oh-uh*
ø	as *ur* in *fur* though without the final *r*

Incidentally, the Faroese capital, Tórshavn, is pronounced *toe-ush-hown*.

Grammar

Faroese **nouns** are divided into three genders: *kallkyn* (masculine), *kvennkyn* (feminine) and *hvørkikyn* (neuter). Like German, they are also declined by case: nominative, accusative, dative and genitive, depending on several factors including their role in the sentence and preceding prepositions. Endings are added to nouns to denote their case. Nouns are qualified by **articles**. The **indefinite article** (*a*) is *ein* (masculine and feminine) and *eitt* (neuter). Like nouns, articles are also declined according to case. *Ein* is conjugated as follows:

Singular	Masculine	Feminine	Neuter
Nominative	ein	ein	eitt
Accusative	ein	eina	eitt
Dative	einum	ein(ar)i	einum
Genitive	eins	einar	eins

Plural			
Nominative	einir	einar	eini
Accusative	einar	einar	eini
Dative	einum	einum	einum
Genitive	eina	eina	eina

When used with an adjective the **definite article** is: masculine: *hin* stóri maðurin – the big man; feminine: *hin* raska konan – the skilful woman; neuter: *hitt* sjúka barnið – the sick child. However, when used without a preceding adjective, the definite article is attached to the end of the noun, in common with the other Scandinavian languages. For example, masculine: *-in* maðurin – the man; feminine: *-in* bygdin – the village; neuter: *-ið* barnið – the child.

Hin and *hitt* are conjugated as follows:

Singular	Masculine	Feminine	Neuter
Nominative	hin	hin	hitt
Accusative	hin	hina	hitt
Dative	hinum	hini	hinum
Genitive	hins	hinnar	hins

Plural			
Nominative	hinir	hinar	hini
Accusative	hinar	hinar	hini
Dative	hinum	hinum	hinum
Genitive	hinna	hinna	hinna

Faroese **adjectives** precede the nouns they describe: ein *grønur* bilur – a green car; hin *grøni* bilurin – the green car, though they can also stand alone: maðurin er *stórur* – the man is big; konan er *stór* – the woman is big; barnið er *stórt* – the child is big.

Adjectives are conjugated by number: ein *stórur* maður (a big man); fleiri *stórir* menn (many big men); by case: ein *stórur* maður sat har – a big man sat there; eg sá ein *stóran* mann – I saw a big man; eg møtti einum *stórum* manni – I met a big man; by gender: ein *stórur* maður – a big man; ein *stór* kona – a big woman; eitt *stórt* barn – a big child; and by comparison: stórur – størri – størstur = big – bigger – biggest (masculine).

Adjectives are **strongly conjugated** when the noun is **indefinite**: ein *sjúkur* maður – a sick man; ein *sjúk* kona – a sick woman; ein *sjúkt* barn – a sick child.

Adjectives are **weakly conjugated** when the noun is **definite**: hin *sjúki* maðurin – the sick man; hin *sjúka* konan – the sick woman; hitt *sjúka* barnið – the sick child. Otherwise the **definite** declension is used: *gamli* Andras – old Andras; Eirikur *Reyði* – Eric the Red.

Pronouns are generally conjugated by numbers, case and gender. The personal pronouns when used in the nominative case in Faroese are:

Eg	I
Tú	you (informal)
Hann	he
Hon	she
Tað	it
Vit	we
Tit	you (plural)
Teir/tær/tey	they (masc/fem/neuter)

Verbs fall into two main categories: those with sound changes and those without. They are conjugated by **tense, number** and **person**. They also use **weak** and **strong** conjugations.

Weak conjugation

Singular	Present	Past
1st person	eg: *skrivi*	eg: *skrivaði*
2nd person	*tú skrivar*	*tú skrivaði*
3rd person	*hann skrivar*	*hann skrivaði*
	hon skrivar	*hon skrivaði*
	tað skrivar	*tað skrivaði*

Plural		
1st person	*vit skriva*	*vit skrivaðu*
2nd person	*tit skriva*	*tit skrivaðu*
3rd person	*tey skriva*	*tey skrivaðu*

Strong conjugation

Singular	Present	Past
1st person	eg: *lesi*	eg: *las*
2nd person	*tú lesur*	*tú last/tú las*
3rd person	*hann lesur*	*hann las*
	hon lesur	*hon las*
	tað lesur	*tað las*

Plural		
1st person	*vit lesa*	*vit lósu*
2nd person	*tit lesa*	*tit lósu*
3rd person	*tey lesa*	*tit lósu*

Vocabulary
The basics

Good morning	*Góðan morgun*
Hello	*Góðan dag*
Good evening	*Gott kvøld*
Good night	*Góða nátt*
Goodbye	*Farvæl*
Bye	*Bei*
Thank you	*Takk (fyri)*
Don't mention it	*Tað var so lítið*
Yes	*Ja*
No	*Nei*
Excuse me	*Orsaka meg*

Useful phrases

My name is …	*Eg eiti …*
How are you?	*Hvussu gongur?*
I'm fine	*Tað gongur væl*
What's your name?	*Hvussu eitur tú?*
Where are you from?	*Hvaðan ert tú?*
Where do you live?	*Hvar býrt tú?*

How old are you? (masculine/feminine)	*Hvussu gamal/gomul ert tú?*
I am ... years old (masculine/feminine)	*Eg eri... ára gamal/gomul*
I (don't) understand	*Eg skilji (ikki)*
I (don't) know	*Eg veit (ikki)*
Where is?	*Hvar er?*
I'd like ...	*Kundi eg fingið ...*
Do you have any rooms free?	*Eru nøkur leys kømur?*
I'm staying for ...	*Eg steðgi í ...*
one day	* ein dag*
two days	* tveir dagar*
How much is it?	*Kvussu nógv kostar tað?*
Can I see it?	*Kann eg sleppa at síggja tað?*
Is breakfast included?	*Er morgunmatur uppi í?*
The bill, please	*Kann eg fáa rokningina?*
Will it be windy/rainy today/tomorrow?	*Verður tað vindur/regn í dag/í morgun?*
When does ... leave?	*Nær fer ...*
the boat/the bus	* báturin/bussurin*
The timetable will be modified on the following days	*Hesar dagar er broytt ferðaætlan*
What's included?	*Hvat hoyrir til?*
I'm vegetarian	*Eg eri vegetarur*
the bill	*rokningin*

Essential vocabulary

beach	*sandur*
beach	*strond*
bus and ferry terminal	*farstøðin*
camera film	*filmur*
coach/bus	*rutubilur*
dentist	*tannlækni*
doctor	*lækni*
Faroese ferry company	*Strandfaraskip Landsins*
guesthouse	*gistingarhús*
hospital	*sjúkrahús*
hotel	*hotell*
library	*bókasavn*
map	*kort*
matches	*svávulpinnar*
money	*pengar*
newspaper	*dagblað*
next week	*næstu viku*
now	*nú*
pen	*kúlupennur*
pharmacy	*apotek*
police	*løgregla*
police station	*løgreglustøð*

post office	*posthús*
a single ticket	*einvegis*
taxi	*leigubilur*
this evening	*í kvøld*
this morning	*í morgun*
ticket	*ferðaseðil*
today	*í dag*
tomorrow	*í morgin*
youth hostel	*vallaraheim*
yesterday	*í gjár*
yesterday evening	*í gjárkvøldið*

Food and drink

breakfast	*morgundrekka*
dinner	*døgurði*
lunch	*morgunmatur*
beef	*neytasteik*
bread	*breyð*
butter	*smør*
carrots	*gularøtur*
cauliflower	*blomkál*
cheese	*ostur*
chicken	*høsnarungi*
fish	*fiskur*
garlic	*hvítleykur*
haddock	*hðsa*
halibut	*kalvi*
herring	*sild*
jam	*súltutoy*
lamb	*lambskjøt*
lamb cutlet	*lambssteik*
meat	*kjøt*
mushrooms	*hundaland*
mustard	*sinoppur*
onion	*leykur*
peas	*ertrar*
plaice	*reyðsprøka*
pork cutlet	*grísasteik*
potato	*epli*
prawns	*rækjur*
rice	*rís*
runner beans	*bønir*
salmon	*laksur*
sausage (hotdog)	*pylsa*
toast	*ristað breyð*

trout	*síl*
whale meat and blubber	*grind o speek*

coffee	*kaffi*
milk	*mjólk*
orange juice	*appelsindjús*
sugar	*sukur*
tea	*te*
water	*vatn*
wine	*vín*

Days and months

Monday	*Mánadagur*	Friday	*Fríggjadagur*
Tuesday	*Týsdagur*	Saturday	*Leygardagur*
Wednesday	*Mikudagur*	Sunday	*Sunnudagur*
Thursday	*Hósdagur*		

January	*Januar*	July	*Juli*
February	*Februar*	August	*August*
March	*Mars*	September	*September*
April	*Apríl*	October	*Oktober*
May	*Mai*	November	*November*
June	*Juni*	December	*Desember*

Numbers

Unfortunately, in Faroese, numbers one, two and three are also declined in all four cases. Numbers above three are unaffected. Examples are as follows:

1, 2, 3 (masculine)	*ein, tveir, tríggir*	18	*átjan*
1, 2, 3 (feminine)	*ein, tvær, tríggjar*	19	*nítjan*
1, 2, 3 (neuter)	*eitt, tvey, trý*	20	*tjúgu*
4	*fýra*	21	*einogtjúgu*
5	*fimm*	30	*tretivu*
6	*seks*	40	*fjøruti*
7	*sjey*	50	*hálvtrýss*
8	*átta*	60	*trýss*
9	*níggju*	70	*hálvfjerðs*
10	*tíggju*	80	*fýrs*
11	*ellivu*	90	*hálvfems*
12	*tólv*	100	*hundrað*
13	*trettan*	101	*hundrað og ein*
14	*fjúrtan*	200	*tvey hundrað*
15	*fimtan*	1,000	*túsund*
16	*sekstan*	2,000	*tvey túsund*
17	*seytjan*	1,000,000	*ein miljón*

Appendix 2

GLOSSARY OF FAROESE GEOGRAPHICAL TERMS

Faroese	English
á	river, stream
bakki	slope
barð	promontory, headland
botnur	rounded valley, corrie, cirque
brekka	brink, edge
bøur	cultivated infield surrounding a village
dalur	valley
drangur	sea stack
eiði	isthmus
enni	cliff-face, rock wall
fjall	mountain
fjørður	fjord, sound
fossur	waterfall
gjógv	ravine, gorge, gully
hagi	uncultivated outfield
heiði	peat moor, heathland
hálsur	mountain col
heyggjur	hill
hólmur	island
høvdi	promontory, headland
kambur	mountain ridge
kinn	mountain slope
klettur	rock pinnacle
klubbi	rounded hill
knúkur	mountain summit
múli	promontory
nakkur	sharp-edged promontory
nes	point, headland
nípa	protruding mountain ridge
oy, oyggj	island
pollur	cove, anchorage
ryggur	ridge, hill line
sandur	sandy beach
skarð	narrow mountain col (pass)

stakkur	sea stack
steinur	stone, rock
sund	sound
tangi	eroded headland, tongue of land
tindur	pyramidal peak
tjørn	mountain tarn, lake
trøð	allotment
vágur	cove, small bay, inlet
vatn	large lake
vík	V-shaped bay or inlet
vøllur	pasture or grassland in cliff-face

For a glossary of weather terms, see page 24.

Cotton grass

Appendix

FURTHER READING

English-language books on the Faroe Islands are remarkably scant. The books listed below are the pick of a meagre crop. Some of the titles are more readily accessible in the Faroes than elsewhere and are marked accordingly.

General

Day, David *Faroes UK: Faroese People at Home in the UK* Guillemot Publishing. An unusual account of Faroese life outside the Faroes, predominantly in Scotland where seemingly no Faroese household is complete without a stuffed puffin as a reminder of home.

Jackson, J *The Faroes: Faraway Islands* Robert Hale. An excellent contemporary account of Faroese life written within the past decade which attempts to finally put the Faroes on the map and explain what makes these remote islands so unusual yet so appealing.

Kjørsvik Schei, Liv and Moberg, Gunnie *The Faroe Islands* Birlinn Ltd. Although certainly the established authority on all things Faroese, this tome makes dry and stodgy reading. If you're looking for offbeat facts about the islands, the chances are you'll find them here. Illustrations are by the Faroese artist, Tróndur Patursson.

Miller, James *The North Atlantic Front: The Northern Isles at War* Birlinn Ltd. During the two world wars, the Faroes, along with Orkney, Shetland, and Iceland, linking Europe to North America, acquired great significance. This work tells of operations along this northern front, and gives an insight into how the Faroe Islands came to be occupied by Britain whilst the rest of Denmark was under Nazi command.

Millman, Lawrence *Last Places* Houghton Mifflin. A humorous and quirky account of a visit to the Faroes as part of a North Atlantic journey. Millman seems obsessed with whale hunts and blubber – however, it's definitely one of the best contemporary reads on the Faroes, although it is around 15 years out of date.

York-Powell, F *Færeyinga Saga: the Tale of Thrond of Gate* Llanerch Press. A must-read for anyone interested in the flamboyant characters who lived in the Faroes during medieval times. This Icelandic saga deals essentially with the long-standing and ultimately fatal rivalry between Tróndur í Gøtu and Sigmundur Brestisson. With this book in hand you'll gain an altogether more realistic appreciation of some of the villages where history was played out to the full.

Young, G V C *From the Vikings to the Reformation: Chronicle of the Faroe Islands to 1538* Shearwater Publishing. Readily available in the bookshops in Tórshavn, this is the definitive historical account of early Faroese life from the time of the settlement to the Reformation.

Language

Lockwood, W B *An Introduction to Modern Faroese* Føroya Skúlabókagrunnur. The only English-language grammar and reference book to the Faroese language. It's hard going but if you're intent on learning the language, you won't be able to manage without it. Available in specialist language shops outside the Faroes (ie: Grant and Cutler in London) and in the bookshops in Tórshavn.

WEBSITES

www.visit-faroeislands.com	The official Faroese tourism site
www.dmi.dk/dmi/index/ faroerne/femfaro.htm	Five-day weather forecast for the Faroes
www.faroearts.com	Summary of the Faroese arts scene and information on the country's leading artists
www.faroeweb.com	News and information about the Faroes
www.football.fo	The Faroe Islands football association with details on fixtures of the national team
www.framtak.com	Facts and figures about the Faroes as well as language information
www.hagstova.fo	Statistics about the Faroe Islands
www.ssl.fo	Timetables and fares for Faroese public transport
www.stamps.fo	Everything about Faroese stamps for the philatelist
www.tutl.com	A chance to buy Faroese music online
www.uf.fo	Faroese Radio offering a summary of Faroese news in English
www.whaling.fo	Pro-whaling information issued by the Faroese government

Bradt Travel Guides is a partner to the 'know before you go' campaign, masterminded by the UK Foreign and Commonwealth Office to promote the importance of finding out about a destination before you travel. By combining the up-to-date advice of the FCO with the in-depth knowledge of Bradt authors, you'll ensure that your trip will be as trouble-free as possible.

www.fco.gov.uk/knowbeforeyougo

Bradt Travel Guides

Africa by Road	£13.95	Kabul Mini Guide	£9.95
Albania	£13.95	Kenya	£14.95
Amazon	£14.95	Kiev City Guide	£7.95
Antarctica: A Guide to the Wildlife	£14.95	Latvia	£12.95
The Arctic: A Guide to Coastal		Lille City Guide	£5.95
Wildlife	£14.95	Lithuania	£12.95
Armenia with Nagorno Karabagh	£13.95	Ljubljana City Guide	£6.95
Azores	£12.95	London: In the Footsteps of	
Baghdad City Guide	£9.95	the Famous	£10.95
Baltic Capitals: Tallinn, Riga,		Macedonia	£13.95
Vilnius, Kaliningrad	£11.95	Madagascar	£14.95
Bosnia & Herzegovina	£13.95	Madagascar Wildlife	£14.95
Botswana: Okavango Delta,		Malawi	£12.95
Chobe, Northern Kalahari	£14.95	Maldives	£12.95
British Isles: Wildlife of Coastal		Mali	£13.95
Waters	£14.95	Mauritius	£12.95
Budapest City Guide	£7.95	Mongolia	£14.95
Cambodia	£11.95	Montenegro	£12.95
Cameroon	£13.95	Mozambique	£12.95
Canada: North – Yukon, Northwest		Namibia	£14.95
Territories	£13.95	Nigeria	£14.95
Canary Islands	£13.95	North Cyprus	£12.95
Cape Verde Islands	£12.95	North Korea	£13.95
Cayman Islands	£12.95	Palestine with Jerusalem	£12.95
Chile	£16.95	Panama	£13.95
Chile & Argentina: Trekking		Paris, Lille & Brussels: Eurostar Cities	£11.95
Guide	£12.95	Peru & Bolivia: Backpacking &	
China: Yunnan Province	£13.95	Trekking	£12.95
Cork City Guide	£6.95	Riga City Guide	£6.95
Croatia	£12.95	River Thames: In the	
Dubrovnik City Guide	£6.95	Footsteps of the Famous	£10.95
East & Southern Africa:		Rwanda	£13.95
Backpacker's Manual	£14.95	St Helena, Ascension,	
Eccentric America	£13.95	Tristan da Cunha	£14.95
Eccentric Britain	£11.95	Serbia	£13.95
Eccentric Edinburgh	£5.95	Seychelles	£12.95
Eccentric France	£12.95	Singapore	£11.95
Eccentric London	£12.95	South Africa: Budget Travel Guide	£11.95
Eccentric Oxford	£5.95	Southern African Wildlife	£18.95
Ecuador, Peru & Bolivia:		Sri Lanka	£12.95
Backpacker's Manual	£13.95	Sudan	£13.95
Ecuador: Climbing & Hiking	£13.95	Svalbard	£13.95
Eritrea	£12.95	Switzerland: Rail, Road, Lake	£12.95
Estonia	£12.95	Tallinn City Guide	£6.95
Ethiopia	£13.95	Tanzania	£14.95
Falkland Islands	£13.95	Tasmania	£12.95
Faroe Islands	£13.95	Tibet	£12.95
Gabon, São Tomé & Príncipe	£13.95	Uganda	£13.95
Galápagos Wildlife	£14.95	Ukraine	£14.95
Gambia, The	£12.95	USA by Rail	£12.95
Georgia with Armenia	£13.95	Venezuela	£14.95
Ghana	£13.95	Your Child's Health Abroad	£9.95
Iran	£12.95	Zambia	£15.95
Iraq	£14.95	Zanzibar	£12.95

WIN £100 CASH!
READER QUESTIONNAIRE

**Send in your completed questionnaire for the chance to win
£100 cash in our regular draw**

All respondents may order a Bradt guide at half the UK retail price – please
complete the order form overleaf.

(Entries may be posted or faxed to us, or scanned and emailed.)

We are interested in getting feedback from our readers to help us plan future Bradt
guides. Please complete this quick questionnaire and return it to us to enter into
our draw.

Have you used any other Bradt guides? If so, which titles? . . . .
. . . .

What other publishers' travel guides do you use regularly? . . . .
. . . .

Where did you buy this guidebook? . . . .

What was the main purpose of your trip to the Faroe Islands (or for what other
reason did you read our guide)? eg: holiday/business/charity etc. . . . .
. . . .

What other destinations would you like to see covered by a Bradt guide?
. . . .

Would you like to receive our catalogue/newsletters?

YES / NO (If yes, please complete details on reverse)

If yes – by post or email? . . . .

Age (circle relevant category)   16–25   26–45   46–60   60+

Male/Female (delete as appropriate)

Home country . . . .

Please send us any comments about our guide to the Faroe Islands or other Bradt
Travel Guides. . . . .
. . . .
. . . .
. . . .

Bradt Travel Guides
19 High Street, Chalfont St Peter, Bucks SL9 9QE, UK
Telephone: +44 (0)1753 893444 Fax: +44 (0)1753 892333
Email: info@bradtguides.com
www.bradtguides.com

CLAIM YOUR HALF-PRICE BRADT GUIDE!

Order Form

To order your half-price copy of a Bradt guide, and to enter our prize draw to win £100 (see overleaf), please fill in the order form below, complete the questionnaire overleaf, and send it to Bradt Travel Guides by post, fax or email. Post and packing is free to UK addresses.

Please send me one copy of the following guide at half the UK retail price

Title		*Retail price*	*Half price*
. . .	. . . .	. . . .	. . . .

Please send the following additional guides at full UK retail price

No	*Title*		*Retail price*	*Total*
. . .	. . . .	. . . .	. . . .
. . .	. . . .	. . . .	. . . .
. . .	. . . .	. . . .	. . . .

Sub total . . . .
Post & packing outside UK . . . .
(£2 per book Europe; £3 per book rest of world)
Total . . . .

Name . . . .

Address. . . . .

Tel . . . .   Email . . . .

☐ I enclose a cheque for £ . . . . made payable to Bradt Travel Guides Ltd

☐ I would like to pay by VISA or MasterCard

   Number . . . .   Expiry date . . . .

☐ Please add my name to your catalogue mailing list.

Send your order on this form, with the completed questionnaire, to:

Bradt Travel Guides/FAR
19 High Street, Chalfont St Peter, Bucks SL9 9QE
Tel: +44 (0)1753 893444 Fax: +44 (0)1753 892333
Email: info@bradtguides.com
www.bradtguides.com

Index

Page numbers in bold indicate main entries,
those in italics indicate maps.